The Politics of the New Germany

The Politics of the New Germany takes a new approach to understanding politics in the post-unification Federal Republic. Assuming only elementary knowledge, it focuses on debates and issues in order to help students understand both the workings of Germany's key institutions and some of the key policy challenges facing German politicians.

Written in a straightforward style by four experts, each of the chapters draws on a rich variety of real-world examples. In doing so, it highlights both the challenges and opportunities facing policy-makers in such areas as foreign affairs, economic policy, immigration, identity politics and institutional reform. The book also takes a bird's-eye view of the big debates that have defined German politics over time, regardless of which political parties happened to be in power. It pinpoints three key themes that have characterised German politics over the last sixty years; reconciliation, consensus and transformation.

The book is a comprehensive, yet highly accessible, overview of politics in twenty-first century Germany and should be essential reading for students of politics and international relations, as well as of European and German studies.

Simon Green is Senior Lecturer in German and European Politics at the European Research Institute and Deputy Director of the Institute for German Studies, University of Birmingham. He has written widely on German politics and especially on immigration and citizenship policy in Germany.

Dan Hough is Senior Lecturer in Politics at the University of Sussex. He has published widely on parties and party systems, devolution and constitutional change and German politics. He recently co-wrote (with Michael Koß and Jonathan Olsen) *The Left Party in Contemporary German Politics* (Palgrave, 2007).

Alister Miskimmon is Lecturer in European Politics and International Relations and Director of European Studies at Royal Holloway, University of London. His research interests are in the field of German foreign policy, as well as wider European and global security issues.

Graham Timmins is Professor of Politics at the University of Stirling. His research areas cover European integration and security, and German politics. Recent publications include *Russia and Europe in the Twenty-First Century: An Uneasy Partnership*, co-editor Jackie Gower (Anthem, 2007).

The Politics of the
New Germany

Simon Green, Dan Hough,
Alister Miskimmon
and Graham Timmins

LONDON AND NEW YORK

First published 2008
by Routledge
2 Park Square, Milton Park, Abingdon, Oxon OX14 4RN

Simultaneously published in the USA and Canada
by Routledge
270 Madison Avenue, New York, NY 10016

Transferred to Digital Printing 2008

Routledge is an imprint of the Taylor & Francis Group, an informa business

Typeset in Times New Roman by
Keystroke, 28 High Street, Tettenhall, Wolverhampton
Printed and bound in Great Britain by
TJI Digital, Padstow, Cornwall

British Library Cataloguing in Publication Data
A catalogue record for this book is available from the British Library

Library of Congress Cataloging in Publication Data
The politics of the new Germany/Simon Green . . . [et al.].
    p. cm.
    Includes bibliographical references and index.
    1. Germany—Politics and government—1990– 2. Germany—Economic
conditions—1990–   I. Green, Simon, 1971–
JN3971.A58P593 2008
943.088—dc22   2007021224

ISBN 10: 0–415–35365–3 (hbk)
ISBN 10: 0–415–35366–1 (pbk)
ISBN 10: 0–203–34681–5 (ebk)

ISBN 13: 978–0–415–35365–6 (hbk)
ISBN 13: 978–0–415–35366–3 (pbk)
ISBN 13: 978–0–203–34681–5 (ebk)

Contents

Acknowledgements

Books, of course, do not see the light of day because of the efforts of their authors alone. Many other people and institutions make vital contributions. This book is no different. First, we have all received help and assistance from our academic institutions – the Universities of Birmingham, Sussex, Royal Holloway and Stirling. Second, we would also like to thank Craig Fowlie and his colleagues at Routledge for showing faith in us as authors and also for their (at times almost limitless) patience!

We would also like to record our thanks to a number of friends, family and colleagues who have, in their own ways, made their contributions to this book being written: Nils Bandelow, Nicola Corkin, Emma Gittus, Michael Koß, Christian Nolte, Hans-Heinrich Nolte, Insa Nolte, Ying Lin, William Paterson and Martin Seeleib-Kaiser.

Illustrations

Map

Tables

Figures

Boxes

Principal abbreviations

AA	*Auswärtiges Amt* (Foreign Ministry)
APO	*Außerparlamentarische Opposition* (extra-parliamentary opposition)
AStA	*Allgemeiner Studentenausschuss* (student union; collectively, these played a key role in the student movements of the 1960s)
BA	*Bundesagentur für Arbeit* (Federal Labour Agency)
CDU	*Christliche-Demokratische Union Deutschlands* (Christian Democratic Union of Germany)
CFSP	Common Foreign and Security Policy of the European Union
CSU	*Christliche-Soziale Union* (Christian Social Union)
DGB	*Deutscher Gewerkschaftsbund* (German Federation of Unions)
DM	*Deutsche Mark*
DVU	*Deutsche Volksunion* (German People's Party)
ECB	European Central Bank
ECSC	European Coal and Steel Community
EEC	European Economic Community
EMU	Economic and Monetary Union
EP	European Parliament
EPC	European political co-operation
ESDP	European Security and Defence Policy
FDP	*Freie Demokratische Partei* (Free Democratic Party)
FRG	Federal Republic of Germany
GDP	Gross Domestic Product
GDR	German Democratic Republic
HVA	*Hauptverwaltung Aufklärung* (the Stasi's foreign affairs department)
MfS	*Ministerium für Staatssicherheit* (East Germany's Ministry for State Security, Stasi)
NATO	North Atlantic Treaty Organisation
NöS	*Neues ökonomisches System* (New Economic System)
NPD	*National-Demokratische Partei Deutschlands* (National Democratic Party of Germany)
NSDAP	*National-Sozialistische Deutsche Arbeiterpartei* (National-Socialist German Workers' Party)
NVA	*Nationale Volksarmee* (National People's Army of the GDR)
OSCE	Organisation for Security and Co-operation in Europe

PDS   *Partei des demokratischen Sozialismus* (Party of Democratic Socialism), the successor party to the East German communist party (SED)

RAF   *Rote Armee Fraktion* (Red Army Faction)

SDS   *Sozialistischer Deutscher Studentenbund* (German Association of Socialist Students)

SED   *Sozialistische Einheitspartei Deutschlands* (Socialist Unity Party of Germany)

SPD   *Sozialdemokratische Partei Deutschlands* (Social Democratic Party of Germany)

TEU   Treaty on European Union

THA   *Treuhandanstalt* (the state-owned agency charged with privatising the GDR economy)

VAT   Value Added Tax

WASG   *Wahlalternative für Arbeit und Soziale Gerechtigkeit* (Electoral Alliance for Labour and Social Justice)

Glossary of key terms

9/11 The terrorist attacks on New York and Washington on 11 September 2001

Agenda 2010 Package of measures introduced by Chancellor Gerhard Schröder in 2003 to modernise the German welfare state system

Alleinvertretungsanspruch West Germany's claim to speak for all Germans in East and West Germany

Bundesbank German central bank

Bundesrat Chamber of the German Parliament representing the sixteen federal states (*Länder*)

Bundestag Directly elected chamber of the German Parliament

Bundeswehr Germany's armed forces

Bündnis 90/Die Grünen **Alliance 90** The Greens founded in 1993 as merger between western German ecologist party (*Die Grünen*) and eastern German civil rights organisations (*Bündnis 90*). Referred to in this book simply as 'Greens'

Bündnis für Arbeit 'Alliance for Jobs' formed under Chancellor Kohl, continued under Chancellor Schröder

Die Linke 'Left Party' founded in 2007 in a merger between the ex-communist PDS and the western German WASG

Eurozone EU member-states participating in the single currency (the Euro)

Fraktionsvorsitzende(r) Elected leader of a political party's membership in a municipal, *Land* or the federal parliament; at federal level, incumbents are usually among the most influential figures in their party

Fundis Members of the Green movement who were not willing to compromise Green political ideology in order improve their party's electoral prospects

Gastarbeiter Temporary foreign workers recruited by Germany to meet labour shortages

Grundgesetz Basic Law – Germany's Constitution

Hallstein Doctrine West German policy not to recognise diplomatically any state which itself maintained diplomatic relations with East Germany

Hartz IV The fourth, and best-known, series of measures introduced by the SPD–Green government to tackle long-term unemployment

Jugendweihe The secular coming-of-age ceremony that thirteen- and fourteen-year-olds in the GDR underwent; it was supposed to replace the Christian Confirmation ceremony

Konzertierte Aktion Tripartite macro-economic co-ordination body, 1967–77

Land, pl. *Länder* One of sixteen federal states (1949–90, ten states)

Länderfinanzausgleich The fiscal equalisation scheme among federal states

Leitkultur German 'leading culture', used in the context of the integration of immigrants into German society

Mitbestimmung System of 'co-decision' in German industrial relations between unions and employers

Mittelstand Small to medium-sized businesses

Modell Deutschland The German economic model

Ostpolitik West Germany's policy towards the East, most closely associated with Willy Brandt and Egon Bahr

Parteienstaat Literally 'party state'; refers to the permeation of state and administrative structures by political parties

Parteienverdrossenheit Disenchantment with parties

Politikverdrossenheit Disenchantment with politics

Realos Members of the Green movement who were willing to compromise on the idealism of some party policies in order to enhance their chances of electoral success and, ultimately, government participation

Reformstau Reform blockage in the economic and political system

Ressortprinzip Principle of ministerial independence

Richtlinienprinzip Right of the Federal Chancellor to set the overall parameters for government policy

Sonderweg Notion that Germany has undergone a unique political development as a nation

Soziale Marktwirtschaft Social market economy, combining market competition with generous welfare benefits

Sozialversicherungspflichtige Beschäftigung Wage-earning employment in which full contributions to statutory welfare insurance schemes are made by employers and employees

Standortdebatte Debate on Germany's economic position in a globalised world

Stasi East German secret police

Stunde Null Zero Hour – the end of the Second World War when Germans began to recover from the devastation of Nazi Germany

Volkskammer The GDR's parliament

Volksparteien Germany's 'catch-all' parties, i.e., those which gather support from across traditional class and religious divides – the CDU/CSU and the SPD

Wehrmacht German armed forces pre-1945

Westintegration Adenauer's policy of integrating into the West

Wirtschaftswunder West German economic miracle in the 1950s

Zuwanderungsgesetz Immigration Law

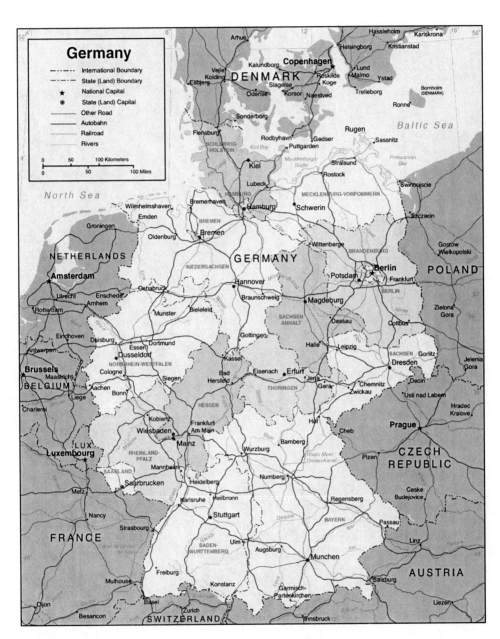

Map of Germany

Introduction

Studying Germany can frequently be a bewildering experience. Germany remains an economically affluent and politically influential country at the core of the European Union (EU). The German economy has been, and still is, a powerhouse that remains remarkably resilient. German companies lead the field in such sectors as pharmaceuticals, state-of-the-art industrial products and cars (one need not think too long before stumbling on leading German global brands such as Audi, BASF, Bertelsmann, BMW, Bosch, Daimler-Chrysler, ThyssenKrupp, Siemens and Volkswagen). Germans are for the most part, as was amply illustrated during the hugely successful Football World Cup of 2006, tolerant, open and welcoming; in Germany welfare provision is broad and comprehensive, public transport functions exceptionally well, and civil society flourishes; the general quality of life is high (no matter how it is measured), crime rates are low and social dislocation, again for the most part, nowhere near as obvious as is the case in Britain, France or Italy. Germany, so it would appear to the naked eye, is a place with a lot going for it. Table 1 provides a general overview of the country compared with other key European states.

Yet a significant number of Germans – and many commentators who write on the country – can also, if they so wish, paint a much darker picture (e.g., Steingart, 2004). The German economy, they argue, is no longer producing the growth rates that it did in the immediate post-war period; unemployment, particularly in eastern Germany, is worryingly high; balancing the books remains difficult in a country that spends so much on supporting the less well off and the ever-increasing number who are no longer of working age; the spectre of neo-Nazi violence lurks below the surface in significant parts of the country (most prominently in eastern Germany); and 'uniting' two populations from East and West Germany has been much more time-consuming, problematic and expensive than anyone anticipated when the Berlin Wall fell in 1989. Furthermore, and in the immediate unification period in particular, Germany's partners were also acutely aware that a newly empowered Federal Republic might perhaps abandon its 'civilian power' approach to foreign policy, choosing instead to throw its increased weight around rather more freely in the international arena. Would the new 'Berlin Republic' therefore be a much more outgoing, and potentially troublesome, partner than the 'Bonn Republic' had been before it (for more on the foreign policy of the 'Berlin Republic', see Sperling, 2003)? Germany's rather hasty decision to recognise the independence of Croatia and Slovenia from the state of Yugoslavia in 1991, for example, did little to calm international nerves (Hodge, 1998). A significant minority wondered out loud whether the forty-five-year period between 1945 and 1990 would prove, given time, to be nothing more than a peaceful and prosperous interlude in Germany's otherwise unhappy history.

Table 1 Germany in a comparative context

	Germany	France	UK	Italy	EU-25
Population (2005, millions)	82.5	62.4	60.0	58.5	461.3
Population density (2004, population/km²	231	98*	244*	197	118
Economic growth (2005, per cent)	0.9	1.2	1.9	0.0	1.7
Inflation (2005, per cent)	1.9	1.9	2.1	2.1	2.2
GDP per person (2005, compared with EU average)	109.3	108.8	116.6	102.6	100.0
Labour productivity (2005, compared with EU average)	101.5	119.1	106.6	108.1	100.0
Balance of trade (exports – imports, billion Euros)	158	–30.2	–102.5	–10.0	–105.8
Population development (births and immigrants minus deaths and emigrants, 2004, thousands)	–30,900	+386,000	+334,700	+574,200	+2,324,900

* 2003

Source: Statistisches Bundesamt, 2006b

Although the doomsayers who predicted a post-unification lurch back to political conditions that resembled those of the inter-war years have been proven wrong, it is still clear that contemporary Germany is indeed rich and yet discontented; it is open and tolerant, yet there are tinges of ethnocultural exclusivity thrown in; it is legally united but psychologically very much divided. Such contradictions are not, of themselves, uniquely German preserves. Italy, for example, has been constitutionally united since 1871, and yet the northern and southern parts of the country appear to exist in different socio-economic worlds; the French state may well be indivisible and the values of the republic unquestioned by the vast majority, but this has not prevented serious worries about increasing social dislocation – seen most visibly in regular urban riots – from becoming one of the most prominent themes in contemporary French politics. Even in the generally tranquil United Kingdom, tangible economic divides between the northern and southern parts of country and increasing ethnic and social tensions in a number of (primarily northern) cities, such as Bradford, Blackburn and Oldham, have led to increasing worries about the cohesion of British society. The particularly German twist comes from the country's uniquely gruesome past and the effect that it inevitably has had on con-temporary political life, complicating political discourse in a way that is not the case elsewhere.

This book takes a new approach to understanding the challenges and dilemmas of contemporary German politics. It focuses on key debates and issues to help shed more light on Germany's key institutions and policies and to identify the principal problems and challenges faced by German policy-makers. Each of the issues under consideration is phrased as a question; moreover, each topic is structured similarly, with sections examining the background, issues and debates in turn. The chapters draw on a rich variety of real-world examples, illustrating that governing Europe's biggest country is a task that is fraught with difficulty. The book also takes a bird's-eye perspective of the big debates that define German politics over time, regardless of which party happens to be in power, and pinpoints three key themes of reconciliation, consensus and transformation. We hope that the book therefore provides a comprehensive, yet still highly accessible, overview of where Germany is as it approaches the end of the first decade of the twenty-first century.

These three general themes appear (in different ways) throughout the course of this analysis. First, since the end of the Second World War there have been systematic attempts to learn from Germany's past mistakes and to ensure that the country never goes back to its old destructive, militaristic ways. This overt attempt at *reconciliation* has not always been easy, but, after an initial period of reluctance, significant progress has clearly been made. Worries about the dangers of extremism have led post-war policy-makers to stress the importance of *consensus* politics, and this is the second recurrent theme running through our analysis of what drives politics in Germany. The 'politics of centrality' is characterised by political institutions and political actors working together to find consensual solutions in the knowledge that a lurch to the left or right can have destabilising and ultimately destructive consequences (Smith, 1976). The need to find and cultivate consensus has served Germany well over most of the Federal Republic's history, although when politicians seek to implement rather more radical policy changes the interlinked institutional structures can provide plenty of barriers that need to be overcome. The third theme is one that has been particularly prevalent in recent times; it is one of *transformation* and adaptation to changed (and changing) circumstances. Germany has had to adapt to a new role as a unified state in an ever-deeper and -wider European Union. In recent times it has found itself expected to take on more responsibility and also to adapt to a set of difficult internal policy dilemmas. In a consensus society that is wary of taking risks that may lead to political instability, this is no easy task. Together, these three themes – reconciliation, consensus and transformation – underpin much of the writing in the chapters to come.

The first chapter analyses German history and, more specifically, how the post-war generation has attempted to deal with the legacy of Germany's unhappy past. This is important for a plethora of reasons. Put simply, Germans remain obsessed with what it means to be German, and numerous authors have attempted to analyse, define and critique the notoriously slippery concept of 'Germanness' (for a discussion of this, see Stevenson and Theobald, 2000). Given the crimes that were committed in its name between 1933 and 1945, can (or, indeed, should) Germany ever be viewed as 'normal' by the international community or even by Germans themselves? In Germany this is not simply a debate for historians; it affects everyone as well as the (very successful) system of government that has been created post-1945. And it is for this reason that this book begins by addressing issues of Germany's historical legacy. It does so by briefly outlining key stages in Germany's past, before addressing the way in which the past has been dealt with in post-1945 West Germany. Although there are clearly no hard and fast answers to difficult questions of how past experience should shape contemporary political activity, Chapter 1 indicates that German history is highly significant when attempting to understand how and why Germany's institutional framework was created, and how German politicians seek to answer complex, real-world problems today.

Chapter 2 attempts to map out the historical development of the West German state and its institutions by illustrating the role that the past played in guiding political actors when shaping Germany's institutional architecture. It shows how West Germany sought to rehabilitate itself after the disaster of Nazi rule in political, economic and international terms. And, by any standards, this process of rehabilitation was extraordinarily successful and stands in stark contrast to the development of the GDR, with its crumbling economy and complete lack of popular legitimacy. But Chapter 2 also identifies some of the key trends that reappear later in the book. By as early as the mid-1980s, there were fears that West Germany was living beyond its means, and that labour and welfare costs were simply too high in international terms. Immigration had exploded on to the political agenda in 1980, and it has remained there ever since. The arrival of the Green Party heralded a change in both the structure and ideological composition of the party system. Corruption and political scandals were becoming more commonplace. Together, they constitute some of the challenges of transformation facing Germany in the twenty-first century.

Chapter 3 turns its attention to life in the GDR more specifically, before discussing how its regime collapsed and the unification of the two German states took place. It then moves on to analyse both the legacy of this unification process, especially in economic terms, and identity politics in post-unification Germany. The experience of living in the GDR, of seeing it collapse and then of entering a new state contributed to many citizens of what was East Germany developing (perhaps subconsciously) rather different sets of attitudes, values and interests to their western German counterparts. These have come together to make what some authors believe is a unique eastern German identity. This chapter assesses what this identity may be and what – if anything – it means for contemporary German politics.

Chapter 4 analyses one of the most distinctive elements of the German political system that in recent years has come under increasing strain: federalism and the institutions of government. The decentralisation of power that led to the creation of a federal system with inbuilt checks and balances has made governing Germany a much more difficult task than is the case in other states. The *Bundesrat* retains significant veto powers and the 'blockaded' political system has caused many to wonder whether Germany's unwieldy institutional framework is making it ungovernable.

Chapter 5 shows that the two-and-a-half-party system that characterised German politics for the majority of the post-war era is now a thing of the past. Two medium-sized (CDU/CSU, SPD) and three smaller (FDP, the Greens and the Left Party) parties now garner enough votes to make coalition formation – and consequently governing in general – a much more complex task than it used to be. Processes of dealignment (in western Germany) and partial alignment (in eastern Germany) ensure that voters have become more volatile and the traditional supporter bases of all the parties more fragile. Although unification did not spawn all of these developments, it has certainly exacerbated them and has contributed to the fragmentation of the party system and to an increasing diversity of electoral outcomes.

Chapter 6 considers two key changes to the composition of Germany's population both in recent and future decades. First, Germany has been one of the main destinations for immigration in the European Union; and, second, Germans themselves are living longer and having fewer children. The combination of these factors has created a number of difficult political challenges surrounding issues such as Germany's identity, integration and the future of the welfare state, many of which have now been on the political agenda for more than twenty-five years. At the same time, it has not been easy to develop new solutions to some of these challenges because of Germany's long-established self-perception as a 'non-immigration country'.

Chapter 7 moves on to analyse the much-vaunted 'German Model' of economic management. For much of the post-war period, this model was held up as a success story, not only in terms of reconstruction after 1945 and the development of Germany into a major economic power, but also for the consensual nature of industrial relations. This chapter outlines the main characteristics of the German Model and examines pressures on the institutional framework of economic management in post-unification Germany, focusing on industrial relations, corporate governance and European integration. In sum, it asks to what extent the German Model remains 'fit for purpose' at the start of the twenty-first century.

Chapter 8 then discusses the problems and challenges surrounding the traditionally generous German welfare state. The comparatively high level of benefits was seen as an integral element of the social market economy and *Modell Deutschland*. However, for a range of reasons (although cost was very much paramount amongst them), pressure on this system has been building ever since the 1970s, and especially since unification. But the political challenge of reforming Germany's welfare provisions has been extremely difficult to manage, as political parties have had to impose unpalatable cuts on an electorate accustomed to generous unemployment benefits, comfortable pensions and comprehensive health insurance. The resulting political disputes have not only been some of the most contentious of recent years but are set to define much of German politics in the future.

Chapter 9 illustrates how the European Union has played a central role in the development of the German state since the 1950s. European integration provided Germany with an institutional framework to rebuild its economy, regain its international standing and establish lasting ties with its European neighbours. Along with the obvious benefits that EU membership has brought Germany, it has also presented a number of challenges. In particular, the chapter discusses to what extent Germany has, in recent years, adopted a more interest-focused position in its engagement with European integration.

Chapter 10 analyses German foreign and security policy since 1949. It shows that it has been dominated by the need to redefine Germany's role in the world after the mistakes of the first half of the twentieth century. It has been characterised by a firm commitment to co-operation within multilateral institutions and by a rejection of the use of aggressive military force as a tool of foreign policy. German foreign policy has, however, changed radically since unification, with Germany taking on more responsibility in attempting to secure international stability.

The book concludes with a summary of where Germany has come from and the challenges that it is likely to face both now and in the future.

1 Germany and the burden of history

Summary

Germany is a country where history looms larger than it does in most other places. This chapter sets the scene for the book as a whole by linking what has been, for the most part, an unhappy history with some of the main political debates in post-1945 and contemporary Germany. It begins by discussing the development of Germany from its beginnings as a *Kulturnation* ('cultural nation') through to the end of the Second World War. It then examines how post-war German politicians dealt with the legacy of this tumultuous history. Originally, they made little attempt to engage actively with Germany's past, and it was only from the 1960s onwards that Germans really began to work through their country's difficult heritage. By the mid-1980s, debates about how Germany's history should be understood became much more mainstream. Unification in 1990 complicated matters further by introducing another dimension to the debate, that of how best to understand and interpret the history of the German Democratic Republic. The chapter concludes by highlighting why an appreciation of German history is vitally important if contemporary political life in the Federal Republic of Germany is to be understood adequately.

Introduction

Even the most cursory of glances at the way in which Germany functions will reveal that the burden of history has been very significant in shaping the contemporary political system. Many historians have traditionally debated issues about Germany's role in the world, position at the heart of Europe and difficulty in feeling at ease with itself by highlighting what is frequently known as the 'German Question'. However, debates about what that question actually is have been almost as lively as what the possible answers to it might be (see Box 1.1).

Some analysts have stressed that there is a uniquely German political path (the so-called *Sonderweg*). Germans 'failed' to create a nation-state in the Middle Ages and, as a result, the cultural and political conflicts that took place around the time of the Reformation helped to institutionalise Germany into a myriad of smaller units, all with predominantly German-speaking populations. A genuinely German state therefore took

BOX 1.1 THE GERMAN QUESTION

The term 'German Question' can have a number of different meanings depending on context (see Wolff, 2003). It was first articulated in literary circles in 1797 when the influential German thinkers Johann Wolfgang von Goethe and Friedrich Schiller asked, in the simplest of terms, what Germany was, and where it could be found. They asked this for two reasons. First, Germany's territorial borders were a matter of some controversy (among Germans and non-Germans alike). This remained so long after Goethe and Schiller had died, largely as the country does not benefit from natural boundaries (such as seas and mountain ranges) in the way that states such as the USA, UK and France do. A further complication was that German nationality was, until very recently, understood as being granted on the basis of blood lineage (see Chapter 6). 'Germans' living many miles apart therefore felt some allegiance to one another through the prism of what came to be known as the *Kulturnation* ('cultural nation'). Resolving to everyone's satisfaction issues of where a German state, incorporating as many Germans as possible, should actually be therefore proved immensely difficult. The problem was not resolved even when Otto von Bismarck created the first German nation-state in 1871, as many millions of Germans continued to live outside of its borders.

The German 'problem' in this form is therefore best understood as the difficulty of reconciling where Germany is (or should be) in geographical terms with where German-speakers live and have lived. It should, then, not come as too much of a surprise that the question of how to resolve this has kept appearing – if in slightly different forms – ever since those two great German thinkers first articulated it over two centuries ago. Post-1945, the division of Germany into two states provided a preliminary answer to the 'German Question'. The final, official, answer came in the form of German unification, together with the recognition under international law of Germany's borders. Since 3 October 1990 we now know precisely where Germany is, thus defusing at least one of the traditional issues that contributed to making the 'German Question' so controversial.

The nature and meaning of the 'German Question' changed post-1945. It took on one of four forms, again depending on context:

*   How should Germans seek (or have sought) to overcome the division of Germany into two states?
*   How should Germans (have) relate(d) to territories in Central and Eastern Europe formerly belonging to Germany and/or inhabited by members of German minorities?
*   How should millions of refugees, expellees and ethnic Germans from Central and Eastern Europe (have) be(en) integrated into German society?
*   Finally, and probably most significantly in the contemporary period, what role, post-1990, should a unified and fully independent Germany play in the post-Cold War world order?

The first three of these variants took precedence pre-1989 but the fall of the Berlin Wall and the granting of complete independence to Germany post-1990 soon pushed the fourth point to the forefront of discussions.

an awful long time to come into existence and, even then, the circumstances of its birth ensured that it adopted decidedly militaristic and expansionist poses (Fulbrook, 2002). Germany's historical uniqueness subsequently came in its *Kleinstaaterei* (literally translated as 'small-statedness'). The British, French (and even, in many ways, the Americans), meanwhile, imposed – at a much earlier stage – statehood on their populations from the top down and they now celebrate historic achievements, disastrous failures, lingering legacies and missed opportunities that their respective states have experienced over a number of centuries.

The absence of a German nation-state should not blind us to the fact that the collective beginnings of what could plausibly be understood as a German national identity can nonetheless be traced back a long way in history, perhaps even to the Germanic tribes' famous defeat of the Romans in the Teutoburger Forest in AD 9. But agreeing on what constituted 'Germanness' was more tricky, and it was only towards the end of the eighteenth century that Germans began to seriously consider what this meant in practice. At this point German people lived, for the most part, in the Holy Roman Empire (AD 800 to 1815). However, defining and describing what the Holy Roman Empire was is also no easy task. At its simplest, it was a collection of territories united under an emperor who was elected by various Germanic states. It was not, though, a nation-state in the modern sense of the term and could never have become one due both to its internal structures and the differing sets of interests that existed within it. A patchwork of small states, imperial cites, free cities, principalities, monarchies and duchies existed alongside each other. In more centralised countries, such as the UK and France, they would no doubt have long since disappeared.

From Holy Roman Empire to the Weimar Republic

This Holy Roman Empire therefore existed in spite of the fact that its people possessed little allegiance to it. It was characterised by both religious heterogeneity and strong territorial distinctiveness. It is not by chance that the names of some of contemporary Germany's *Länder* (such as Saxony and Bavaria) reflect this historical territorial diversity, their names resonant of the long histories that they enjoy. The main (and for many only) common factor across the territory was the German language. Inhabitants of this diverse political landscape were also linked through various other phenomena that had their roots in this common tongue: German literature, German culture and a shared sense of a history of the German-speaking peoples all existed long before Germany existed as a political entity. Germany was a cultural nation, stressing linkages through shared customs, shared language and blood lineage. This ethos underpinning this understanding of 'Germanness' is something which remained (and in some ways remains) prominent in some aspects of contemporary politics, particularly when issues of immigration, nationality and citizenship are discussed (see Chapter 6).

This is not to say that there were no attempts to create a unified German state. There were, and they occurred periodically across the thirty-eight German territories that comprised the German Confederation (formed after the Congress of Vienna in 1815). The most famous of these movements came in 1848 when repeated calls were made for political freedoms, genuine democracy and national unity. Increases in nationalist rhetoric were noticeable as newspapers such as *Deutsche Zeitung* (*German Paper*) increased in circulation, nationalist songs such as the *Deutschlandlied* by the poet Hoffmann von Fallersleben (later to become Germany's national anthem) were written, and worries about possible advances by the French (on the Rhineland) and Danish (on Schleswig-Holstein in the north) grew. Liberalism also gained political ground, and significant liberal pressures (such as calls for more individual rights and greater press freedoms) spread across the German-speaking lands. The increasing economic strength of Prussia led to the eventual creation of a customs union as more tangible feelings of economic interdependence spread across the German-speaking states. All of these factors nevertheless led each of the territories to experience what was to become an attempted revolution in slightly different ways. Some monarchs, fearing the fate of Louis-Philippe of France (who abdicated in 1848), accepted (albeit temporarily) some of the demands of the revolutionaries. Others defended their corner and rejected them out of hand. In the more southerly and westerly parts of Germany there were mass demonstrations as well as the creation of large popular assemblies.

No matter what form this dissent towards aristocratic rule took, the masses made similar claims: they wanted a free press, the freedom of assembly, and a parliament representing the German citizens instead of the federal council representing only the monarchs of the German states. That they ultimately failed in these aims can be attributed to a number of factors. First, the national parliament that was created in Frankfurt suffered from both weak leadership (mainly from Heinrich von Gagern, who was the most significant member) and the tendency to intellectualise and prevaricate. Second, the revolution enjoyed no military support. Third, there was a major divide between those who favoured a *Großdeutschland* (Greater Germany, which would have included Austria) and those who were happy with Austria to remain outside the state's borders, while there were also regular disagreements over a range of matters between Prussia and some of the southern German states. Finally, the fact that there were no political parties involved did not help in facilitating agreement and channelling interests into compromise solutions. By late 1848 plans to institutionalise German unity were starting to crumble as the military and the aristocracy began to regain their composure and subsequently the political upper hand. By 1851 almost all of the achievements of the revolutionaries across Germany had been revoked, the national assembly had disintegrated and the old order had been restored.

Germany had to wait another twenty years before Otto von Bismarck, a long-time schemer involved in the failure of the 1848 revolution, changed all this to create a fully fledged nation-state. Bismarck was a conservative politician from Prussia, the strongest of all the German territories. He was determined to unite the German states into a single empire (with the exception of Austria) with Prussia at its core. Beginning in 1884, Germany also began to ape Europe's traditional Great Powers by acquiring several colonies in Africa, including German East Africa, and the territories that are now Namibia, Togo and Cameroon.

As Bismarck was initially unable to persuade all of the German states to join him in forging this new and more powerful empire under Prussian leadership, he provoked war with France as a way of uniting them. His plan worked, and following Prussia's crushing victory in the ensuing conflict, the *Deutsches Kaiserreich* (German Empire) was declared in Versailles in 1871, with Wilhelm I of Prussia as *Kaiser* (Emperor) and Berlin as the new capital. As 'Chancellor' of the new Germany, Bismarck concentrated on building a powerful state with a unified national identity (see Pulzer, 1997). To this end, and given Prussia's Protestant religious profile, he targeted the Catholic Church (in the *Kulturkampf*), which he believed had too much influence (particularly in southern Germany); indeed, the sectarian divisions between Catholics and Protestants still retain occasional relevance in German politics today. He also aimed to prevent the spread of socialism, partly by introducing national health insurance and pensions, thereby laying the foundations of the modern welfare state, not only in Germany but throughout Europe (see Chapter 8).

In the early period following the first unification of Germany, Emperor Wilhelm I's foreign policy secured Germany's position at the forefront of international affairs by forging (sometimes uneasy) alliances with neighbours and purposefully using diplomatic means to isolate France. Under his successor Wilhelm II, however, Germany, like a number of other European powers, became more overtly imperialist, and this contributed to Europe slipping towards war. Many of the alliances that German leaders crafted were not renewed over time. New alliances between other states also slowly began to exclude Germany. France, Germany's traditional foe in Central/Western Europe, even established new relationships with its traditional enemies, such as the United Kingdom (most notably in the 'Entente Cordiale' of 1904) and Russia. As war became ever more likely, Germany found itself on the same side as Austria-Hungary, Bulgaria and the Ottoman Empire in an alliance that came to be known as the Central Powers (on the basis that they were all located between the Russian Empire in the East and France and the UK in the West).

The assassination of Austria's crown prince, Archduke Franz Ferdinand, on 28 June 1914 ultimately triggered the opening of hostilities in what became the First World War. The unsuccessful Central Powers, headed by Germany, suffered defeat against the Allied Powers in what was up to then the bloodiest conflict of all time. Eventually, a revolution broke out in November 1918 in Germany and Wilhelm II and all the German ruling princes abdicated their thrones. An armistice putting an end to hostilities was signed on 11 November 1918 and Germany was compelled – in June 1919 – to sign the Treaty of Versailles in the very building where Bismarck had called the German Empire into existence forty-eight years previously. The treaty was perceived by many in Germany as a humiliating continuation of the war by other means and its harshness is often cited as having facilitated the later rise of Nazism.

The Weimar Republic and the rise of Nazism

The proclamation of a republic in the immediate aftermath of the First World War led to the meeting of a constitutional convention in the sleepy town of Weimar in what is now the eastern German state of Thuringia. The constitution of the 'Weimar Republic' was in many ways an exemplary document, offering Germany the opportunity to distance itself from its militaristic and imperial past and recast itself as a liberal, democratic state in the tradition of older democracies such as France, the UK and the USA. However, as is well known, what looked good in theory proved much less impressive in practice and the new political system's democratic credentials failed to stand the test of time.

One of the reasons why the Weimar Republic failed was the desolate economic situation from which Germany never really recovered after 1918. Like other countries, the war almost bankrupted Germany, and this, when combined with the high levels of reparations imposed in the Treaty of Versailles, left the republic very economically vulnerable. But worse was to come. In the early 1920s, and partly as a result of the war, Germany was struck by gradually worsening hyperinflation. This culminated in late 1923, by which time the value of its currency was depreciating on an almost daily basis. In a famous picture of the time, a woman is depicted using paper currency to heat her home, as this was cheaper than buying firewood. The effects of hyperinflation were devastating, and it destroyed any remaining wealth not already lost in the ravages of the First World War, leaving millions in poverty (Feldman, 1997). This left a deep and unmistakable scar on German society.

During the mid-1920s the German economy recovered somewhat, and many parts of the country enjoyed both economic and cultural revivals. Berlin, in particular, experienced what came to be known as the 'Golden Twenties', in which – for a short period – the more well-off residents appeared to be enjoying an exciting, extremely vibrant and positively hedonistic lifestyle. Although this period lasted little more than a decade, sophisticated and innovative approaches to architecture and design (notably the *Bauhaus* school) prospered across Germany, and literary figures (such as the poet Bertolt Brecht), film-makers (such as the Austrian Fritz Lang, director of *Metropolis*), artists, fashion designers and musicians all excelled. Although Berlin was the centre of this movement, once the hyperinflation catastrophe had been overcome the diffuse and diverse forces involved spread throughout the country. But the movement did not last long. Those on the right of the political spectrum were highly suspicious of what they perceived as a socially disruptive and dangerous development, and with the increasing influence of right-wing parties through the late 1920s and early 1930s came increasing intolerance towards such alleged decadence. When the economy was once again hit hard by the Great Depression of the early 1930s (which spread following the 1929 Wall Street Crash) the Golden Twenties came to an abrupt end.

The erratic nature of the economy allowed anti-system parties of both the left and right to dominate political discourse and, before long, Germany found itself once again slipping towards authoritarianism. By 1932, the combined shackles of the Great Depression, the harsh peace conditions dictated by the Treaty of Versailles and a long succession of unstable and ineffectual governments caused Germans increasingly to question the efficiency and efficacy of their political system. Parliamentary democracy was seen as permitting foreign governments to control Germany and to prevent it from regaining any form of self-respect. The far left (communists) and particularly far-right (ultra-conservatives and Nazis) chose, in their different ways and for their different reasons, to oppose the system and to attempt to overthrow it (Fulbrook, 2002). These feelings of dissatisfaction were exacerbated by a widespread right-wing, partly monarchist, partly ethnic (or *völkisch*), partly Nazi *Dolchstoßlegende* (or 'stab in the back'), a political myth which claimed that Germany lost the First World War because of the betrayal of mainstream democrats and not because of military defeat. Radical left-wing communists, such as the Spartacus League, on the other hand, wanted to abolish capitalism altogether, preferring to install a *Räterepublik* (state based on councils). Paramilitary organisations abounded and politically motivated murders became ever more frequent. Pushed by right-wing advisers and following a succession of unsuccessful cabinets, President Paul von Hindenburg – a decorated First World War general – saw little alternative but to appoint, on 30 January 1933, the leader of the National Socialists, Adolf Hitler, as Chancellor of Germany.

The Third Reich, 1933–45

The history of the Third Reich is well known and need not detain us long here. Hitler's reign began shortly before a mysterious fire in the Reichstag on 27 February 1933, for which a Dutch anarchist, Marinus van der Lubbe, was officially convicted. Van der Lubbe was the scapegoat that the NSDAP (National-Socialist Party of Germany, otherwise known simply as 'the Nazis') needed in order to convince the German people that the Communist Party was trying to take over and that it had to be stopped. It gave them an excuse to act against the thousands of anarchists, socialists and communists scattered throughout the country, many of whom were sent to concentration camps, quelling much of the natural opposition to Nazi politics. Furthermore, Hitler proceeded to abrogate by emergency decree a significant number of democratic rights more or less immediately. A so-called Enabling Act – which only the Social Democrats voted against – then gave Hitler's government full legislative powers, facilitating his aim of creating a centralised, totalitarian state where he was in complete control. The Act also authorised the government (and thus effectively the Nazi Party) to deviate from the provisions of the constitution for four years.

By June 1933 the Social Democrat and Communist parties had been banned, while the German Nationalists, German People's Party and German Democratic Party had all been forced to disband. In July 1933 the Catholic Centre Party chose to disband itself and on 14 July Germany officially became a one-party state with the passing of a law against the formation of parties. Further consolidation of power was achieved on 30 January 1934 when the federal structure of the Weimar Republic was officially transformed into a centralised state. State parliaments were wiped off the political map and the sovereign rights of the states were all transferred to central government in Berlin. This process of *Gleichschaltung* affected not just the territorial structure of Germany, but the societal structure, as youth groups, unions, courts and even the motorists' organisation were brought under direct Nazi control.

The creation of a secret police, the much-feared Gestapo, acting outside of any civil authority, highlighted the Nazis' intention to use powerful, coercive means to control German society directly. Soon, perhaps 100,000 spies and infiltrators operated through-out Germany, reporting the activities of any critics or dissenters to Nazi officials. Most ordinary Germans, happy with the improving economy and better standard of living, remained quietly obedient, but many political opponents, especially communists and some socialists, were imprisoned and in many cases tortured and killed.

Once he had stabilised his power position within Germany, Hitler took back the demilitarised Rhineland (in 1936) before proceeding to create a Greater Germany by annexing parts of what is now the Czech Republic. In September 1939 Germany's increasingly nationalist and militarist policies led it to attack Poland, an event that prompted, two days later, declarations of war by both the UK and France. Although initially the German army enjoyed much the upper hand in the conflicts with its enemies, it soon found that its surprise attack on the Soviet Union and the difficulty of dealing with a war on two fronts stretched its forces too far. Subsequently, the German army retreated on the Eastern Front and eventually, on 8 May 1945, it was defeated completely and surrendered to the victorious Red Army in Berlin.

During the Nazis' period in power approximately six million European Jews were killed in the Holocaust. This was a programme of deliberate extermination of allegedly inferior peoples and races that was meticulously planned and executed by Hitler's regime. Large numbers of Slavs, Roma, homosexuals, religious opponents and the disabled, among others, were also systematically murdered. The Nazis planned their murderous activities to take place in stages. Legislation outlawing Jews from taking part in everyday German life was enacted years before the outbreak of the Second World War, while as the Third Reich expanded eastwards, ghettos were established to contain and eventually eliminate victims. In Western European countries occupied by the Nazi regime, Jews were interned before being deported to death camps such as Auschwitz–Birkenau in southern Poland, where murder was conducted on an industrial scale. When the Nazi state finally collapsed approximately fifty million people had died (see Fulbrook, 2002, for more detail on this period in German history).

History and its effect on post-1945 Germany

The very abnormality of Germany's history, and the crimes that were committed in its name, meant that questions of what could, and should, be done with post-war Germany were at the forefront of the minds of not just German policy-makers but also of the wider international community. Later chapters in this book analyse in more detail what this meant in practical terms. Initially, Germany was (unsurprisingly) a country in complete turmoil. The Allied powers divided – at a conference in Potsdam in August 1945 – Germany into four military zones that they proceeded to occupy: the British were in the north, in the modern-day states of Schleswig-Holstein, Hamburg, Lower Saxony and what is now North Rhine-Westphalia; US forces were in Bavaria, Hesse and the northern parts of what is now Baden-Württemberg (the ports of Bremen and Bremerhaven in the north were also put under US control); the French occupied a smaller zone including the Saarland and Baden in the very south-western corner of the country; and the Soviets held sway over what was to become the German Democratic Republic.

The former German provinces east of the Oder and Neisse rivers (Eastern Pomerania and Silesia) were transferred to Poland while East Prussia was split between Poland and the Soviet Union, effectively shifting Germany's eastern border hundreds of miles westwards. Roughly fifteen million displaced persons and expellees suffered great hardships in the years between 1945 and 1949 during their flight and at times enforced expulsion from these former German territories towards their newly demarcated state. Of the roughly twelve million Germans who in 1944 were living in territory that was soon to become part of Poland, an estimated six million fled or were evacuated before the advancing Red Army reached them. Of the remainder, up to 1.1 million died, 3.6 million were expelled by the Poles, a further million were designated as Poles, and 300,000 remained regardless (Beschloss, 2002: 233). Thousands starved and froze to death while being expelled in slow and ill-equipped trains (Petrov, 1967: 228–9). Conditions in Germany itself were better, although they were hardly pleasurable. Many soldiers from the Eastern Front returned home traumatised and there were significant numbers of home-based casualties. Most larger German cities were in ruins and industrial production had collapsed because of the non-availability of raw materials. The country's transport infrastructure had suffered widespread damage. Financially, Germany was on its knees and the East in particular was being pillaged by its Soviet occupiers.

The speed of Germany's post-war economic recovery and the stabilisation of the country as a democratic state soon ensured that, perhaps surprisingly, it became rather easy to forget over debates about Germany's past. For one thing, there was no such debate going on in one of the two post-war German states, namely the GDR. 'Anti-fascism' remained the state ideology and the repressive state apparatus prevented any genuine discussion both of what this meant and of how Germans should attempt to deal with the evils of fascism that they had just experienced. The GDR simply *was* anti-fascist, end of story, and its leaders declared that it was for the FRG to deal with the aftermath of the Nazi period. Indeed, the GDR did not see itself as a legal successor of the Third Reich and consequently made no attempt to come to terms with the significance of 'dealing with' the crimes committed during this era.

In West Germany, meanwhile, citizens simply got on with the job of trying to rebuild their lives. They had no time or inclination to dwell on this desperate period in their history; mouths needed to be fed, family members clothed, houses rebuilt and money somehow earned. A cultural escapism developed, which was epitomised by the popularity of the rather saccharine *Heimat* film genre, which depicted an unspoiled, simple world (von Moltke, 2005). At the elite level there was a broad consensus stressing the need to deal – however imperfectly at first – with the evils of the Nazi regime and then to move on. In line with this attitude, the lesson learned from Germany's past was one of reconciliation. The newly formed Federal Republic of Germany should be absorbed into the Western alliance and should actively look to embed itself in the institutions of the international community. However, this did not mean that Germans quickly and seamlessly recognised that they may have played unsavoury roles during the period of Nazi rule. Initially there was a tendency in German society to put the blame for war crimes on just a small number of Nazi leaders. Germans wanted to look forward, to forget and move on, not to pose awkward questions of what they knew of the Nazi period and, even more delicately, what they themselves may have done in the service of the state during this era. But the process of coming to terms with such a damning legacy takes time, much head-scratching and no small amount of anguish.

As early as the 1950s, intellectuals were raising their voices in protest against the all too rapid (re)appearance of normality within the Federal Republic, stressing the apparently seamless rehabilitation of many who had worked for, and to some extent may well have believed in, what the Nazis did. The increasing affluence of Germany, successful post-war reconstruction and the apparent willingness to brush the Nazi period under the carpet of history worried many and a group of influential intellectuals began to encourage citizens to ask themselves what roles they, or their friends and family, played during this terrible period. Their ideas and arguments were greeted with particular interest by a new generation of Germans – people who were born near the end of, or even after, the war had concluded and were now making their way through Germany's education system. Such unease with the historical settlement took time to disseminate through society, but by the student protests of the late 1960s at the very latest, sections of the public at large were making it clear that some sort of genuine confrontation with the Nazi past was central to Germany establishing itself as a 'normal', liberal, democratic regime.

The student unrest of 1968 (discussed further in Chapter 2) triggered a sea-change in Germany's willingness to 'work through' its past. The open revolts that students across Germany's university campuses led were largely reactions against the perceived authoritarianism and hypocrisy of the German (and other liberal, democratic) government(s), as well as what many regarded as the poor conditions that students in the Federal Republic had to endure. The protests, some of which turned violent, were fuelled by strong reactions by the police and marked a significant shift to the radical left of previously conservative student politics.

Although the students were protesting over a large number of issues, ranging from the Vietnam War to the need to reform campus life, one of the core motivating forces behind the rebellion was their conviction that German elites had not dealt with the fallout from fascism in anything like a sufficiently thorough way. And there is little doubt that their fears were at least partially justified. Although 'denazification' had been a top priority for the Allies, and despite the Nuremberg war trials from 1945–8, many Nazis at all levels of authority simply slipped through the net (Frei, 2003). Konrad Adenauer himself, although a proven opponent of the Nazi regime who spent much of the war in prison, was prepared to include ex-Nazis in his government so long as they expressed committment to democracy. Most notoriously, he chose Hans Globke, one of the author's of Nazi Germany's anti-Jewish legislation, as a key adviser; elsewhere, the Minister for Refugees and Expellees during the 1950s, Theodor Oberländer, had served with execution squads on the Eastern Front. West Germany's intelligence apparatus consisted almost entirely of wartime military intelligence officers, under the leadership of the shadowy General Reinhard Gehlen. One post-war Chancellor, Kurt-Georg Kiesinger, had even himself been a member of the Nazi Party until 1945. Universities too came under fire, and many senior faculty members, especially in the field of medicine, had proven links to the Nazi regime. Even though the *Bundestag*, in a landmark debate in 1965, had voted to extend the twenty-year statute of limitations on murders committed under the Nazi regime, the leaders of the student movement considered West German society's attitudes towards its recent past to be complacent in the extreme.

While the students failed to overthrow the status quo, the effects of the student movement are still visible today. The students were the first in Germany to articulate the need to address Germany's past publicly. They were also the first to use demonstrations, sit-ins and other forms of direct action as tools against the Establishment. They also promoted the first thorough investigations of Germany's past, provoking a sea-change in the way that the Third Reich was discussed in public. No longer was it an issue to be avoided; on the contrary, interest in the Nazi period blossomed like never before.

Attempts to analyse, digest and learn to live with their country's past through a process of *Vergangenheitsbewältigung* (literally 'working through the past') received further impetus when one of Germany's most impressive Federal presidents, Richard von Weizsäcker, made a seminal speech in May 1985 to mark the fortieth anniversary of the end of the Second World War (Weizsäcker, 1985). He referred to this moment not as a day when Germany was defeated by the Allies, but as a liberation from the inhuman system of Nazi tyranny. Von Weizsäcker therefore consciously helped to redefine the meaning of this event as a positive landmark in German history rather than as a point of agony and national defeat, as it had often been referred to before. His words appeared to many to be the final step in a long process of liberation from the guilt associated with Nazism and, somewhat unexpectedly, they helped promote one of the stranger public spats of recent years: the 'Historians' Dispute'.

The Historians' Dispute

Increased interest in Germany's recent past naturally provoked controversial interpretations of what precise lessons Germans should learn from the period. Although the public at large began to take an interest in such questions, these discussions for the most part took place between historians. Normally, such debates would be confined to the ivory towers of university campuses; not in Germany in the 1980s. The so-called 'Historians' Dispute' (*Historikerstreit*) was big news. It was essentially an intellectual and political controversy about the way the Holocaust should be interpreted. Although historians had been arguing about this before it really caught the public imagination, the main thrust of the debate took place between 1986 and 1989 (see Brockmann, 1990).

A new breed of more left-wing historians began to criticise the post-war consensus that underpinned the traditional understanding of Germans' behaviour during the Nazi period. Nazism was conventionally seen as a totalitarian movement that represented only the work of a small criminal clique. Germans therefore were, for the most part, victims of Nazism, and the Nazi era represented a major aberration in German history. A younger generation of historians such as Fritz Fischer began to challenge this assessment in the 1960s, arguing that Nazism was a logical endpoint of the unique nature of German history. Linked with this came further claims that medium- and lower-ranking German officials were not just obeying orders, but actively engaged in the making of the policies that led to the Holocaust. These 'functionalists' thereby cast blame for the Holocaust more widely than had been done previously. This in turn prompted a reaction from more conservative German historians who strongly disliked the implications of both the *Sonderweg* conception of history and the implications of the functionalist analysis. Both of these came to be identified with the left and were, in different ways, seen as being derogatory towards Germany.

This debate took on a new dimension in the mid-1980s. By then, conservative German historians were starting to feel that enough time had passed and Germans could and should start celebrating their history again. Michael Stürmer's article 'Land without History', which was published in the conservative *Frankfurter Allgemeine Zeitung* in April 1986 and bemoaned the absence of a 'positive history' in which Germans could take pride, is a paradigmatic example of this (Stürmer, 1986). The fact that Stürmer was serving as an adviser and speechwriter to the then Chancellor, Helmut Kohl, made his remarks all the more contentious. But the name more closely linked to the *Historiker-streit* is that of the historian Ernst Nolte. On 6 June 1986 he published an article, again in the *Frankfurter Allgemeine Zeitung*, in which he argued that the 'race murder' of the Nazi death camps was a 'defensive reaction' to the 'class murder' of Stalinism. Nolte declared that the gulags were the original, and greater horror, and that faced with of the threat of Bolshevism it was reasonable that the German people had turned to a form of fascism (Nolte, 1986). The left-wing philosopher Jürgen Habermas quickly responded in a more liberal weekly newspaper, *Die Zeit*. He rejected this position, arguing that it could be seized upon as 'a kind of cancelling out of damages' for the Holocaust (Habermas, 1986). In this article Habermas also complained that certain historians, such as Nolte and Stürmer, were too keen to draw a curtain over Germany's troubled past, and that, in itself, was inherently dangerous. After further exchanges by various commentators in the conservative and liberal press (documented in Augstein *et al.*, 1987), the debate did eventually die down and the historians retreated to their campuses. But the effects of this debate were quite clear: German history was put firmly back into the public sphere just as the GDR was collapsing and the issue of German unity was back on the political agenda.

Post-unification Germany and the double legacy of history

The picture now, at the beginning of the twenty-first century, has therefore turned full circle from what it was as late as the early 1960s: few countries in the world are more aware of where they have come from, the mistakes that they have made and the lessons that need to be learned. But even as Germany reunified and the 'unnatural' division was overcome, issues of history refused to disappear. In fact, they reappeared in slightly different guises. With unification in 1990, attitudes to Germany's past proceeded to gain both new relevance and new salience. Germany's neighbours became intensely interested in the self-image of the largest nation in Europe. As stated earlier, they became worried that the much-vaunted 'German Question' was likely to need answering once more. And the Germans themselves were at first very uncertain how they should deal with their newly won political freedom and the larger responsibilities that this inevitably brought with it. Should the self-restrictions that were taken for granted during the division of the country continue? These questions have definitively been answered with Germany's participation in the NATO campaign in Yugoslavia in 1999, but discussions of whether the *Bundeswehr* should go to Afghanistan, Iraq and the Congo illustrate that the past remains important in determining contemporary foreign policy. The fact that it was a centre-left government that took the first steps in this direction is even more noteworthy (see Chapter 10).

Normality and collective memory

Trying to make sense of the role that historical memory plays in shaping contemporary affairs is not a straightforward task. But, in essence, there are two distinct ways in which memories of the past are transmitted between societal groups and between generations, and both have had profound effects on contemporary German politics. On the one hand, communicative memory is a shared memory of the recent past. This is obtained through the social interaction of citizens who remember the events concerned. The scope and extent of communicative memory of the Nazi period is therefore naturally on the wane, while recollections of life in the GDR, for example, remain strong and relevant in shaping the contemporary attitudes of those affected. Cultural memory, on the other hand, is a much more formally constructed version of past events – and it is this type of memory that is intrinsically open to manipulation by groups within society (Assman, 1999; Pearce, 2007). As indicated above, the management of memory in the Federal Republic has periodically come to be seen as controversial and this has become even more so since 1990. Germany found itself compelled to come to terms with the legacies of not just one but two (the Nazi and the East German) dictatorial regimes. Although the dictatorships had fundamentally different ideological goals and adopted different methods in attempting to fulfil them, they both restricted freedoms, denied civil liberties, eliminated the democratic process and, to different extents and in different ways, disposed of their enemies. The challenge of dealing with their different legacies was huge. Post-1990, this was particularly so in eastern Germany, where many citizens (unexpectedly) found their biographies under close examination by many of their western German counterparts (see Chapter 3). The debate has often been tinged with bitterness and recrimination and easterners have found themselves having to defend their existences pre-1989 in a way that many never expected they would have to at the time of unification. Easterners have also openly reflected on the characteristics in their past that *differentiate* them from westerners – in an attempt to relegitimise their own lived experiences (see Chapter 3).

Communicative memory in eastern Germany remains informal, non-structured and inclusive, occurring and recurring through the everyday interaction of eastern German citizens. Cultural memory, which younger eastern Germans are more likely to possess, is much less spontaneous than communicative memory, and relies on *perceptions* of the past rather than *experience* of it. Memory is, by its very essence, a creative process, deliberately selective and often conditioned through the prism of an individual's attitude to current reality – hence the GDR that easterners possess in their minds will be unique to them, rather than a true reflection of reality. Eastern Germans across the age spectrum are in possession of pictures and assumptions about all aspects of the GDR, even if they differ from reality, from the perceptions of other easterners and, most importantly, from western Germans – on account of westerners having no or much reduced linkages to the GDR. Given this, it is not difficult to see why interpretations on the past can differ so much – and therefore why they can prompt such political controversy. (This is discussed with regard to the GDR in Chapter 3.)

Post-1990 Germany also explicitly recognised that the passing of time should not cause one of the darkest moments in human history – the Holocaust – to be erased from public consciousness. But with what means and in what form should memory of it be guarded? In the late 1980s there had been talk of erecting a central monument to remember those who had died at the hands of the Nazi regime in the centre of Berlin. The federal government and the Berlin city government even sponsored a competition to design such a memorial, but the controversy that surrounded the results simply proved how difficult it was to do justice to the memory of such crimes in terms of a single monument. After much head-scratching the architect Peter Eisenman eventually won the right to design the new memorial, in a location right in the heart of the German capital, next to the Brandenburg Gate, emphasising the importance of recalling Germany's darkest hour. It was finally completed in December 2004 and consists of a 19,000-square-metre site covered with 2,711 concrete slabs, arranged in a grid pattern on a sloping field. The slabs are all 95 centimetres wide and vary in height from 20 centimetres to 4.8 metres. According to Eisenman, they are designed to produce an uneasy, confusing atmosphere, and the whole sculpture aims to represent a supposedly ordered system that has lost touch with human reason. An underground museum beneath the memorial holds the names of all known Jewish Holocaust victims, obtained from the Israeli Yad Vashem Museum. The memorial remains the most poignant sign of Germany's willingness – no matter how painful – to confront and defeat the ghosts of its past in order to avoid allowing history to have even the slightest opportunity of repeating itself.

Yet, as time has passed, Germans have also begun to analyse critically some of the more controversial aspects of German history. The evils of the Nazi dictatorship remain at the forefront of Germans' historical understanding, but there has also been a greater willingness to look into, and articulate the interests of, *German* suffering during this period. Public discussions of such prickly issues rarely occurred in pre-1989 Germany. Post-1989 something therefore appears to have changed. This is certainly not a revisionist attempt to rewrite history, but, for example, ongoing debates on a proposed Centre against Expulsions (*Zentrum gegen Vertreibungen*) in Berlin perhaps indicate a willingness to engage more critically with complex historical matters that do not always paint the Germans in an expressly bad light. The centre is intended to analyse expulsions and ethnic cleansing wherever they occur, but there is likely to be a particular emphasis on German expulsions from Central and Eastern Europe following the end of the Second World War. A centre documenting the sufferings of a significant group of people would probably not be particularly controversial in most countries, but one focusing on German suffering at the point in history just after millions of people had been murdered by the Nazi regime obviously provokes strong reactions. Two further examples can be cited. First, Jörg Friedrich, in his characterisation of the bombing of Germany during the war as the 'politics of extermination' (Friedrich, 2002: 93), deliberately equates Allied tactics with the actions of the Nazis. Second, the release of the film 2004 film *Downfall* (*Der Untergang*), directed by Oliver Hirschbiegel and the first German production ever to feature Adolf Hitler as the main character, not only portrayed the dictator in a human light but depicted ordinary Germans as victims in the inferno of Berlin in April 1945. By contrast, a study by the American scholar Daniel Goldhagen (1997) caused a renewed bout of soul-searching in Germany in the late 1990s by claiming that ordinary Germans had participated willingly and actively in the Holocaust. Similarly, an exhibition of the extent of the regular army's involvement in war crimes during the Second World War, the so-called *Wehrmachtsausstellung*, caused intense controversy in the late 1990s by puncturing the hitherto established narrative of the ordinary soldier's integrity in contrast with the atrocities committed by the SS. To be sure, even more than sixty years after the event, such debates over Germans as either perpetrators or victims remain highly controversial, both within Germany and internationally.

Conclusion

The discussion in this chapter has sketched out how Germany has developed in broad historical terms and provided some examples of how, in more recent times, historical memory has been very much at the forefront of public discussions of what it means to be German. Although there are clearly no hard and fast answers to difficult questions of how past experience should shape contemporary political activity, the chapter has indicated that German history is significant when attempting to understand how and why Germany's institutional framework was created and how German politicians seek to answer complex, real-world problems today.

The chapter sets the scene for the book as a whole by linking what has been, for the most part, an unhappy history with some of the main political debates in post-1945 and contemporary Germany. It discussed the development of Germany from its beginnings as a *Kulturnation* through to the end of the Second World War and illustrated that post-war German politicians have not always found it easy to deal with the legacy of this tumultuous history. Originally, they made little attempt to engage actively with Germany's past, and it was only from the 1960s onwards that Germans really began to work through their country's difficult heritage. By the mid-1980s, debates about how Germany's history should be understood became much more mainstream, and although unification, and the accession of the GDR to the Federal Republic in 1990, complicated matters, Germans remain more aware of the need to assess their past critically than do citizens of many other nations. That this is not always an easy task should not be surprising. Equally, however, the fact that Germans appreciate its importance and so are willing to undertake it should afford a quiet reassurance that Germany really has learned the lessons of its difficult history.

Questions for discussion

1 **What is/was the German Question and why has it proven to be so controversial?**
2 **Are Germans victims or perpetrators?**
3 **What impact has the Holocaust had on contemporary German politics?**

Further reading

Dahrendorf, R. (1968), *Society and Democracy in Germany* (London: Weidenfeld & Nicolson). Despite its age, this remains a defining analysis of West Germany's social structure.

Elias, N. (1996), *The Germans: Power Struggles and the Development of Habitus in the Nineteenth and Twentieth Centuries* (Cambridge: Polity Press). One of the most impressive studies of the German nation, encompassing imperial, Weimar, Nazi and West Germany.

Fulbrook, M. (2002), *History of Germany, 1918–2000* (Oxford: Blackwell). A thorough and readable account of German history through the twentieth century.

Pulzer, P. (1997), *Germany, 1870–1945: Politics, State Formation and War* (Oxford: Oxford University Press). A highly accessible discussion of Germany from first unification to collapse.

2 Germany's post-war development, 1945–89

Summary

Germany emerged from the devastation wrought by the Second World War in a desolate state. Many millions were dead and the country itself had been destroyed and discredited, as well as occupied. The end of the war therefore represented *Stunde Null* ('Zero Hour') – the end of the horrors of Nazi Germany and the beginning of West Germany's rehabilitation and gradual reintegration into the European society of states. This chapter outlines the establishment and post-war history of East and West Germany and provides the background for the subsequent chapters dealing with political, economic and social developments in contemporary Germany.

Introduction

The capitulation of Nazi Germany on 8 May 1945 constitutes a complete break in the country's history. After more than five years of war, Germany was completely, and in almost every respect, destroyed. It had, at terrible human cost, been defeated in the most comprehensive of manners. The country was occupied militarily by the victorious Allied nations – the USA, the UK, the Soviet Union and France – and divided into four zones of occupation; the capital, Berlin, was also under four-power government. Millions of homes had been devastated as a result of area bombing, and entire cities such as Hamburg, Cologne and Dresden were little more than accumulations of rubble. Germany's transport infrastructure, as well as industrial and agricultural production, had effectively collapsed. Some twelve million refugees from the eastern territories of East Prussia, Silesia and Pomerania needed to be clothed, fed and housed. Perhaps most devastatingly, Germany as nation was morally bankrupt. For these reasons, May 1945 really does constitute 'Zero Hour' in German history, marking both the end of Nazi rule and the beginning of Germany's long path to rehabilitation.

This development was to take place in difficult circumstances. The emerging stand-off between the USA and the Soviet Union in the context of the Cold War ultimately forced the division of Germany into the Federal Republic, or West Germany, and the German Democratic Republic, or East Germany. Henceforth, the two countries followed quite different paths. Over the course of the 1950s and 1960s, West Germany re-established a liberal, democratic system of government and underwent a remarkable economic recovery. Internationally, it quickly sought to integrate itself both into the Western defence alliance, the North Atlantic Treaty Organisation (NATO), and into the fledgling process of European integration. This contrasted with the GDR, where a communist dictatorship had been established at the outset and where economic development quickly fell far behind that of the West, never to catch up.

This chapter traces the development of Germany during the period 1945–90. Although it also considers the development of the GDR, its primary focus lies on West German post-war history because of the continuity between this and post-unification Germany. This can be subdivided into four distinct eras. The first encompasses the formative period of reconstruction and the establishment of the Federal Republic under its first Chancellor, Konrad Adenauer (1949–63). The second marks the economic recovery by Adenauer's heirs as Chancellor, Ludwig Erhard and Kurt-Georg Kiesinger (1963–9). The third era includes the successive administrations of Willy Brandt and Helmut Schmidt (1969–82), whose periods of office saw the first real attempts to ease tensions between East and West Germany. The fourth corresponds to Helmut Kohl's time in office (1982–1990), leading up to German unification.

Certainly, this chapter does not claim to provide anything other than a summary of post-war German history, so for more in-depth discussion the reader is referred to the multitude of definitive volumes available on this topic (e.g., Pulzer, 1995; O'Dochartaigh, 2003; Fulbrook, 1997 and 2002; Görtemaker, 2004; Jarausch, 2006). In the context of this book, the chapter has two central purposes. First, it indicates how Germany was rehabilitated after the disaster of *Stunde Null*. Second, by outlining the principal axes of political development, it sets the scene for the challenges of transformation which will be discussed in detail in the remainder of the book.

The creation of the West German state, 1945–9

The Federal Republic of Germany emerged as much as a result of the political calculations of the Western Allied powers – the USA, the UK and France – as because of the efforts of the founding fathers of the 'Bonn Republic' in Germany. At the 1945 Potsdam Conference, the USA, the Soviet Union and the UK agreed common goals for Germany as a whole: denazification, demilitarisation, democratisation and decentralisation (the so-called 'four Ds'). The West German and East German states did not come into existence immediately after the conclusion of negotiations in Potsdam, but events in the immediate post-war period and particularly the fundamental differences that were appearing between the Soviet Union and the three Western Allies (most notably the USA) soon gave plenty of indications that a two-state solution was likely to be the only viable medium-term option. The 1947 economic merger, partly out of financial necessity, of the British and US zones was a particularly important step along this path, while the June 1948 currency reform – introducing the new *Deutsche Mark* into the Western zones – also sent a clear signal that economic integration in those zones was going to take place on the basis of market economics, regardless of what the Soviets thought. The currency reform set in motion a chain of events that helped facilitate the much-vaunted West German 'economic miracle' (*Wirtschaftswunder* – see Chapter 7). In response, the Soviet leader, Josef Stalin, imposed a land blockade on the Western sectors of Berlin – which lay deep inside the Soviet zone – between 1948 and 1949. For their part, the Western Allies resolved not to give up Berlin and decided to supply their sectors of the city by air in the so-called Berlin Airlift (*Luftbrücke*). Visions of a solution to Germany's division involving one unified state were now all but pipe dreams.

By summer 1948 relations between the Soviet Union and the three Western powers had effectively broken down. On the invitation of the Allied powers the Minister-Presidents of the newly reconstituted *Länder* in the French, British and American zones met in Koblenz on 8 July to begin discussions on the measures necessary for the creation of a West German state. The Allies' proposals proved highly controversial and difficult to accept on the German side as this implied reciprocal measures in the Soviet zone – thereby accepting that two German states were going to be established. The leader of the Social Democrats, Kurt Schumacher, was a particularly prominent defender of an all-German political solution, rather than contemplating the emergence of two rival political systems on German soil. However, under Allied insistence and after considerable debate among German political elites, an eleven-member constitutional convention (one representative from each of the *Länder*) met at a castle at Herreninsel im Chiemsee in Bavaria to agree on a blueprint for a *Grundgesetz* (Basic Law). The contents of this Basic Law were to be negotiated by the Parliamentary Council (*Parlamentarische Rat*), made up of sixty-five delegates from *Länder* parliaments and five non-voting delegates from Berlin. As its president it elected the former Mayor of Cologne, the then seventy-two-year old Konrad Adenauer, a member of the newly founded centre-right Christian Democratic Union, who went on to become the Federal Republic's first Chancellor.

After strenuous negotiations a majority of the Parliamentary Council agreed the document before submitting it for ratification by the necessary two-thirds majority in each of the *Länder* parliaments (Bavaria refused to ratify the Basic Law, but still chose to join the new Federal Republic); it also received qualified acceptance from the Allied occupying forces. The Basic Law was subsequently promulgated on 23 May 1949 and came into force the next day. Thus, the Federal Republic was established and its legal basis became a defining feature of the West German state. The term 'Basic Law' rather than a German 'constitution' was deliberate, as the document's authors wished to reinforce the provisional nature of the document *in lieu* of an all-German settlement. Similarly, a provisional capital for the new state was chosen in the form of Bonn, a sleepy town south of Cologne most famous for being the birthplace of Beethoven. The Soviet occupiers followed this lead in their part of Germany, and on 7 October 1949 the GDR was founded. It claimed to be a socialist state within the territory of the Soviet zone, showing allegiance to its brother in the East. This completed the formal, institutional division of Germany, and the structures created then remained in place for over forty years, until unification in 1990.

The Basic Law was an explicit and direct attempt to prevent the mistakes of the past recurring. West Germany's founding fathers sought to make a return to the horrors of Nazism as improbable as they possibly could. The political system of the Federal Republic contained numerous checks and balances on executive power to prevent any future concentration of power in the hands of one person, as had been the case under Hitler (see Chapter 4). As well as these internal checks and balances contained within the *Grundgesetz*, the Western Allies maintained their right to comment on all significant aspects of West German policy, namely foreign policy, questions of security, occupation costs, disarmament and demilitarisation, reparations, foreign trade, exchange rates and economic control of heavy industry in the Ruhr Valley, as well as the structure of large businesses and banks. Day-to-day supervision of these areas fell to the Allied High Commission for Germany. Significantly, the cost of maintaining the Allies' presence in

West Germany fell to the Federal Republic, costing the enormous sum of DM4.5 billion, or 36 per cent of West Germany's entire federal budget at the time.

Manfred Schmidt (2003b: 20–1) pinpoints six main strands of the Basic Law which defined the political, social and legal order of West Germany. It outlined the primacy of the *rule of law*, stipulated that West Germany should be a *republic*, organised according to a *federal system*, and should explicitly be a *human rights-based democracy* with an *active social policy* which should work towards the *unification of Europe*. The central institutions of the West German state outlined in the Basic Law were the *Bundestag* (the lower house of parliament), the *Bundesrat* (the upper house of parliament made up of representatives of the *Länder*), the Federal President, the national government and the Federal Constitutional Court (the functioning of the political system is discussed in greater detail in Chapter 4).

Perhaps the most notable aspect of West Germany's political system was its normative dimension. The explicit intent of the Basic Law to create a human rights-based democracy marked a clear break from the Germany of 1933 to 1945. At the same time, the Federal Republic defined itself as a 'militant democracy' (*streitbare Demokratie*), and the Basic Law included a number of provisions, such as the potential for anti-democratic parties to be banned, to ensure that it would never suffer the same fate as the Weimar Republic. German federalism operated on the normative principle that each *Land* should act in the interests of the wider federation, not just its own (see Chapter 4). In foreign policy, West Germany's commitment to work towards the unity of Europe as outlined in the preamble to the Basic Law was a signal of intent to repair relations with its neighbours and break out of the cycle of interstate violence which had dogged Europe for centuries (see Garton Ash, 1994). Significantly, this normative dimension went beyond formal constitutional provisions. The values of the 'social market economy' combined economic liberalism with a strong sense of social responsibility, which found expression in an extensive welfare state (see Chapter 8). In its political style, and partially reflecting the issues mentioned here, consensus politics quickly became a defining characteristic of the new state.

The theory and practice of the political system contained within the Basic Law, principally via federalism and the practice of coalition government, placed extensive constraints on the federal government. This famously led West Germany to be described as internally 'semi-sovereign', although this semi-sovereignty had a very real external dimension too (Katzenstein, 1987). The Cold War division of Germany and the Occupation Statute meant that there was considerable external influence on West Germany which did not formally end until unification in 1990. West Germany's participation in the development of the European Community also resulted in the deliberate sharing of sovereignty in a number of key economic areas (see Chapter 9).

The Adenauer era, 1949–63

Despite the trauma of division, the 1950s and 1960s witnessed a remarkable upturn in the fortunes of the Federal Republic. This contrasted greatly with events in East Germany. The West German state pinned its recovery and stability on espousing a clear anti-communist stance alongside the goal of achieving economic prosperity. Such a policy helped establish West Germany's legitimacy as well as its prosperity, but it made the likelihood of unification seem ever more distant with each passing year. West Germany's rehabilitation and recovery centred on Chancellor Adenauer's policy of integration into the Western community of nations (*Westintegration*). The *Wirtschaftswunder* – economic miracle – of the 1950s and 1960s bolstered the fledgling West German state and spread a sense of optimism within the country which it lacked in the years immediately following 1945: between 1950 and 1960 average annual growth in GDP was a remarkable 8.2 per cent (see Chapter 7). Central to this economic growth was the export market and the strong performance of such companies as Siemens, BMW and Bayer. In terms of relations with neighbours, West Germany and France, having fought no fewer than three wars in the space of seventy years, also made initial steps towards long-term reconciliation during the 1950s and 1960s, culminating in the 1963 Elysée Treaty.

Meanwhile, the development of East Germany was much more problematic. From the outset, it was characterised by the dictatorial and bureaucratic dominance of the Marxist–Leninist Socialist Unity Party (*Sozialistische Einheitspartei Deutschlands*, SED), which had been formed in 1946 at the behest of the Soviet occupiers through a forced merger between the social-democratic SPD and the communist KPD. The SED-led government under a colourless and dour communist apparatchik, Walter Ulbricht, whose main distinction was his unquestioned loyalty to Stalin, quickly set about establishing state ownership of property, a centrally controlled planned economy and a collectivised system of agriculture in the Stalinist mode (Ross, 2000). Power was thus concentrated within the SED, which controlled all aspects of economic, political and social life under the banner of 'democratic centralism'. The *Ministerium für Staatssicherheit* (Ministry for State Security, or colloquially the Stasi) was founded in February 1950, creating a police state that proceeded to collect information on ordinary East Germans in an effort to ensure widespread ideological adherence to the party's (and therefore country's) aims. All of this was overseen by the Soviet Union, which maintained a keen interest in a socialist East Germany as a counterbalance to the West. In response to the remilitarisation of West Germany in 1955 (see below), East Germany established the NVA (National People's Army) and integrated it into the Soviet Union's equivalent of NATO, the Warsaw Pact. Opposition to the SED was vigorously repressed by the East German state through the Stasi and, where necessary, by Soviet troops. Hopes that Stalin's death in 1953 would result in greater freedom for East Germans were dashed when Soviet troops crushed a popular uprising on 17 June 1953 by East Berlin factory workers calling for better working conditions, free elections and eventually the dissolution of the East German government. Although the uprising was successfully contained by the government and the Soviet Union, it underlined the fragility of the GDR's legitimacy (see Chapter 3; Fulbrook, 2000).

In contrast, West Germany's social market economy boomed during the 1950s and 1960s, spurred on by a powerful sense of purpose among ordinary citizens of the FRG. Ludwig Erhard, the cigar-smoking Economics Minister under Adenauer who was later to succeed him as Chancellor, embodied the optimism and prosperity of this time after the hardships of the immediate post-war years. The success of West Germany's economy helped deliver excellent public services, generous working conditions and an all-encompassing welfare state (see Chapters 7 and 8). As a result, West Germany emerged from the ruins of 1945 to become one of the world's leading economies within just twenty-five years. Crucially, this economic success played a decisive role in legitimising not only the Federal Republic but parliamentary democracy to a population numbed by the experience of total war (see Almond and Verba, 1963). Adenauer's CDU, together with its Bavarian sister party the CSU, was the principal political beneficiary of this: in the 1957 federal election the CDU/CSU secured an absolute majority of valid votes cast – a feat not repeated before or since. West Germany's famous victory at the 1954 Football World Cup in Switzerland, when it came from behind to beat Hungary in the final (*Das Wunder von Bern*; see the film of this title directed by Sönke Wortmann in 2003), further symbolised the fact that the country was back on its feet again.

But equally, the importance of European integration in West Germany's reconstruction cannot be ignored. Bulmer and Paterson (1987) rightly note that without West Germany's political integration into the European Community, the country's economic success would have been viewed with suspicion, if not seen as a threat. In 1952 West Germany was a founding member of the European Coal and Steel Community and in 1957 it was a signatory to the Treaty of Rome. These moves were greeted enthusiastically by the founding fathers of European integration, the Frenchmen Robert Schuman and Jean Monnet, who also saw these bodies as vehicles for forging stronger Franco-German ties. At the forefront of French calculations was that France would take the political leadership in European integration and West Germany would provide the economic clout for Europe's recovery. European integration thus provided West Germany with a forum to return to international respectability. The success of German European policy also reinforced in the minds of successive generations of German policy-makers the advantages of multilateral co-operation and the clear limitations of unilateral German endeavours. These crucial points will be discussed further in Chapter 9.

Rehabilitation in the international community as a consequence of Germany's political and economic integration into the European Community was mirrored in West Germany's gradual reacquisition of partial sovereignty. Under the Bonn Agreement (*Deutschlandvertrag*) of 26 May 1952 between the Federal Republic and the Western Allies, the occupation status was formally ended, and (with minor exceptions) full sovereignty in internal and external policy conferred on West Germany. Of course, in reality, the Allied powers retained significant influence over West Germany both politically and through the stationing of large numbers of troops on German soil. At its heart, the treaty called for the remilitarisation of West Germany to play a part in the defence of Western Europe as a member of a European Defence Community. However, efforts to create this were dashed in 1954 by the decision of the French parliament not to endorse supranational defence co-operation, making integration into NATO structures the obvious alternative. The amended *Deutschlandvertrag* came into force in 1955 and accompanied West Germany's integration into NATO. The reacquisition of sovereignty was completed when the Saarland, which borders France and had been under independent French administration since 1945, was returned to West Germany on 1 January 1957 following a referendum.

Throughout the Cold War, West Germany was more a consumer than a producer of security. Despite this, Adenauer's conviction in his policy of *Westintegration* and his concern to contribute to Western security through membership of NATO necessitated German remilitarisation, even though, coming so soon after the end of the Second World War, this was highly contentious in the domestic arena. Indeed, many West Germans hoped that their country would remain completely demilitarised in light of the two world wars that it had begun. Ultimately, though, Adenauer's argument that Germany must contribute to its own defence won out. West Germany's military command was, however, fully integrated into NATO command structures and there were strict constitutional limitations on the use of the new armed forces from 1955. More specifically, they were to be used solely for the defence of German soil and of the NATO area. These safeguards were designed to reassure West Germans and Germany's allies that the *Bundeswehr* would only be used for the good of NATO. Efforts were made to integrate the *Bundeswehr* into West German society as *Staatsbürger in Uniform* – citizens in uniform – through the introduction of compulsory military service and by placing the armed forces under strict parliamentary control. Thus, the central principle of the remilitarisation of Germany ensured that the new armed forces were clearly distinguishable in ethos and organisation from the *Wehrmacht* of Nazi Germany.

In stark contrast to West Germany's policy of *Westintegration*, its relations with the GDR remained decidedly icy. In March 1952, Stalin offered to permit the reunification of Germany on the basis that it remained a neutral state. This offer was rejected as untrustworthy by both the Western Allies and Adenauer. West Germany simply refused to accept the GDR's legitimacy and considered itself to be the only legal successor to pre-1945 Germany – which encompassed the GDR. This even stretched to refusing to use the term 'GDR' in official news bulletins: West Germans were informed of events in the 'Soviet Zone of Occupation' until the 1970s. Known as the *Alleinvertretungsanspruch*, West Germany's claim to speak for all Germans, including those Germans living under the East German regime, affected not only its citizenship policy (see Chapter 6), but its diplomacy. Under the 1957 Hallstein Doctrine, West Germany refused to conduct bilateral relations with states which recognised the GDR. By 1962, the physical division of Germany, in the form of the so-called 'Iron Curtain' on the inner-German border, was complete – the construction of the Berlin Wall began on 13 August 1961 and constituted the last element of this process, following which East Germany was hermetically sealed off from the capitalist West. Nonetheless, Adenauer did work to improve relations with the Soviet Union after Stalin's death, visiting Moscow in 1955, as a result of which the last German prisoners-of-war who were held in the Soviet Union were released. Elsewhere, he also promoted reconciliation with Israel, principally in the form of financial compensation of almost DM3.5 billion in 1952.

Erhard, Kiesinger and the Grand Coalition, 1963–9

Konrad Adenauer's tenure as Chancellor came to an end in 1963 not long after one of his pivotal successes – the signing of the Franco-German Elysée Treaty. On the face of it, his successor, Ludwig Erhard, should have been a symbol of continuity in German politics as he was a member of the same political cadre and was seen to represent the principles which had guided West Germany to recovery. However, Erhard's fame as the father of West Germany's economic miracle was greatly contrasted by his weakness in foreign policy, which was epitomised by his inability to combine a pro-American Atlanticism with a close relationship with France's President Charles de Gaulle in the same way that his predecessor had done. Thus, he found himself caught between the United States and France over the American President John F. Kennedy's proposal to establish a Multilateral (nuclear) Force (MLF) between the USA and Western Europe, which was opposed by France and ultimately led to its withdrawal from NATO operational structures in 1966. Yet, at the same time, Erhard was unable to work constructively with de Gaulle over the reinvigoration of European integration after the 1965 'Empty Chair Crisis', when France boycotted the European Community in protest over the pace of integration. More broadly, Erhard failed to take advantage of the thawing of relations between the USA and the Soviet Union in the aftermath of the Cuban Missile Crisis of 1962 in order to seek improvements in relations between the two German states.

Overall, therefore, the early 1960s did not represent a particularly successful period for West Germany in terms of foreign policy.

Both social attitudes and the general composition of German society began to change during the 1960s. One of the most significant aspects of this was the 'guest worker' (*Gastarbeiter*) programme initiated by the federal government from the 1950s onwards to address the shortage of low-skilled labour in the West German economy. The idea behind the programme was that workers would come to Germany for a fixed term to fill a gap in the labour market before returning to their countries of origin. However, with the slowdown in the world economy from the early 1970s onwards, all recruitment was ended in November 1973. Nonetheless, some four million foreigners, most of whom were *Gastarbeiter* and their families, remained in West Germany after the end to recruitment and today they form the rump of its immigrant population. This and subsequent sources of immigration prompted long-running debates over citizenship and identity, and above all over the question of whether (West) Germany is a country of immigration (*Einwanderungsland*). These issues are discussed in depth in Chapter 6 (see also Green, 2004).

Meanwhile, the 1960s also saw the GDR's economic system come under enormous pressure as the FRG's economy continued to far outstrip that of the East. Between 1949 and 1961, some 2.7 million East Germans, many of whom were young, skilled craftsmen, fled the GDR, leaving its economy desperately short of key workers. The construction of the Berlin Wall in 1961 stemmed the flow of refugees, but the economy remained significantly weakened. In response, Ulbricht developed a 'new economic system' (*Neues Ökonomisches System*) in an attempt to boost productivity by decentralising some decision-making, thereby bending the Marxist–Leninist principles of democratic centralism on which the state had been founded. Although these reforms did generate some success, enabling the GDR by 1970 to become the second-strongest economy in the Eastern Bloc, it continued to lag far behind West Germany on more or less every level. When combined with the fact that Ulbricht's economic reforms effectively called into question the absolute supremacy of the SED, the failure of the GDR to keep up with the FRG sparked a heated ideological discussion both within the SED itself and between the GDR and the Soviet Union. On top of this, the West German government's *Ostpolitik* (see below), together with a general thawing in relations between the superpowers, served to isolate Ulbricht's unbending refusal to contemplate change. On 3 May 1971 he was forced to resign under pressure from leading figures within the SED. He was replaced by Erich Honecker, who was to lead the GDR until its final days in late 1989.

Despite a resounding success at the 1965 federal election, the CDU/CSU–FDP government was split by domestic and foreign policy problems which ultimately would bring Erhard's chancellorship and the entire coalition to a premature end. In 1966 the catalyst proved to be the federal budget for the following year, which the liberal FDP rejected; it then decided to withdraw from government altogether. The CDU/CSU was, however, unwilling to call fresh elections after just one year – after all, the frequency of elections in the early 1930s had been one of the factors behind the Weimar Republic's loss of credibility. Instead, they formed a government with the only other party in parliament, the SPD. Because this consisted of the two largest parties, it became known as the 'Grand Coalition' and, under the leadership of a new Chancellor, Kurt-Georg Kiesinger (of the CDU), it enjoyed a massive majority in both chambers of parliament. It also marked the first time in West Germany's political history that the SPD participated in the federal government. The Grand Coalition's first task was to address a prospective recession which hit during 1967 and saw the economy contract for the first time since 1949. Moreover, unemployment rose to nearly 700,000 – an almost inconceivably high figure at that time. These economic problems were, however, swiftly overcome, and real GDP growth rose rapidly again in 1968 and 1969, hitting 5.5 and 7.5 per cent, respectively.

More broadly, the absence of any effective parliamentary opposition proved a real challenge to West German parliamentary democracy. This took two main forms. On the one hand, the extreme-right *Nationaldemokratische Partei Deutschlands* (National Democratic Party of Germany, NPD), which had been founded in 1964 as a successor to other neo-Nazi groups, was able to make some electoral headway in the late 1960s. During this period, the NPD had significant electoral success in state elections in Rhineland-Palatinate, Schleswig-Holstein, Lower Saxony and Bremen, the pinnacle of which came when it scored 9.8 per cent of the vote in the 1968 *Land* election in Baden-Württemberg. However, in the 1969 federal election it narrowly failed to secure the 5 per cent of the vote necessary for representation in the *Bundestag*, and after that returned to its relatively inconsequential position on the outer reaches of the party system (see Chapter 5).

The other challenge came from the left, in the form of the so-called 'Extra-parliamentary Opposition' (*Außerparlamentarische Opposition*, APO). This was a highly diffuse coalition of interests, but was largely associated with the West German student movement of the late 1960s, which itself emerged within the context of student protests in France and the United States. In West Germany, however, the issue of generational change was particularly significant: the '68ers' (as they came to be called) were the first generation to have been too young to have had any direct memories of either Nazi Germany or the Second World War. As this generation grew up, it became disillusioned with what it saw as the failure of the Federal Republic to address its Nazi past, as well as with the apparent impunity with which many ex-Nazis continued to live in the country (see Chapter 1, pp. 14–15).

Beyond this, the APO and the students also had a number of other grievances, in particular a fear that West Germany was about to relapse into an authoritarian state. In that context, the passing of laws in 1969 under which civil liberties could be suspended in national emergencies (*Notstandsgesetzgebung*) seemed to provide further evidence that the Grand Coalition was seeking to quell dissenting voices within society. In addition, the students strongly disagreed with West Germany's foreign policy and the government's support of American involvement in the Vietnam War. The student movement also campaigned against the conservative publisher Axel Springer's dominance of the West German press, and notably the influence of Europe's largest-selling tabloid, the *Bild Zeitung*. Nobel Prize-winning playwright Heinrich Böll's 1974 work *Die verlorene Ehre der Katherina Blum* (*The Lost Honour of Katharina Blum*) was an expression of this view that Springer-published newspapers were dangerously influential in West German society.

The intellectual basis of the APO was neo-Marxist. Its exponents included the philosophers Herbert Marcuse, Karl Jaspers and Jürgen Habermas, as well as Böll and fellow-author Günter Grass. This 'New Left' sought to advance Marxist policies without the ideological baggage of the Cold War stand-off and proved to be the breeding ground for many of Germany's future leading centre-left politicians. The student movement was organised largely around a loose amalgamation of the various University student unions (AStA). Other key organisations included the *Sozialistischer Deutscher Studentenbund* (SDS) and its leaders, Rudi Dutschke and Bernd Rabehl. West Berlin, where conscription was not practised and which thus became a Mecca for draft dodgers, emerged as the main hot-bed of activity.

The process of radicalisation of the student movement is usually linked to one particular event in June 1967 at the *Deutsche Oper* in West Berlin, when a student, Benno Ohnesorg, was killed by a police officer while protesting against a visit by the Shah of Persia. Thereafter, student protests became more radical, often resulting in street violence. This ultimately led to a split within the movement with those advocating violence going underground and forming their own organisations, and the more peaceful students joining the ranks of the SPD and the fledgling ecologist movement in an attempt to change the political system from within. The Red Army Faction, a group of left-wing urban guerrillas who espoused violence and kidnapping as legitimate means to bring down the West German state, was the most prominent legacy of this split (the Foreign Minister from 1998 to 2005, Joschka Fischer, flirted with this violent fringe during his youth in Frankfurt, when he was often involved in street battles with the police). Left-wing terrorism subsequently became a major issue in domestic politics during the 1970s and will be returned to below.

Consolidation under the SPD–FDP coalition, 1969–82

The SPD's rise to become the senior partner in government following the 1969 election owes much to the political opportunism of its then leader, Willy Brandt, and the impulses towards co-operation that had emerged between the SPD and the FDP during the late 1960s in the last months of the Grand Coalition. Brandt saw in the FDP a party with which the SPD could do business for three specific reasons. First, the FDP had been supportive of the nomination of the SPD's candidate, Gustav Heinemann, as Federal President in 1969. In addition, it had gone through a process of reassessing its policy on relations with the GDR and the East – something that appealed to Brandt in particular as this was an issue where he held particularly strong views. Lastly, Brandt had governed with the FDP during his time as Mayor of Berlin, and this had largely proven to be a positive experience. For these reasons, he formed a coalition with the FDP following the SPD's strong showing at the 1969 election. If the 1968 student protests marked a defining moment in German society, the SPD's rise to power must be seen in the same context, as a clear signal of change in the Federal Republic – in other words, a new era in West German politics.

Ostpolitik, West Germany's policy towards the East, was to be the defining policy of Willy Brandt's period as Chancellor. At its heart lay the decision to construct better relations between the two German states. The intellectual visionary of *Ostpolitik*, Brandt's foreign policy adviser Egon Bahr, had advocated a policy of *Wandel durch Annäherung* – 'change through proximity' – since July 1963. Brandt and Bahr achieved this through, first, the pursuit of improved relations between Bonn and Moscow. This facilitated Brandt's attempts to establish better relations with other Central European states before he could tackle relations with the GDR. The pursuit of Brandt and Bahr's *Ostpolitik* was undertaken under the strictest conditions of secrecy for fear of alarming West Germany's allies. In October 1969, the same month in which the SPD–FDP coalition took power, Brandt made the tentative suggestion that West Germany would be willing to establish diplomatic relations with East Germany, thus legitimising at least in practice the existence of a second German state and breaking a previously held taboo of West German politics. He followed this by meeting Willi Stoph, the East German Prime

Minister, in the East German town of Erfurt on 19 March 1970. This emotional first contact was followed by a meeting between the two leaders in Kassel in West Germany on 21 May. These discussions were early steps in 'normalising' relations between both German states and included initial tentative negotiations for a treaty between the two. Only after Brandt had clarified relations with the Soviet Union (in the Moscow Treaty of 12 August 1970) and Poland (in the Warsaw Treaty of 7 December 1970, which confirmed Poland's western border) were East and West Germany able to conduct full negotiations on their own bilateral treaty (*Grundlagenvertrag*), which began in 1972. Establishing such an agreement between East and West Germany was complicated by suspicions between the two states caused by renewed Cold War tensions, but also because the Western Allied powers and the Soviet Union retained significant influence over East and West German affairs. Thus, relations between East and West Germany and Brandt's wider attempts to forge better East–West relations were a delicate balancing act between achieving German aims and not fuelling fears of German motives.

Brandt came under intense pressure on account of *Ostpolitik*, particularly from the CDU/CSU, who claimed that, rather than smoothing the way to eventual unity, the Basic Treaty had forestalled all hope of unification. Indeed, as a result of *Ostpolitik*, a number of FDP parliamentarians defected to the CDU/CSU, to such an extent that, by April 1972, Brandt had formally lost his parliamentary majority. The opposition CDU/CSU then tried to topple him by means of a 'constructive vote of no-confidence', which allows a government to be replaced by another but without new elections (see Chapter 4). However, in a moment of the highest political drama, Brandt survived the vote. Subsequently, it was alleged that the East German Stasi had bribed certain CDU parliamentarians to vote with the SPD-led government. Following this vote, Brandt did call an early election, and in probably the most passionately contested poll in post-war German history, in which turnout exceeded 90 per cent, the SPD won handsomely in a ringing public endorsement of *Ostpolitik*. The signing of the *Grundlagenvertrag* on 21 December 1972 facilitated a genuine relaxation in FRG–GDR relations. As well as establishing de facto diplomatic relations between the two countries, the agreements eased mail and telephone traffic, agreed road transit routes between West Germany and West Berlin and promoted co-operation between the governments on such issues as the economy, health, science and technology, culture and sport. In a sign of the new era of détente, East and West Germany finally met on the football pitch in a game in the 1974 World Cup finals in Hamburg. East Germany famously won 1–0, but West Germany eventually went on to win the World Cup itself. The new era in FRG–GDR relations was epitomised by both countries' admittance to the United Nations in 1973, and by their participation in the landmark Conference on Security and Co-operation in Europe (CSCE) between 1973 and 1975.

The *Grundlagenvertrag* also marked a personal triumph for Brandt: he was awarded the Nobel Peace Prize in 1971 and *Ostpolitik* remains the key legacy of his chancellorship. Ironically, though, it also proved to be the cause of his downfall, when he was forced to resign in 1974 after his close adviser, Günter Guillaume, was revealed to be a Stasi informer. His successor was Helmut Schmidt (also of the SPD), a highly capable politician who quickly earned a reputation for skilful crisis management.

In domestic politics, a number of developments were notable. First, the issue of left-wing terrorism dogged the SPD–FDP government throughout the 1970s. By 1972, its initial leaders, Andreas Baader and Ulrike Meinhof, were both behind bars. However, a new generation of RAF activists and sympathisers arose to conduct a campaign of violence against German and US military targets during the mid-1970s, including an assault on the German Embassy in Stockholm in 1975 and the assassination of the Federal Prosecutor Siegfried Buback in April 1977. This culminated in the so-called *Deutscher Herbst* of 1977, when the RAF kidnapped the leader of the national employers' organisation, Hanns-Martin Schleyer, with the aim of securing the release of eleven RAF members and ultimately bringing down the West German government. The federal government refused to negotiate, which in turn prompted a Palestinian terrorist cell to hijack a Lufthansa jet with the same demands. However, the federal government decided to order the storming of the jet by West German special forces on 18 October 1977 in the Somali capital of Mogadishu, where it had landed. That same night, the main RAF leaders in jail, including Andreas Baader, committed suicide. Schleyer's body was found in France shortly thereafter (see Aust, 1998).

Although the RAF was never again to challenge the authority of the federal government so directly, it continued to operate for another twenty-one years, notably assassinating the head of the Deutsche Bank, Alfred Herrhausen, in 1989, before it finally disbanded in 1998. However, even today its activities and role remain very much an open scar on German society. On the one hand, the government was criticised for overreacting to the threat of terrorism, by for instance limiting the amount of contact time between terrorist suspects and their lawyers – something that RAF sympathisers seized upon as evidence of the inherently fascist nature of the West German state. On the other hand, the early release of Brigitte Mohnhaupt in 2007, who as leader of the RAF's so-called 'second generation' played a pivotal role in the events of 1977, provoked highly polarised reactions in Germany, especially as most of the terrorists' murders remain technically unsolved. More broadly, the principles of the 1968 generation remain a theme in German political culture to this day, with many leading left-wing politicians having cut their political teeth in the radical left milieu of the 1960s and 1970s. For instance, a further key figure on the political left, Otto Schily, who was Federal Interior Minister from 1998 to 2005, was active in the SDS during in the 1960s and went on to defend Gudrun Ensslin, one of the leading RAF members who committed suicide in 1977.

In economic and social policy, the SPD–FDP governments of the 1970s extended welfare provision considerably, leading to a significant increase in public expenditure (see Chapter 7). In social policy, the government passed a landmark abortion law in 1975, but only after a heated debate and a challenge in the Constitutional Court. Economically, West Germany's rates of growth failed to reach the dizzy heights of the 1950s and early 1960s, as the economy encountered a number of significant difficulties. These included another recession during 1975 and an unemployment rate that exceeded one million people for the first time in twenty years.

Despite these pressures and as a way to try to confront the challenges facing Germany, the SPD–FDP government in 1976 put in place a much wider definition of co-determination (*Mitbestimmung*), which subsequently became one of the defining pillars of the social market economy (see Chapter 7). The role of the state in the German economy continued to grow during the 1970s largely on account of worsening economic conditions that stemmed from the oil crisis of 1973. In January 1976, unemployment stood at a record 1,351,000 or 5.9 per cent of the German workforce.

The late 1970s also witnessed a sharp deterioration in East–West relations which threatened to undo the successes of the *Grundlagenvertrag*. The Soviet Union's decision to invade Afghanistan in 1979 led first President Carter and then President Reagan to increase US military spending. On top of this, both superpowers decided to station medium-range nuclear missiles in Europe, thereby increasing fears in West Germany that it would be a target in a strategic nuclear war. The NATO 'Dual-Track' decision of 12 December 1979 outlined the deployment of 108 Pershing II missiles in Europe to counter the Soviet SS-20 deployment but also called for new arms reduction talks with the Soviet Union. However, in light of the Afghanistan invasion, the US Senate refused to sanction the pursuit of arms reduction talks. Chancellor Schmidt was therefore faced with a significant foreign policy dilemma. The SPD–FDP government faced growing opposition from the West German peace movement over the Dual-Track decision, but it needed to demonstrate its loyalty to NATO in this period of significant cooling of East–West relations. In the end, Schmidt decided to consent to the Dual-Track decision despite the domestic criticism. In light of intense US pressure and despite West German peace demonstrations, Pershing II mid-range nuclear weapons arrived on German soil in November 1983, after Schmidt's successor, Helmut Kohl (of the CDU), confirmed their deployment.

The uncertainty caused by the Cold War stand-off subsequently played a major role in galvanising left-wing social movements within West Germany, ultimately leading to the foundation of the anti-establishment, radical Green Party (*Die Grünen*) in 1980. These new social movements, which developed largely out of the 'New Left', embraced alternative lifestyles, women's rights and especially the right to abortion, ecological issues, pacifism and opposition to nuclear power. The Dual-Track decision presented the Greens with a rallying cry against renewed nuclear build-up in Europe. After its founding by figures such as Petra Kelly, Otto Schily (who would leave the party for the SPD in 1989) and Joschka Fischer, the Green Party took only three years to gain representation in the *Bundestag*. Its emergence represented a significant development in the German party system and a shift in the political concerns of the electorate (see Chapter 5). The emergence of social movements was a phenomenon witnessed not only in West Germany but in the GDR, albeit to a lesser extent. Indeed, as will be discussed in Chapter 3, these new social movements played a central role in overthrowing the SED in East Germany.

Ultimately, it was differences on economic policy which brought the SPD–FDP government to an end and led the FDP to pursue coalition negotiations with the CDU/CSU after Helmut Schmidt lost a vote of confidence in the *Bundestag* on 5 February 1982. On 1 October 1982, following a successful constructive vote of no confidence, he was replaced by Helmut Kohl at the head of a new CDU/CSU–FDP administration.

The Kohl era and the road to unification, 1982–9

The CDU/CSU therefore returned to federal government after thirteen years in opposition. Its leader, Helmut Kohl, saw himself as the direct heir of Adenauer's legacy – socially conservative, economically liberal and pro-European integration. Indeed, in his statement to the *Bundestag* outlining government policy in 1983, Kohl famously referred to the change in government as a '*geistig-moralische Wende*' ('spiritual and moral reorientation').

However, in domestic policy there was little in the way of substantive change and indeed considerable continuity with the policies of the previous government (Katzenstein, 1987). One of the self-declared aims of the new government was to reduce immigration, which had become a major political issue in the 1980 federal election campaign. But despite introducing a scheme for voluntary repatriation, it was unable to achieve its goal of reducing the number of foreign residents by one million. Instead, the pressure to address the legal status of immigrants, for instance through citizenship, increased as the residence periods of non-nationals lengthened (see Chapter 6).

Economically, West Germany made a tentative recovery after a further recession in 1982, although real growth rates remained below 3 per cent until 1988. With traditional heavy industry struggling to compete with Asian economies, unemployment also remained high, and stood at just over two million in 1989. During the 1980s, West Germany's gradual economic slowdown to a relatively low level led to debates about the country's long-term viability as a production location (*Standortdebatte*). Much of this debate focused on whether labour and welfare costs were simply too high to be competitive internationally. Yet the unions chose to politicise the issue of a reduction in working time, with the main union, IG Metall, fighting (and failing) in 1985 to secure a standard thirty-five-hour working week. It was also a period of welfare retrenchment, as social spending as a percentage of GDP fell from almost 31 per cent in 1982 to just under 28 per cent in 1990 (see Chapter 8). In other areas of policy, the environment continued to gain in importance as a political issue, and following the Chernobyl nuclear accident in 1986 the Federal Ministry for the Environment was founded.

Domestically, the Kohl government was completely overshadowed by one of the most spectacular episodes in recent West German history: the so-called Flick Scandal. In 1983 it emerged that the industrialist Friedrich Karl Flick had been making illegal donations to all of the main parties except the Greens. This raised the spectre of endemic long-term corruption in the German political system, and several key protagonists, including Kohl, revealed themselves under questioning to have extraordinarily poor memories of any such donations. Although no link between Flick's money and government policy was ever proven, the affair shook public confidence in the political class. The issue of illegal political donations was to return in 2000, when a network of undeclared funds was uncovered within the CDU. Chapter 5 discusses corruption and public disaffection with the political system in more detail.

In foreign policy, Kohl held firm to traditional principles through his dual commitment to European integration and close German–US relations. He enjoyed harmonious relations with the American President Ronald Reagan, although he courted controversy by escorting Reagan in 1985 to a cemetery in Bitburg in which Waffen SS soldiers had been buried as well as US troops. He also struck up a warm relationship with the French President François Mitterrand, and the Franco-German alliance became the motor of European integration once more. During the 1980s, great strides forward were taken, principally the 1986 Single European Act which provided the framework for the completion of the internal market by the end of 1992.

Meanwhile, the GDR was stumbling from crisis to crisis. Although the economic reforms of the 1960s had delivered some improvements in its economic situation, consumer goods remained extremely scarce. The demand for housing too remained acute; much of the housing stock outside Berlin had scarcely seen any renovations since before the Second World War and it was by now literally crumbling. More immediately pressing, the GDR was heavily hit by the increase in world oil prices post-1973, after which the Soviet Union, which supplied most of the GDR's energy needs, stopped subsidising its oil, coal and gas sales. In response, the SED government expanded domestic production of brown coal for use in its power stations. But this in turn had the disadvantage of being extremely damaging environmentally, and during the 1980s many East German cities were covered with a semi-permanent blanket of brown coal smog. Crucially, with energy costs rising, and spending on consumer goods, social welfare and internal security unable to be cut for political reasons, industrial investment slowed to a trickle, thereby further reducing economic output. The fragility of the country's infrastructure was cruelly exposed in the winter of 1978–9, when unusually cold weather caused, first, the entire transport system to collapse and, then, domestic electricity production to collapse, leaving the GDR in a blackout.

By the late 1970s, therefore, the GDR was caught in spiral of rising expenditure demands and falling industrial output. It attempted to close the gap through loans, principally from West German financial institutions and guaranteed by the West German government. In return, the GDR was forced to open itself gradually to the West, for instance by allowing more family visits and exchanges between the two countries. In 1987, in a reflection of the GDR's growing financial dependency on West Germany, Honecker made his first and only state visit to the Federal Republic. By 1989, the GDR's indebtedness to West Germany was estimated to amount to almost DM50 billion in prices of the day. Given the deterioration in the real exchange rate between the GDR's currency and the 'hard' *Deutsche Mark*, servicing the interest payments on this debt became ever more difficult, and by 1989 the GDR was, to all intents and purposes, bankrupt (see Kopstein, 1997).

The GDR's international context was changing, too. The Soviet Union had already refused to bale out the SED government economically via lowering energy prices. But under its new leader Mikhail Gorbachev, who took power in 1985, the hard-line Stalinist regime in East Berlin also lost its political protection, as Gorbachev promoted internal restructuring of the Soviet Union in an (ultimately forlorn) attempt to stabilise its economy. This included a more open approach to the West. Gorbachev's reforms encouraged the embryonic peace and ecological movements in the GDR to become more vocal in their calls for change. However, the SED leadership refused to countenance any real reforms and, by 1989, in the light of changes in Hungary, Czechoslovakia and Poland, Honecker was increasingly isolated within the Eastern Bloc.

Conclusion

This chapter has shown broadly how West Germany sought to rehabilitate itself after the disaster of Nazi rule in political, economic and international terms. By any standards, this process of rehabilitation was extraordinarily successful and stands in stark contrast to the development of the GDR, with its crumbling economy and complete lack of popular legitimacy.

The chapter has also identified some of the key trends which will reappear later. As early as the mid-1980s, there were fears that West Germany was living beyond its means and that labour and welfare costs were simply too high in international terms. Immigration had become a hot political topic, and it has remained so ever since. The arrival of the Green Party heralded a change both in the structure and ideological composition of the party system. Corruption and political scandals were becoming commonplace. Although largely hidden from public view, the GDR's economy was in a parlous state and much weaker than most in the West believed. All of these themes will be discussed in greater detail in subsequent chapters. Together, they form the challenge of transformation facing Germany in the twenty-first century.

Questions for discussion

1 Why did Konrad Adenauer espouse a policy of integration with the West?
2 What was the impact of the student movement of the late 1960s on West German society?
3 What are the main reasons behind the emergence of constitutional patriotism in West Germany?

Further reading

Fulbrook, M. (1997), *Anatomy of a Dictatorship: Inside the GDR, 1949–89* (Oxford: Oxford University Press). Standard English-language text on the German Democratic Republic.

Jarausch, K. (2006), *After Hitler: Recivilizing Germans, 1945–1995* (Oxford: Oxford University Press). Offers a cultural analysis of post-war German society.

Katzenstein, P. (1987), *Policy and Politics in West Germany: The Growth of a Semisovereign State* (Philadelphia, Penn.: Temple University Press). A landmark analysis of German politics up to and including the mid-1980s.

Winkler, H. (2002), *Der lange Weg nach Westen* (Munich: C.H. Beck). A magisterial treatment of German history.

3 Towards German unity?

Summary

This chapter has three purposes. First, it analyses life in the GDR before discussing, second, how East Germany collapsed and the unification of the two German states took place. It then moves on to analyse both the legacy of this unification process, especially in economic terms, as well as identity politics in post-unification Germany. The experience of living in the GDR, of seeing it collapse and of entering a new state contributed to many former citizens of the GDR developing (perhaps subconsciously) rather different sets of attitudes, values and interests to their western German counterparts. These have come together to create what some authors believe is a unique eastern German identity. This chapter assesses what this identity may be and what – if anything – it means for contemporary German politics.

Introduction

'The [Berlin] Wall', former East German leader Erich Honecker proclaimed on 19 January 1989, 'will be standing in 50 and even in 100 years if the reasons for it are not removed.' Those 'reasons' included, according to Honecker, the need 'to protect our Republic from thieves, not to mention those who are prepared to disturb stability and peace in Europe' (quoted in Hamilton, 1989: 176). Little did he know that within barely ten months the Berlin Wall would be consigned to history. Honecker was not the only person who failed to foresee the collapse of his dearly beloved GDR, and he certainly was not alone in failing to predict the rapid speed with which East and West Germany united. This chapter analyses how these events came to pass. In late 1989, as Easterners were dancing on top of the Wall and enjoying what for many was their first taste of life in the capitalist West, most people expected that – after a few teething problems – Germans would unite and prosper in one state.

In many ways, as is illustrated throughout this book, this has indeed happened: despite a number of economic and political difficulties very few people openly seek to undermine Germany's constitutional framework and even fewer people want to return to the GDR. A lurch towards ideological extremism the like of which took place in the Weimar years has not taken place. But this does not mean that there have been no difficulties. Economic problems, the inability to push through political reforms in important areas such as pensions, social spending, immigration and federalism, and an increasing general disaffection with politics have all become much more prevalent in recent years. Furthermore, the question of whether Germany has enough 'inner unity' (Veen, 1997) has arisen. The social, political and particularly economic divides between the eastern and western *Länder* have prompted many people to wonder if the constitutional unification of Germany is masking genuine divides between a much poorer, moody and dissatisfied east and a richer, less moody and more phlegmatic west.

In order to make sense of these differences we have to start by analysing what came before unification. Chapter 2 concentrated primarily on explaining how West Germany developed in the years 1949–89, as well as sketching out the main stages of the GDR's historical progression. This chapter turns the analytical focus on to the GDR and examines a number of the most important aspects of life in East Germany before moving on to discuss how the state collapsed and then how unification took place. Only when these processes have been adequately understood can we move on to analyse not just the socio-economic challenges that these two parts of Germany face (which will be outlined here but are explored further in subsequent chapters) but the role that identity politics now plays in this. The experience of living in the GDR (or in West Germany), of experiencing (or observing from afar) it collapse and then of entering a new state (or of having lots of new people become citizens of your own) have contributed to the crystallisation of different self-understandings. Many citizens of what was East Germany developed (perhaps subconsciously) rather different attitudes, values and interests to their western German counterparts, and they were disappointed with what they perceived as the reluctance of some West Germans to embrace them (Roberts, 1991). These differences have come together to form what some authors believe is a unique eastern German identity. This chapter concludes by assessing what – if anything – these multiple identities mean for contemporary German politics.

Background

As was discussed in Chapter 2, both West and East Germany were established in 1949. The FRG was created in the Western zones of occupation in May, while the GDR was founded in the Soviet zone on 7 October. East Berlin was named the latter's capital. It was declared fully sovereign by the Soviet Union in 1955, although Soviet troops remained in the country on the basis of the Four-Power Agreement signed at Potsdam for the remainder of its history, only completely withdrawing in 1994.

Following the Second World War, most of the early leaders of the GDR returned to Germany from exile in the Soviet Union. They came as true believers in the Soviet model of governance and they wasted little time setting up a Stalinist-type system in the newly created state. Although Wilhelm Pieck, a trusted ally of Stalin who fled to Russia in 1935, was President of the GDR from 1949 to 1960 (the position was abolished on his death), the Leipziger Walter Ulbricht quickly rose to be the most prominent politician in East Germany, taking on the positions of General Secretary of the SED's Central Committee (from 1950) and later First Secretary (from 1953) (see Box 3.1).

Ulbricht and his colleagues realised that if East Germany was ever going to gain any sort of popular legitimacy then it had to convince its citizens that the first attempt to create socialism on German soil would see the GDR competing with West Germany in terms of generating economic wealth and ensuring peace and prosperity. But it became clear from an early stage that this was going to be an exceptionally difficult task. The

---

BOX 3.1 THE GDR

Established	7 October 1949
Treaty on Final Settlement (i.e., Unification Treaty) signed	25 September 1990
Unification Day	3 October 1990
Capital	East Berlin
Heads of State	
• 1949–60	Wilhelm Pieck
• 1990	Sabine Bergmann-Pohl
First Secretaries/General Secretaries of the Central Committee	
• 1950–71	Walter Ulbricht
• 1971–89	Erich Honecker
• 1989	Egon Krenz
Area	108,333 km^2 (41,828 sq. miles)
Population (1990, estimate)	16,111,000
Currency	East German Mark

---

increasing gap between the social, economic and political lives of East and West German citizens soon led many Easterners to look enviously at the progress that their neighbours were making (see Chapter 2). Unsurprisingly, many citizens of the GDR quickly became disillusioned with a number of aspects of their own lives, and a steady stream of them – between 2.5 and 3 million between the years 1949 and 1961 – chose to flee to the West. This ongoing emigration of East Germans worried the party leadership immensely. Although the inner-German border was largely closed by the mid-1950s, the borders between the sectors in Berlin were relatively easy to cross. Due to the lure of higher salaries in the West, many skilled workers (such as doctors) crossed into West Berlin, causing a veritable brain drain in the East. East German troops were eventually told to seal the border between West and East Berlin and, on 13 August 1961, the most famous landmark of the Cold War, the Berlin Wall, was built to keep East Germans hemmed in their own country.

Life in the GDR

The official rhetoric of the GDR was that it was a socialist state of workers and farmers. It had broken with the destructive forces of capitalism and it based its development on detailed planning and the command economy. The state, and therefore SED apparatchiks, established production targets and prices. They allocated resources, and set all of their decisions down in a comprehensive five-year plan, the first of which was introduced in 1952. The means of production were almost entirely state owned. In 1985, for example, state-owned collectives earned 96.7 per cent of total net national income. To secure consistent prices, the state bore around 80 per cent of the costs of basic supplies such as bread and housing.

The GDR remained the USSR's most loyal pupil in both domestic and international affairs. Although the Soviets stripped the GDR of much of its industrial base in the late 1940s, a consistently pro-Moscow regime relentlessly expressed its loyalty to the Soviet-led socialist cause. The East German citizenry was much less enthusiastic and it did not take it long to realise that the road to socialist utopia was, at best, going to be a long and tricky one. In the immediate aftermath of war, there is little doubt that a significant number of East Germans *did* believe in the aims of their government – they were desperate not to repeat the mistakes of the past and saw egalitarian societal structures and careful economic planning as the means to achieve both peace and prosperity. By 1953, at the latest, however, many realised that the state was clearly not delivering on its aims. Elections to the GDR parliament, the *Volkskammer*, were nothing more than shams, and democratic competition and freedom of speech were stifled. The positive narrative that the government produced through newspapers such as *Neues Deutschland* and the electronic media seemed, for many, to be far removed from the reality of persistent shortages and little visible sign of economic progress that they were experiencing themselves. Citizens also became increasingly aware that criticising the government could lead to difficulties for the individual concerned and avenues to articulate dissent became ever more restricted – as was illustrated most graphically by the crushing of a workers' uprising in 1953 (see Chapter 2, p. 25). In May 1953, the SED regime increased the work quotas for East German industry by 10 per cent. On 16 June, between sixty and eighty construction workers in East Berlin went on strike after their bosses announced a pay cut if they failed to meet their respective work goals. News of this quickly spread and, remarkably, a general strike and a series of protests were called for the next day. One hundred thousand protesters gathered in East Berlin alone and stoppages and protests of some sort took place in most of East Germany's larger cities.

The original demands of the protesters, such as the reinstatement of the previous lower work quotas, turned into political demands. Initially, SED functionaries took to the streets and began arguing with small groups of protesters. Eventually, though, the workers demanded the resignation of the government, which consequently decided to use force to stop the uprising, turning to the Soviet Union for military support. It is still unclear how many people died during the uprising, and through the death sentences that followed. The official number of victims is fifty-one, but research conducted post-1989, when more official documents became available, indicated that the true figure was well over a hundred. The extent of the propaganda disaster for the GDR government remains, of course, unquantifiable, but suffice it to say that a possible repetition of the uprising remained the ultimate nightmare for the SED during the life of East Germany.

The Berlin Wall

A government sending troops in to shoot its own citizens should have been more than enough evidence of the GDR's moral and ethical bankruptcy. Even though logistical reasons meant that leaving the GDR was not an option for many, events such as those in the summer of 1953 were important milestones in creating a 'virtual identity' as Easterners looked increasingly westwards when evaluating their own lives. The widespread jubilation that was evident in the GDR in 1954, for example, when the West German football team won the World Cup in Switzerland, was particularly strong evidence of this. Many East Germans were able to adjust their antennas and watch West German TV (only citizens in the south-east corner of the GDR, around Dresden in the so-called *Tal der Ahnungslosen* – 'Valley of the Clueless' – were, by virtue of their disadvantageous geographical position, denied this privilege) and therefore were well informed about how badly their state was lagging behind its western neighbour.

However, even those who were still prepared to defend the regime's actions in June 1953 (normally in the name of defending the socialist cause) found themselves doubting their position when, on 13 August 1961, the SED regime started to build a wall right through the centre of Berlin. In official discourse, and in a clear attempt to give the impression that they were 'protecting' their citizens from the disruptive forces of West Germany, the authorities always referred to the ninety-six-mile-long Wall as an 'anti-fascist protection barrier' (*anti-faschistischer Schutzwall*). Despite claiming as late as June 1961 that they had no intention of building any such thing, the idea was nonetheless conceived by Ulbricht's administration and approved by Soviet leader Nikita Khrushchev in a clear attempt to stop the daily drain of labour. And, regardless of the moral bankruptcy of the policy, it did its job, with only 5,000 citizens able to escape the GDR by any means between 1962 and 1989. The other side of the coin was that almost 1,000 people lost their lives trying to breach the state's maze of defences.

The erection of the Wall convinced many East Germans that, for better or worse, they had to find some sort of accommodation with the state. This was not evidence of positive identification with the GDR, more a reluctant acceptance of reality. 'Exit' was no longer a viable option (unless huge risks were taken) and 'voice' had long since been throttled by the dictatorial regime (Hirschman, 1993). Some form of 'conditional loyalty' in order simply to get by and make life bearable therefore became the norm (Grix, 2000b). Although most GDR citizens never came to possess positive feelings towards 'their' state, they realised that in return for mouthing support in public and keeping criticisms of their leaders to their own private sphere, the state would leave them in peace to shape their lives as they wished. This 'social contract' enabled East Germans to forget about political realities and live in smaller, more personalised 'niches' (Lindenberger, 1999). These 'niches' were not completely independent of state influence – the ubiquitous secret police, the Stasi, was remarkably good at infiltrating even the most innocuous of groups, as some of the harrowing post-1989 evidence from their many files revealed – but they were arenas where citizens could talk at least a little more freely.

Striving to catch-up: attempts at economic revival

Despite the slow distancing from Stalinism that was taking place in Khrushchev's Soviet Union, the GDR made little attempt to move in a similar direction. It remained very much a case of Stalinism or bust. An SED party congress in July 1956, for example, acted as if nothing had happened in the USSR, confirming Ulbricht's position at the head of the party and state, and presenting the second five-year plan (1956–60). The plan-writers gave the document the slogan 'Modernisation, Mechanisation and Automation', empha-sising what they hoped would be a new focus on technological progress. The intention to develop nuclear energy was announced, and the first nuclear reactor in East Germany was indeed activated in 1957. The government increased industrial production quotas by 55 per cent and there was a renewed emphasis on heavy industry. The plan committed the GDR to accelerating its moves towards agricultural collectivisation (in 1958 there were still 750,000 privately owned farms, containing 70 per cent of all arable land) and a complete nationalisation of the industrial sector. By mid-1960, nearly 85 per cent of all arable land was incorporated in more than 19,000 co-operatives; state farms comprised another 6 per cent.

Unsurprisingly, the second five-year plan encountered difficulties, and the regime soon replaced it with a seven-year plan (1959–65). This aimed, somewhat fancifully, at achieving West Germany's per capita production by the end of 1961, set yet higher production quotas, and called for an 85 per cent increase in labour productivity. Yet still the annual industrial growth rate declined steadily. In 1963 Ulbricht decided to introduce a 'New Economic System' (*Neues ökonomisches System*, NöS), an economic reform programme providing for some decentralisation in decision-making and the consideration of market and performance criteria. But it too failed to bring any significant advances in economic development.

By the early 1970s, and with Erich Honecker now at the helm, the SED launched yet more propaganda programmes, re-emphasising Marxism–Leninism and the international class struggle. 'Consumer socialism' was introduced in an attempt to magnify the appeal of socialism by offering special consideration for the material needs of the working class. Wage policy was overhauled and more attention was given to increasing the availability of consumer goods. The regime also accelerated the construction of new housing and the renovation of existing apartments; 60 per cent of new and renovated housing was allotted to working-class families with extremely low rents. Because women constituted nearly 50 per cent of the labour force, childcare facilities, including nurseries and kindergartens, were provided for the children of working mothers. Women in the labour force also received salaried maternity leave which ranged from six months to one year. The legacy of this policy is still visible in post-unification Germany, where the availability of childcare in the east far outstrips that in the west (see Chapter 8).

The Stasi

Overseeing all of these programmes and all of the plans that the SED concocted was the infamous Stasi. This was widely regarded as one of the most effective intelligence agencies in the world. Its motto of 'Shield and Sword for the Party' made its intentions explicit: to defend the interests of the SED above all else, including the rights of GDR citizens if need be. It was founded on 8 February 1950 and modelled on its Soviet counterpart, the KGB. Although Wilhelm Zaisser was the first Minister for State Security, it was his deputy whose name became synonymous with the institution: Erich Mielke, who became head in 1957. Also in 1957, Markus Wolf became head of the *Hauptverwaltung Aufklärung* (HVA), the foreign intelligence section. Wolf was remarkably successful in placing East German informants in the inner sanctums of foreign regimes as well as the political and business circles of West Germany. As noted in Chapter 2, the presence of one of his spies, Günter Guillaume, even led to the fall of West German Chancellor Willy Brandt in 1974. For many years it was claimed (erroneously, as it turned out) that Western authorities were not even sure what Wolf looked like. In reality, Säpo, Sweden's national security service, claimed to have taken the first picture of him while he visited their country in 1978 (the CIA has since revealed that it identified Wolf as early as 1959 from photos of attendees at the Nuremberg trials). It was also claimed that Wolf was the inspiration for John le Carré's spymaster Karla in a number of his novels – something that the author himself strongly denies. Similarities nevertheless appear to abound.

The Stasi influenced almost every aspect of life within the GDR. A civilian network of informants known as the *Inoffizielle Mitarbeiter* (Unofficial Collaborators) kept close tabs on thousands of GDR citizens by filing reports on them that were all carefully checked and stored. This Stasi efficiency meant that studying it became something of a boom industry in the early 1990s (see Dennis and LaPorte, 2003). By the time of unification, it was estimated that 91,000 full-time employees and 300,000 informants were employed by the organisation. Some more recent estimates are considerably higher.

The GDR did not collapse in 1989 because the Stasi did anything in particular 'wrong'. It continued to do its job until the very end, although as it became clear that the state it served was falling apart, panicking Stasi officials attempted – in the final days of 1989 – to shred the files containing their most sensitive documents, first using paper shredders and then tearing them by hand when the machines collapsed under the load. The hastily stored bags of paper fragments were found soon after and confiscated by the new government. In 1995 the German government hired a team to reassemble the documents; six years later, the three dozen archivists commissioned on the project had managed to work their way through only 300 bags (Schomaker, 2006). Following a declassification ruling imposed by the reunited German government in 1992, the Stasi files were also slowly opened both to the public at large and to individuals keen to find their own documents. Some of the most fascinating books on Germany in recent times have arisen as a direct product of this process (see, for example, Garton Ash, 1997).

The collapse of the GDR and unification

The GDR did not collapse for any single reason. As Chapter 2 has indicated, a number of internal and external factors came together to prompt the rapid unification of Germany. First, the ripple effect of Mikhail Gorbachev's domestic policies in the Soviet Union set the context. Gorbachev realised that, in order to survive, communism within the Soviet Union needed to embrace more openness (*'glasnost'*) in the way that its political and economic systems functioned and that the political structures which underpinned Communist Party control needed to be fundamentally restructured (*'perestroika'*). Gorbachev had no intention of unleashing processes of reform that would lead to the eventual dissolution of the USSR, but he did realise that the Soviet Union as it was constituted in 1985 was not a viable long-term entity. It was economically stagnant and if it were to have any chance of 'keeping up' with the USA, reform was necessary. A number of the Soviet Union's satellite states embraced the ideals that Gorbachev embodied, the most notable being Poland, where the Solidarity trade union held round-table talks with the government in February 1989. The GDR, however, was not one of them, as Kurt Hager, one of the SED's chief ideologues, illustrated with characteristic arrogance when he claimed that it was not necessary for the GDR to put new wallpaper in its home just because one of its neighbours was doing so. The GDR leadership made no attempt to diffuse feelings of dissatisfaction that grew through the 1980s, even contradicting the USSR in public on a number of occasions, and the SED's leaders were thus caught completely unprepared as public unease broke into the open in the autumn of 1989.

Second, and importantly for the GDR, it was not long before its other neighbours began to join the reform movement that Poland led. Solidarity's discussions with the communist leadership led to the nomination of a non-communist Prime Minister with no noticeable negative reaction from Moscow. There were no tanks in the streets and no coups to restore the old order. This paved the way for further democratisation –

something that worried a baffled GDR regime immensely. In August 1989 Hungary's reformist government took the unprecedented step of removing its border restrictions with Austria – the first breach of the Iron Curtain and an open invitation to citizens of the Eastern Bloc to flee. Given that 'exit' had now become an option, 13,000 East Germans managed to escape to the West through Hungary in September 1989 alone. Thousands more tried to reach the West by staging sit-ins at West German diplomatic missions in other Central European capitals, most noticeably in Prague. The GDR regime realised that bringing these citizens back 'on side' was out of the question so it first imposed visa restrictions on GDR citizens wishing to leave the country and then, in utter desperation, ceremonially 'expelled' those citizens camped in the grounds of foreign embassies and labelled them irresponsible traitors to the socialist cause as well as selfish criminals. The GDR subsequently announced that it would provide special trains to carry these refugees to West Germany, depriving them of their GDR identities as the trains passed through East German territory, thereby hoping to give the (completely implausible) impression that as and when the traitors wished to return they would be unable to do so. Riots ensued at Dresden station as thousands of East Germans attempted to board the trains to freedom; it was only a considerable military presence that prevented the trains from being stormed (Maier, 1997).

Third, as events such as these illustrate, the GDR's leaders were wholly unable to provide leadership. Politburo members around the woefully inept Erich Honecker had always been good at following orders and they were experts in the bureaucracy of government. As long as the message from Moscow was clear, they saw their job as simply putting that message into practice. As soon as the message became ambiguous (as it did when Gorbachev took over), muddled or even contradictory, they were at a loss as to what to do next. The events of the fortieth anniversary of the GDR on 7 October 1989 illustrated this perfectly. Gorbachev flew to East Berlin, oversaw the traditional military parade and shortly afterwards made the famous claim that 'those who arrive too late are punished by history' – a thinly veiled warning to the GDR leadership to take East Germany's, and therefore its own, predicament seriously. Despite the subsequent resignation of Honecker (in traditional communist style – he voted himself out of office in a unanimous decision of the Politburo on 18 October) and the more conciliatory tone of his successor, Egon Krenz, by now it was too late and the GDR was collapsing around its leaders ears.

Fourth, the GDR was pushed towards the edge by its own economic failure (see Chapter 2 and Kopstein, 1997). Given that the state had little external, and even less internal, legitimacy, it was vital that if it were to survive it should provide its citizens with a comparable standard of living to that which West Germans enjoyed. In this the GDR failed miserably. It falsified its economic statistics, but the reality was clear for all but the most die-hard SED-supporting citizen to see. Staple products were cheap and plentiful, but obtaining anything above this either took an exceptionally long time or was simply impossible. Even though, for example, over three million of the rickety Trabant cars – one of the main symbols of East German material disadvantage – were made in Zwickau, Saxony, it sometimes took ten to fifteen years on a waiting list before a motorist actually obtained one. Regular attempts by the GDR government to improve the country's economic situation failed and all Easterners needed to do was look to West German TV to see what (they perceived) they were missing.

Finally, and in many ways most significantly, the mass protests that occurred throughout the country in late 1989 hastened the demise of the GDR. Led by groups of dissidents, often linked loosely with Protestant churches, hundreds of thousands of East

Germans marched through the streets on Mondays through the autumn of 1989, campaigning for greater freedom of expression and for reform of their country (Joppke, 1995). Despite the threat of police intervention, and with the gruesome behaviour of the Chinese government in Beijing's Tiananmen Square a few months previously no doubt still fresh in many minds, the GDR's citizens bravely articulated dissatisfaction with their government's behaviour. This was not an instantaneous move towards unification but first and foremost a call for improved conditions in the GDR. Only later, towards the end of this process, once the Wall had fallen, were calls for unification heard.

Despite the pressures described above, the jubilant breaching of the Berlin Wall on 9 November 1989 still surprised virtually everyone. The GDR regime realised that the rules of the game had – even if not on paper – changed overnight, and they themselves had to bear a considerable responsibility for this. A liberalising of travel restrictions for East Germans to go to the West had originally been planned for 10 November but a confused press conference by Politburo member Günter Schabowski on the evening of the 9th led many to believe not only that they were going to be liberalised immediately, but that 'liberalisation' meant the complete abolition of all controls. Chaos ensued. Many people flocked to the Wall, where the border guards – faced with thousands of excited citizens telling them that Schabowski had just announced that they could go freely to the West – opened access points and allowed them through. Emboldened, many Germans on both sides began to tear down sections of the Wall itself, and it was not long before people were singing and dancing on the very construction which had once prompted so much fear.

West German leader Helmut Kohl was initially unsure how to react, and it was only after consulting with close domestic advisers that he announced, on 28 November, a ten-point plan for the peaceful unification of the two Germanies. This was to be based on free elections in East Germany and a unification of the two states' economies. In December, the East German parliament removed the SED's right to control power, and the entire Politburo and Central Committee – including Krenz – resigned. The new Minister-President, Hans Modrow, headed a caretaker government which shared power with the newly formed, democratically oriented parties. This government agreed to hold free elections in May 1990 and to rewrite the East German constitution. On 28 January 1990 all the parties agreed to bring the election forward to 18 March, primarily because of an erosion of state authority and because the exodus was continuing apace: more than 117,000 left in January and February 1990 alone.

In early February 1990, the Modrow government made one last attempt to exert some influence on proceedings when it proposed that Germany should be a unified and neutral state. This was roundly rejected by Kohl, who affirmed that a unified Germany must be a member of NATO and that neutrality was not an option. His discussions with Gorbachev had reassured him that there would be no Soviet opposition to this, providing that no NATO troops were stationed on what had been the territory of the GDR. This was codified in the Treaty on the Final Settlement with Respect to Germany, which came to be known as the 2+4 Treaty. The FRG and GDR, plus all four Allied powers that had occupied Germany at the end of the Second World War, signed the treaty in Moscow on 12 September 1990, paving the way for unification formally to take place. Under the terms of the treaty, the four powers renounced all rights they had formerly held in Germany, permitting the newly unified country to become fully sovereign on 15 March 1991. Even before the treaty had been signed, however, it was obvious that unification was happening. As a consequence of the first and only free elections in the history of the

GDR the new government received a clear mandate to negotiate unification and abolish not only itself but the state that it governed.

The first major practical step towards this goal occurred with the establishment of economic, monetary and social union between the two countries on 1 July 1990. In practice, this meant not only that the *Deutsche Mark* became the GDR's legal currency, but that West Germany's entire system of economic management, including its welfare state, was transferred wholesale to the GDR (Jacoby, 2000; see also Chapters 7 and 8). Moreover, the rate of exchange used in the currency union was effectively 1:1 for cash, wages, rents and pensions; only savings and debts above a certain level were converted at a rate of one *Deutsche Mark* to two East German Marks. Certainly, the decision to adopt this exchange rate was motivated by political rather than economic considerations. There was a very real sense within the West German government that anything other than a parity exchange rate would only further fuel the already strong flow of GDR citizens westwards. 'If the DM does not come to us, we will go to it' was one of the slogans among GDR citizens at the time.

Economically, though, this decision had disastrous consequences. The black market (i.e., real) exchange rate between the two currencies was more like one *Deutsche Mark* to five East German Marks; in other words, the 1:1 exchange rate inflated the value of the East German economy by a factor of five. What this meant was that industrial production in the GDR became unviable almost overnight – the (comparatively low) levels of productivity of eastern German workers simply did not justify the real value of wages they earned after 1 July 1990. When combined with the simultaneous collapse of the GDR's former export markets in Eastern Europe, this made large-scale de-industrialisation and unemployment almost inevitabilities. The long-term impact of the currency union for Germany's economic situation, which will be returned to below, cannot be overstated.

The process of unification was officially completed on 3 October 1990 when the five re-established federal states of the GDR – Brandenburg, Mecklenburg–Western Pomerania, Saxony, Saxony Anhalt and Thuringia – as well as Berlin (formed by uniting the two halves of the formerly divided city) formally joined the Federal Republic. As East Germany acceded to the FRG in accordance with the (then-existing) Article 23, the area in which the Basic Law served as the constitution was simply extended to include them. The alternative would have been for East Germany and West Germany to unite formally, but if this option had been chosen then, among other things, under Article 146 of the Basic Law, a new constitution for the newly established country would have to have been written. Though the option chosen was simpler, it has been responsible for some sentiments in the east of being 'occupied' or 'annexed' by the old Federal Republic (Dümcke and Vilmar, 1996).

To facilitate this unification process and to reassure other countries, some changes were subsequently made to the Basic Law. Once the five new eastern states and Berlin had joined, the Basic Law was amended to indicate that there were no other parts of Germany that existed outside of the newly unified country. On 14 November 1990 the German government also signed a treaty with Poland, finalising Germany's boundaries as permanent along the Oder–Neisse Line and thus ending any claims to territories that lay either in Poland or to its east. The following month, the first all-German free election since 1932 were held, resulting in an increased majority for the coalition government of Chancellor Helmut Kohl.

Issues

As 1990 wore on very few Germans foresaw too many serious issues in terms of the process of unification. Most East Germans were happy to be joining West Germany; they saw it as a matter of time before they enjoyed the material benefits of the Federal Republic's social market economy and the social and personal benefits of the individual freedoms that West Germany's democratic structures offered them. West Germans, for their part, were rather less enthusiastic about unification than were Easterners, but they still thought – once an initial potentially tricky transitional period had passed – that a larger Federal Republic would carry on much as before. Within a few months, though, it had become clear these issues were rather more complicated than many had envisaged.

The collapse of the eastern German economy

First and foremost, the economic implications of unification were much more serious than initially anticipated. In the immediate aftermath of unification, the economy of the new *Länder* contracted sharply: between 1990 and 1993, almost four million jobs were lost (Jacoby, 2005: 29; see also Table 3.1). Many of these new unemployed were simply removed from the labour market and put into early retirement, the implications of which are the subject of further discussion in Chapter 8. With their poor economic prospects, the new *Länder* have also experienced significant population decline of around two million, or one-eighth, since 1990.

Yet, astonishingly, this development took the federal government almost completely by surprise. Many Western analysts more-or-less believed the East German official statistics which made it the tenth-largest economy in the world; as late as 1990, Chancellor Kohl famously predicted that the new *Länder* would quickly become a 'flourishing landscape' (*blühende Landschaften*). Only after unification did the true extent of the GDR's economic malaise come to light. The degree of miscalculation is illustrated by the story of the *Treuhandanstalt* (THA). This organisation had been set up by the East German parliament in June 1990 with the aim of privatising the roughly 8,500 firms, with initially over four million employees, which constituted the state's holdings in the GDR. Certainly, the THA went about its task with some vigour, and its operations drew heavy criticism for what some claimed was the unnecessary closure of what could have been profitable businesses. But of all its areas of activity, its financial record was the most damaging of all. Initially, the expectation was that the sale of assets by the THA would generate some DM600 billion at early 1990s prices, which could then be reinvested into the economy in order to create a self-sustaining boom. But by the time that its operations ended in 1994, it had *lost* between DM260 and 270 billion. In return for this, most of eastern Germany had been de-industrialised and unemployment in the eastern states was up to 25 per cent.

Crucially, the astronomical costs of unification have largely had to be borne by the public purse, in the form of state investment in infrastructure such as the road and rail network, and in the huge transfer payments to cover the costs of unemployment and early retirement. Even today, total transfers between the old and new *Länder* are estimated to run to around €100 billion a year – the equivalent of the entire budget for the European Union. In 2003, the total costs of unification were estimated to be around €1.3 trillion since 1990 – an absolutely staggering amount of money, in the light of which it is easy to see how reunification has been a heavy burden on the German economy in general. As well as some significant tax increases, especially in terms of contributions to social

Table 3.1 GDP growth and unemployment in eastern and western Germany, 1991–2006

	1991	1992	1993	1994	1995	1996	1997	1998	1999	2000	2001	2002	2003	2004	2005	2006
Real GDP growth (%)																
• all Germany	2.8	2.2	−1.2	2.9	1.9	1.4	2.2	2.8	1.4	3.2	0.6	0.2	−0.2	1.2	0.9	2.7
• east	2.5		8.5	7.2	5.3	2.0	1.6	2.1								
• west	2.8		−1.8	2.4	1.6	1.3	2.2	2.9								
• EU15		1.3	−0.4	2.8	2.6	1.7	2.6	2.9	3.0	3.9	1.9	1.1	1.1	2.3	1.5	2.7
Unemployment (%)																
• all Germany	7.3	8.5	9.8	10.6	20.4	11.5	12.7	12.3	11.7	10.7	10.4	10.8	11.6	10.5	11.7	10.7
• east	10.2	14.4	15.4	15.7	14.8	16.6	19.1	19.2	18.7	18.6	18.8	19.2	20.1	20.1	20.6	
• west	6.2	6.4	8.0	9.0	9.1	9.9	10.8	10.3	9.6	8.4	8.0	8.5	9.3	9.4	11	8.9
Total public sector debt (% GDP)	41	43	47	49.3	60.3	59.8	61	60.9	61.2	60.2	59.6	60.3	63.9	65.7	67.9	66.8
Public sector budget deficit (% GDP)	−3.3	−2.8	−3.5	−2.3	−3.2	−3.3	−2.6	−2.2	−1.5	1.3	−2.8	−3.7	−4.0	−3.7	−3.2	−1.7

Source: Statistisches Bundesamt

insurance schemes (see Chapter 8), the majority of this sum has been financed through debt, which effectively doubled after 1990 to stand at €1.5 trillion by mid-2007 – around 67 per cent of GDP (see Streeck, forthcoming). This itself has created major challenges for fiscal policy in Germany, which will be returned to in the final section of this chapter.

In addition to these economic issues, identity questions remained very much at the forefront of political and popular debate. 'Identity' remains one of the classic contested concepts of social science and there are plenty of disagreements as to precisely what the term means. In political science, it is seen as the labelling of oneself as a member of a particular group. This prompts people to see themselves as members of sometimes very large groups (ranging from, for example, a citizen's allegiance to a home city of, say, Leipzig, to the state where it can be found (Saxony), to the larger region of eastern Germany, to the German nation and also to the people of Europe). It also causes people to identify with tens, hundreds, thousands and/or millions of people whom they have never met. This phenomenon has been described by Benedict Anderson (1991) in his classic study of nationalism as identification with an 'imagined community'. Shared histories, shared cultures, shared symbols, shared traditions and shared language can all come together to foster this type of allegiance.

Although West Germany was formally created only in 1949, it did not take long – in historical terms – for its citizens to begin to identify with it positively. Despite the fact that the state had to overcome a number of burdens in reinventing itself post-1945, it did so – for the most part, as Chapter 2 illustrated – very successfully. The effectiveness of newly created democratic structures, West Germany's embeddedness in the European Community/Union and especially the 'economic miracle' prompted a growing 'constitutional patriotism' (*Verfassungspatriotismus*), which saw citizens cautiously being proud of the institutions and political system of the peaceful and prosperous country within which they now lived (Habermas, 2001; see also Chapter 2).

The term 'proud', however, needs to be used carefully; West Germans were justifiably pleased with much of the post-war development of their state, but they were also well aware of the dangers of complacency, arrogance and any sort of nationalist chauvinism. Cautious optimism did not blind West Germans to the horrors of the past and the dangers that can lie around future corners. West Germans grew up for the most part believing in the virtues of the social market economy, the importance of the supporting the further development of the EC/EU and the dangers of articulating German national interests too vociferously. Yet, as became evident in the post-1989 period, West Germans also continued to define themselves very much as 'Germans' (rather than '*West* Germans'). The semi-permanence of Germany's division did not stop them from regarding their state as the 'real' Germany and therefore from (perhaps subconsciously) viewing their attitudes, sentiments, feelings and thoughts as those of 'real' Germans. In other words, West Germans identified with many of the positive things that were specific to their state, but continued to see themselves as Germans; and as and when issues of 'identity' were discussed, it was nearly always 'German identity' that took centre stage. The challenge of integrating seventeen million Easterners, possessing a vaguely defined but no less tangible sense of 'East German identity', built on very different sets of experiences, into the Federal Republic in 1989 surprised many Westerners and posed one of the more intractable problems of the unification process.

Both post-war Germanies therefore began, consciously and subconsciously, to search for their own unique brand of 'national' identity. This was particularly so for the GDR, given that it was a new state with no previous history. Initially, each professed an identity that went beyond its state borders. It was only when the two German states began to recognise each other in the early 1970s that the GDR began to claim that a separate socialist nation had developed within its borders. The GDR leadership made concerted attempts to create what they termed a 'socialist national consciousness', even embedding the term in the rewritten constitution of 1974 (McKay, 1998). By May 1976, the official narrative considered the GDR's history as being a logical continuation of all the progressive forces evident in German history. The darker, more aggressive and con-servative tenets of Germany's past were to be found in the aberration that was West Germany. The GDR claimed to be the *Land der Dichter und Denker* (Land of Poets and Intellectuals) and unsurprisingly began to lay claim to the heritage of progressive thinkers such as Wilhelm von Humboldt, Johann Wolfgang von Goethe, Martin Luther, Karl Liebknecht and Rosa Luxemburg.

The ruling SED believed that GDR citizens' identity formation could be conceived and planned by officials much like everything else. Yet the very term itself is a misnomer. 'Socialism' is, by definition, an international ideology. It stresses the importance of workers mobilising as one unit with the aim not only of defending their interests against those who would use and abuse their position in the economic system, but – in its more extreme variant – of overthrowing capitalism and creating a new (world) economic order. The internationalism that underpinned the socialist rhetoric was expressed in support for socialist sister states to the east of the GDR and particularly the mother-state of the socialist revolution, the USSR. 'To learn from the USSR', as the much-touted slogan went, 'is to learn to win!' The second part of the prescribed identity in the GDR, 'national', on the other hand, implies something that is inherently more place-specific. The leadership was desperate to grant the GDR legitimacy as a state in opposition to the FRG. They thought that socialist national consciousness could be achieved by creating and relentlessly pushing 'founding myths' such as anti-fascism and proletarian inter-nationalism. But neither really rooted well in East Germany, even if opinion polling post-1990 indicates that many Easterners *did* imbibe more of the anti-fascist rhetoric than they perhaps realised. As McKay (1998) points out, attempts to create a strong sense of identification with the GDR mostly failed. This was in spite of the widespread embrace of myth-creating elements such as the *Jugendweihe*, a secular coming-of-age ceremony for thirteen- and fourteen-year-olds which pre-dated the GDR and has interestingly survived in post-unification Germany. This failure to instil a sense of GDR consciousness contributed to the speedy process of unification in 1989–90 as, given the opportunity, GDR citizens had no hesitation in wishing their state away in order to join the FRG.

East Germans soon realised that the official discourse was nothing more than propa-ganda aimed to foist an artificial reality on them. However, the fact that GDR citizens had little faith in the identity politics of the SED leadership does not mean that a GDR identity did not exist. It did, but not in the way that GDR leaders, or even GDR citizens themselves, perceived. This only really became evident post-1989 and has much more to do with how the GDR *was* and not how its leaders *wanted it to be*.

Ossis and Wessis

Within months of the Wall coming down, citizens of both East and West Germany were coming to realise that forty years of living in different political, economic and social systems had prompted a degree of attitudinal difference to develop. Within a few short weeks Westerners began referring to Easterners as 'Ossis', a slightly derogatory term derived from the German word for east, *ost*. Easterners – almost as quickly – returned the compliment and the term 'Wessi' entered popular parlance. Both terms are considered disparaging by some and their existence has been interpreted as being a reflection of the differences in the culture and mentality of the states from which their inhabitants hailed. Ossis were seen as being all too quick to moan and all too reluctant to take the initiative and improve their own socio-economic fortunes. So the stereotype went, they were very quick to know their rights and yet not so speedy to make good their obligations. It was therefore no surprise that 'Ossi' was quickly extended to 'Jammerossi' – 'moaning Easterner'. The western stereotype was little better: Wessis were seen as being know-it-alls, prone to boss Easterners about purely on the basis of their heritage. They were allegedly very good at pushing themselves forward and at trampling on the rights and interests of others, most frequently Ossis. Whereas the latter allegedly moaned all the time, 'Besser-Wessis' ('know-it-all Westerners') simply could not help but proclaim arrogantly that they knew everything. While rarely used in popular discourse now, the two terms throw some light on the nature of the differing identities that were quickly taking root in eastern and western Germany at the time.

Eastern and western German identities

There is still a feeling in some quarters that separate identities exist in the two territories. This is rather more true of older generations than it is of younger ones, but, difficult though it is to define, *something* appeared to prompt the two halves of the country to become more aware of their differences. Citizens of the eastern states have clearly undergone fundamentally different processes of identity construction. The effects of socialisation in the GDR alone do not adequately explain this difference. It was only when they were coupled with the experience of watching the GDR implode, of enjoying the euphoria of the unification period and the realisation – for many – that life in an expanded Federal Republic was rather more challenging than was originally anticipated that a form of eastern identity crystallised (Grix, 2000a). Easterners remain more interested in issues of social justice and equality of outcomes. This is not solely because they remain – in purely material terms – poorer than their western counterparts, but because they also tend to place higher demands on the state to act to alleviate socio-economic problems. It was, after all, illegal to be unemployed in the GDR; the social support network was broad and all-encompassing, and there was little worry of being flung into socially precarious positions on the whim of a heartless boss. Post-1990, Easterners (correctly) saw themselves as more likely to be unemployed than they were pre-1990, and they are certainly more likely than Westerners to have had to change jobs regularly while generally earning less. In the GDR the state did, for better or worse, everything. Regardless of whether Easterners liked this, they got used to it – and it is a habit which they have found very difficult to kick. From their perspective, the state appears not to do nearly enough, despite the fact that Germany has a highly inter-ventionist political economy with one of the most generous welfare systems in Europe.

Another key tenet of the eastern German identity is the fine eye that many citizens have for political opportunism. Cynicism with politics and with the public sphere has been on the rise in western Germany too, but there is an additional feeling among Easterners that they were fooled once – in 1989–90 – into believing that this new crowd of rulers would be better, and they are not prepared to be fooled again. Easterners are therefore more disillusioned with politics and, as recent election results have shown (see Chapter 5), more likely to support anti-capitalist, left-wing parties (namely the Left Party) or right-wing parties as a protest measure. Some authors emphasise the strong element of *Trotz* (defiance) that is apparent in eastern German consciousness today; Easterners are portrayed as reacting against the prevailing western German norms that shape contemporary life in Germany. This defiance can come out in surprising ways: in the mid-1990s, for example, a group of Easterners launched a campaign to save the *Ampelmännchen*, the small red and green figures who adorned GDR traffic lights. Irritated that more or less everything that stemmed from the GDR was being wiped off Germany's socio-cultural map, these apparently insignificant little figures came to epitomise an eastern German unwillingness to accept western German symbols, processes and practices on the simple basis that they came from there. The *Ampelmännchen* became remarkably high profile and, eventually, a compromise was reached that allowed them to carry on adorning lights in some eastern states (see Duckenfield and Calhoun, 1997).

The campaign to save the eastern traffic light man was not a one-off example of Easterners trying to claim back some of what they perceived as being their cultural heritage. It was merely an early instance of *Ostalgie*, a conflation of the German words for east and nostalgia (see Cooke, 2005). Definitions of '*Ostalgie*' differ almost as much as do opinions of how the phenomenon, which generated much more attention as Germany entered the twenty-first century, should be viewed. Many see it simply as nostalgic feelings towards life in the GDR. The rush to embrace newfound political and economic freedoms initially led to more or less all GDR brands and products disappearing from eastern German stores, to be replaced by Western products, regardless of their quality (although this was, admittedly, generally higher). With the passing of time some East Germans missed specific, comforting aspects of their old lives and *Ostalgie* rose to fill this void, as citizens sought to bring back or rejuvenate parts of their own lived experiences in the contemporary context (see Box 3.2).

Ironically, many of the businesses that moved quickest to exploit the renewed interest in eastern German products hail from western Germany. Eastern Germans had little choice but to express this renewed sense of cultural difference through the market, an institution of which they were paradoxically becoming ever more suspicious in terms of its ability to provide them with economic prosperity (Dornberg, 1996). *Ostalgie* is not, however, all about material goods. It also has a great deal to do with the politics of memory, and particularly the politics of lived lives. Books, films, plays and satires about life in the GDR are not always overtly political in nature, but they do increasingly try to deal with the GDR in a more differentiated way than has previously been the case. This facet of *Ostalgie* aims to show that the GDR was a state where people lived 'normal' lives, where they fell in love, where they drank beer and where they made the same stupid mistakes as citizens of other countries.

It would be wrong to assume that *Ostalgie* reflects a general willingness to return to life in the GDR. Only a very small minority of Easterners would wish to do any such thing. But it does stress that writing off the lives of GDR citizens as having been shaped by '*Stasi, Stacheldraht und Schiessbefehl*' ('Stasi, barbed wire and shoot-to-kill') inevitably misses much of what shaped the everyday existences of East German citizens. The *Ostalgie* phenomenon received a substantial amount of TV air time in the early years of this century, and many Germans are now convinced that the GDR is worth studying in more detail: there are lived experiences to be analysed and biographies to be respected.

And western Germans should not simply ignore them as if they never happened and/or had nothing to do with them.

Despite the recent interest in everyday life in the GDR and the multifaceted phenomenon of eastern German identity, Westerners are much less conscious in their articulation of difference than are Easterners. As was mentioned above, they tend simply to view themselves as Germans. They have long since synthesised West Germany with

---

BOX 3.2 THE GDR IN RETROSPECT

Over the last decade the GDR has begun to make ever more appearances in Germany's entertainment industry. The initial wave of *Ostalgie* found little expression in the arts. But a second trend that started to develop in the late 1990s saw the GDR reappear in a number of different parts of German popular culture.

A number of highly acclaimed films have appeared, with Leander Haußmann's comedy *Sonnenallee* (1999) about life in East Berlin in the 1970s being the first of this new trend. The novel on which the film is based, *Am kurzeren Ende der Sonnenalle*, was written by Thomas Brussig and published in the same year. The plot concerns a group of children who grow up on the short, wrong (eastern) side of the Sonnenallee in Berlin, a street that was cut in half when the Berlin Wall was erected. The film tells of the group's antics, their families, of the West German friends and relatives who come to visit, and of the East German border guards who patrol a few metres away, all serving to illustrate the absurdity of everyday life both on the Sonnenallee and in the GDR in general.

While *Sonnenallee* received plenty of attention, Wolfgang Becker's *Goodbye Lenin* (2003) had an even more striking effect. It was chosen as the best European film at the 2003 Berlin Film Festival and went on to win nine other awards for its warm portrayal of a young East Berliner trying to conceal evidence of the Wall's collapse from his staunchly GDR-loyal mother. Although newly reawakened from a coma, her fragile health forced her son to go to ever more bizarre (and humorous) lengths to cover up the country's impending implosion. But not even *Goodbye Lenin* managed to do what the most recent film of this genre, Florian Henckel von Donnersmarck's *Das Leben der Anderen* (*The Lives of Others*; 2006), achieved, winning an Oscar (for Best Foreign Film) at the 2007 Academy Awards. *The Lives of Others* is a darker and in many ways much more moving portrayal of the way that the Stasi tried to monitor and stifle the cultural scene of East Berlin.

The GDR has not just been making reappearances on the big screen: a retrospective of GDR art filled the new National Gallery over the summer of 2003; RTL, one of Germany's most popular television networks, aired a documentary–talkshow series (*Die DDR Show*) hosted by Katarina Witt, a former GDR ice-skating star and Ossi pin-up; stores throughout Berlin now also sell gifts with strong links to the GDR, ranging from the East German *Ampelmännchen* to GDR football shirts; and ever more novels are being written on East German subject matter. The GDR may be dead, but memories of it are certainly not.

Germany and therefore tend to see the GDR as an aberration from this norm. At its most crass, it can appear that Westerners felt that it was for Easterners to become like them: this is what they appeared to want in 1989–90, and unification offered them the perfect opportunity to do so. While Westerners were not inherently sceptical of unification, they saw it (correctly, in the literal sense) as a case of their state simply being expanded eastwards, so it was up to Easterners to learn the rules of the game anew. The idea of two states coming together as one seemed, to many in the west, somewhat bizarre; the GDR imploded and the FRG expanded to replace it. Many Westerners were subsequently perplexed at Easterners' dissatisfaction with some of unification's outputs. Western taxes had risen, the welfare state that many had worked so hard to create was coming under increasing strain, and billions of *Deutsche Marks* were being ploughed into reinvigorating infrastructure throughout eastern Germany. Yet Easterners *still* were not happy!

Trying to conceptualise exactly what these respective identities are and then trying to quantify them are, as this chapter has shown, tasks fraught with difficulty. Some authors argue that while these tasks may be of interest to academics, any proposed identity cleavage between east and west should not be granted an importance that, in reality, it does not possess. Hans-Joachim Veen (1997), for example, has argued that in an era of multi-level identities Germans should celebrate their unity in diversity. As long as Germans agree on the basic constitutional consensus – which they do – then regional differences simply contribute to the rich tapestry of social and political life that is normality in many states across Europe. Regional divergences in interests, values and attitudes can be articulated through the political process much like other interests can. Veen argues that although the economic differences between east and west are substantial, there is agreement on the basic rules of the political game; as long as that remains so, Germans should not obsess over other differences. Citizens of northern Germany, for example, have always seen themselves as being fundamentally different to Bavarians. Mecklenburgers are also known (or at least perceived to have) a particular view of life – Bismarck once claimed that he would go to Mecklenburg if the world was coming to an end as everything happens a hundred years later there. Veen, therefore, sees the territorial issue as taking on a worrying dimension only when there are clashes over values and the fundamentals of political organisation. Germany, as even the most negative of doomsayers should agree, has not yet reached this point.

Conclusion

The challenge of mastering the legacy of unification is clearly very complex. Undoubtedly, the most significant of these challenges remains economic; despite enormous progress in terms of bringing eastern Germany's infrastructure up to western standards, eastern Germany remains poorer, unemployment is higher and growth rates are lower (see Table 3.1). And despite the huge sums spent by the west, the east is unlikely to achieve economic self-sufficiency for some years yet.

Even more importantly, the weakness of the economy in the new *Länder* has had a major knock-on effect on the federal government's fiscal position. On the one hand, welfare expenditure has shot up, principally through measures to stimulate the labour market and subsidies for the pensions system (Chapter 8). But debt servicing has increased too, and, at around €40 billion annually, constitutes the second-largest item of expenditure (see Streeck, forthcoming). On the other hand, the relatively low levels of economic growth (see Table 3.1) have meant that tax receipts have been low. The solution so far has tended to be for the government to incur even more debt, which in turn has brought Germany into conflict over its responsibilities to fiscal prudence in the context of its membership of the single European currency (see Chapter 7). Indeed, the fiscal crisis of the German state, which was brought about not simply by unification but by the federal government's responses to it, overshadows all other aspects of German politics. It permeates all aspects of government policy-making, from education, transport and the welfare state (Chapter 8) to even foreign and security policy (Chapters 9 and 10). Put differently, understanding the fiscal problems of (in particular) the federal government holds the key to understanding practically all other issues of public policy in contemporary Germany.

The challenge of dealing with the complex history of the GDR is also likely to remain on the agenda for the foreseeable future. After 1989, the behaviour of eastern Germans in the GDR – who said what, acted in what way and why they did so – emerged with unexpected intensity. The result was seen by many as a collective insult to East German self-esteem. The official inquiries that were set up to produce a historical record of life in the GDR were seen by many citizens as too dry and distant, and after initial periods of interest, most citizens grew bored of their uninspiring and academic style (Barker, 2000). The establishment of the Federal Authority for the Archives of the GDR State Security Service (called the Gauck Authority in popular discourse, after Joachim Gauck, its first head) attracted more attention. Its intention was above all to provide those who had been victims of the Stasi's damaging surveillance activities with access to their files. Important and impressive though its work has been, many eastern Germans have long since tired of dealing – both in public and privately – with the legacy of a state that they were forced to accept. Finding a balance between ensuring that the past is remembered, learning from mistakes, ensuring that justice is done and yet avoiding the impression that they more or less permanently have to justify their past behaviour is therefore delicate.

Should Germany also worry about the multiplicity of identities that exists within its borders? One interpretation of post-unification identity politics is quick to point to the challenges and threats that diverse sets of self-understandings can pose. Eastern Germany is destined to remain economically less well developed for many years to come. The brain drain westwards will continue and there is a real danger that Easterners will become further disenchanted with the outputs of both the social market economy and Germany's political institutions. Easterners, so the doomsayers argue, are likely not just to look defensively backwards to the GDR for inspiration but to the appeals of political extremists who make promises that they will never be able to keep. This scenario paints eastern German distinctiveness as a disruptive and disaffecting force, ultimately posing a challenge to the whole ethos on which post-1945 (West) Germany has been built.

However, a more positive and, we would argue, realistic scenario is also thankfully to hand. Eastern Germany remains a territory with serious socio-economic problems, but there is little evidence to suggest that Easterners reject Germany's constitutional consensus, and support for politically extremist parties remains no higher than it is in most other Western European countries. Eastern German distinctiveness tends, if anything, to find political voice in support for the Left Party, which is now well on the way towards political acceptability (see Chapter 5). Unity in diversity has been a trademark of Germany for many years. The *Ostalgie* phenomenon may well be used and abused by groups with vested interests in defending their behaviour in the GDR, but for most people it is a way of linking their twenty-first century existence in the FRG with the pre-1989 existence in what – in almost every way imaginable – was a completely different social, economic and political setting. The challenges of integrating eastern Germany into the mainstream of German society are considerable; but they should not be seen as insurmountable.

Questions for discussion

1 **How did life in the GDR differ from life in the FRG?**
2 **What were the main causes of German unification?**
3 **Why might it be argued that western Germans and eastern Germans classify themselves as different from one another in unified Germany?**

Further reading

Fulbrook, M. (1997), *Anatomy of a Dictatorship: Inside the GDR, 1949–89* (Oxford: Oxford University Press). Standard English-language text on the German Democratic Republic.

Jarausch, K. (1994), *The Rush to German Unity* (Oxford: Oxford University Press). An impressive account of the complex process of German unification.

Veen, H.-J. (1997), '"Inner Unity" – Back to the Community Myth? A Plea for a Basic Consensus', *German Politics* 6/3: 1–15. A dissenting voice, claiming that Germany has already achieved inner unity.

4　A blockaded system of government?

Summary

For almost ten years, commentators have been lamenting the 'reform blockage' in German politics. This chapter reviews the main institutional features of government and governance in Germany, including federalism, and asks whether the current distribution of powers between and among tiers of government is capable of mastering the country's problems.

Introduction

More than any other single area under discussion in this book, Germany's political institutions bear the mark of history. Most obviously, as Chapter 2 discussed, the entire political system was constructed in conscious reaction to the experience of Nazi dictatorship. But the Federal Republic's institutions also reflect the desire to avoid the authoritarianism of imperial Germany and even more so the weaknesses of the Weimar Republic. In that sense, the post-1949 political set-up has proven to be extraordinarily successful, and Germany is now without doubt one of the most stable liberal democracies in the developed world (see Lijphart, 1999).

But in recent years, the focus has been rather different. One of the themes of this book is the scale of challenges Germany currently has to master, many of which are linked directly or indirectly to unification. Yet actual policy reforms, as will become apparent in subsequent chapters, have tended, when they have happened at all, to be decidedly modest in scope, leading to widespread exasperation at the failure of political parties to grasp the nettle. Of course, political parties only reflect broader trends in society, and long-term changes in both parties and key social groupings are explored in more detail in Chapters 5 to 8. But, at the same time, a recurrent question in German public debate has been whether the country's political system itself is to blame, and whether the division of power within the system institutionally dictates political solutions which are, frankly, inadequate when addressing the country's increasing economic and social problems.

This chapter therefore outlines the political institutions of Germany and their patterns of interaction in order to establish whether the reform blockage is due to the political system as a whole, or rather just the result of a lack of political will on the part of key actors. It shows that 'incremental policy change' (Katzenstein, 1987) is a defining feature of politics in Germany. In particular, it pinpoints federalism as a key source of tension, both in terms of articulating interests and in its impact on party politics (see Wachendorfer-Schmidt, 2005).

Background

Structurally, Germany's political institutions are defined by two main principles: first, they reflect that ever since its foundation as a unified country in 1871, Germany has been a federal state, with discrete political and constitutional constructions mirroring the country's geographical, religious and cultural diversity; second, the political institutions, and many other areas of public life, were designed specifically to make a recurrence of totalitarian rule impossible. The political structure of the Weimar Republic – with a weak legislature and a very strong, directly elected president – was widely held to be at least partly responsible for facilitating the rise of the Nazis; so, as Chapter 2 argued, the authors of the Basic Law in 1948 and 1949 were determined not to allow this to happen again. Thus, the Chancellor's position as the head of government was bolstered at the expense of the President, and the legislature's role was also strengthened; furthermore, the Basic Law introduced a strong Constitutional Court into the panoply of German political institutions. The key components of the resulting institutional constellation are outlined in Box 4.1 (see also Schmidt, 2003a).

BOX 4.1 THE POLITICAL INSTITUTIONS OF GERMANY

Germany is a federal country, which is made up of sixteen individual states (*Länder*), of which three (Hamburg, Bremen and Berlin) are city states. Each state has a directly-elected parliament (*Landtag*) and government (headed by a *Ministerpräsident*). The *Länder* have their own competencies (especially education and policing), although their principal task is to implement federal legislation. The *Länder* vary considerably in area, population and economic development (see Box 4.2). Each *Landtag* is elected on a four- or five-year basis. *Land* elections are not usually bundled systematically to coincide with each other or with national elections (in the way for instance that elections in the USA are), although it is common for two *Länder* to go to the polls on the same day. In practice, this means that one or more *Land* elections usually takes place somwhere in Germany every few months.

At federal level, Germany is made up of the following sets of political institutions.

1 The legislature

The *Bundestag* is Germany's national parliament and is based in Berlin. Its regular size is 598 members, although in practice there are frequently more parliamentarians than this. After the 2005 election, it had 614 members, who are normally elected for

---

four-year terms (see Chapter 5 for a discussion of elections). The *Bundestag* elects the Chancellor (*Bundeskanzler(in)*) and is the country's primary legislature. Like in other parliamentary democracies, a lost vote of no-confidence in the Chancellor may trigger early elections; however, in Germany there is the further option of a 'constructive vote of no-confidence' (*konstruktives Misstrauensvotum*), in which the Chancellor is simultaneously replaced by an alternative candidate, thereby providing continuity of power. In the history of the Federal Republic, this vote has occurred only twice, in 1972 (failed – see Chapter 2) and in 1982 (successful).

Subject to the approval of the *Bundesrat* (see below), the *Bundestag* discusses bills and passes laws. Much of its work is done in committees, and it is not a 'debating' parliament in the way that the House of Commons is. Most of the bills it debates are proposed by the federal government, although both the *Bundestag* and the *Bundesrat* have the right of initiative as well. The parties (see Chapter 5) are organised into parliamentary groupings (*Fraktionen*) within the *Bundestag*, each comprising at least 5 per cent of the parliament's membership. Each *Fraktion* elects a leader (*Fraktionsvorsitzende(r)*), who is its principal spokesperson in parliament. Especially for the two larger parties, this is therefore one of the most influential positions in German politics.

In addition, the *Länder* are represented collectively in federal policy-making by means of the *Bundesrat* in Berlin, in which each *Land* has between three and six votes (totalling sixty-nine), depending on its population. The votes of any single *Land* must be cast unanimously. Following the 2006 federalism reform (see below), an absolute majority of the *Bundesrat* (i.e. thirty-five votes) is required to pass laws in about 35 to 40 per cent of cases, including any legislation which incurs significant costs to the *Länder* in their implementation of federal policy. In the case of no agreement being reached between the two chambers, a conciliation committee (*Vermittlungsausschuss*) is instituted to negotiate a compromise. In all other cases, the *Bundestag* may overturn any rejection of a bill by the *Bundesrat*.

2 The executive

The Chancellor heads the federal government (*Bundesregierung*), the executive arm of the political system. In 2007, there were fourteen ministries plus the Federal Chancellery. The ministries are split geographically between Berlin and the former capital, Bonn.

Historically, the federal government has been based on a coalition, usually between one of the two largest parties and one smaller party. Although the Chancellor has a much stronger position under the Basic Law than was the case under the Weimar Republic, his or her main formal power is the ability to set the parameters of policy (*Richtlinienkompetenz*). Individual ministers are independent in the political management of their portfolios (*Ressortprinzip*) (on the power resources of the Chancellor, see Schmidt, 2003b: 27–30; Helms, 2004).

continued

The head of state is the Federal President (*Bundespräsident*), whose role is largely ceremonial, save in exceptional cases such as an early dissolution of parliament (as in 2005). The President is elected every five years by the federal assembly (*Bundes-versammlung*), drawn from the *Bundestag* and the *Länder* parliaments. He or she can serve a maximum of two terms of office.

3 The judiciary

Courts play a major role in German politics. All decisions by any form of state authority, whether at local, regional or national level, can be subjected to judicial scrutiny by administrative courts (*Verwaltungsgerichte*) – a further historically grounded check on executive power.

The highest court in the land is the Constitutional Court (*Bundesverfassungsgericht*), based in Karlsruhe. Its sixteen judges, organised into two courts (or senates) are elected jointly by the *Bundestag* and *Bundesrat* and serve terms of up to twelve years. The Court has the power, upon referral, to review and strike down any legislation passed by the *Bundestag* and *Bundesrat*. In one of the main expressions of Germany's 'militant democracy', the Court may also ban 'anti-constitutional' parties, which it has done twice, in 1952 (the neo-Nazi SRP) and 1956 (the communist KPD).

As Box 4.1 shows, power in Germany's political system is spread across a range of actors, not only within the federal government, but between the federal level and the *Länder*. The principal axes in which this fragmentation of power takes place are federalism, the dynamics of coalition politics and the impact of the Constitutional Court (Katzenstein, 1987). These dimensions are so important to understanding how German politics work that they need to be explained briefly in turn.

Federalism

First, German federalism is relatively unusual compared to other federal systems. Elsewhere, the purpose of federalism is to help manage diversity (often in geographically extensive countries such as the USA, Canada or Australia). In the Federal Republic, the constitutional aim of federalism has been to create unity, at least in financial terms, between the various component federal states. Moreover, before the 2006 reform (discussed below), there was no strict delineation of competencies between the national and sub-national levels. For instance, Article 73 of the Basic Law laid down those areas where the federation had exclusive rights of legislation, and Article 75 areas in which the federal government could issue so-called 'framework legislation' (*Rahmengesetzgebung*). But Article 74 specified a range of so-called 'concurrent' legislative competencies, to include such significant areas of public policy as regulation of the economy and labour law. These were areas in which the *Länder* were free to legislate, but only in the absence of federal legislation. In practice, these areas saw a gradual encroachment of federal law over the decades and by the beginning of the new millennium, the only significant areas of public policy remaining in the sole competence of the *Länder* were education, law enforcement and public broadcasting. In fact, the principal task of the *Länder* was and remains to implement federal legislation (the so-called *Bundesauftragsverwaltung*); accordingly, the majority of civil servants (*Beamte*) in Germany are employed by the *Länder*, with only a small minority in the direct service of the federal government.

German federalism also differs from that of other countries in that the *Länder* do not possess independent tax-raising powers. Instead, there is an intricate division of taxes between the federation, the *Länder* and local municipalities (*Kommunen*). While the income from some taxes is wholly allocated to particular levels (for instance, petrol tax is exclusively a federal tax), most tax revenues, including those from the two main taxes (income tax and VAT), accrue to all three levels, but in varying proportions depending on the tax in question. Crucially, although the federation can unilaterally decide to raise its taxes, no *Land* and no municipality can do the same independently, even in the case of those taxes which accrue solely to these two levels. There are only very limited exceptions to this rule, such as the ability of municipalities to vary the level of administrative charges, like parking fines. This means that while the *Länder* and municipalities bear full responsibility for their expenditure, they are unable to raise taxes to cover any shortfalls in revenue (or excess expenditure), which in times of slow economic growth therefore tend to be covered by borrowing. Indeed, because most expenditure is fixed (for instance, salaries and pensions of public servants, the majority of which are in *Länder* employment), neither can the *Länder* do much to reduce outgoings. A similar situation befalls the municipalities, significant elements of whose expenditure (such as childcare provision) have in the past been prescribed by *Land* or federal governments *without* the input of the municipalities themselves. Given this institutionalised trend towards meeting shortfalls between expenditure and revenue through public borrowing, it comes as no surprise that most *Länder* and municipalities are heavily indebted (see Table 4.3).

In addition to the interconnections between the federal level and the *Länder* as a group, there are a range of political and financial mechanisms linking the *Länder* to each other. The most important of these is the horizontal fiscal equalisation scheme between the *Länder* (*Länderfinanzausgleich*), which amounted to €6.9 billion in 2005. This system aims to deliver equal levels of per capita income across them in accordance with the constitutional goal of creating equal living conditions throughout Germany (Article 72 of the Basic Law). In 2005, eleven of the sixteen *Länder* were beneficiaries, including all the *Länder* on the territory of what used to be the GDR. The horizontal equalisation scheme is supplemented by vertical equalisation payments from the federal government, amounting to over €14.6 billion in 2005, which went to the same eleven states as the horizontal payments (see Table 4.3 below). Significantly, neither of these systems existed when the Federal Republic was founded in 1949; both developed over time.

German federalism produces political interdependencies, too. The *Länder* are collectively represented in the federal policy-making process via the *Bundesrat* (as shown in Box 4.1), which must be consulted on all legislation, even that which lies in the federal government's exclusive range of competencies. While the *Bundestag* can overrule any opposition from the *Bundesrat* in such laws, the latter wields a veto in over one-third of legislation, including the most significant bills, such as tax reforms. This is a considerable reduction from the 60 per cent or so of legislation over which the *Bundesrat* could collectively exercise a veto prior to the 2006 federalism reform (of which more below), but the *Bundesrat* remains the most visible 'veto point' in German politics, and thereby casts a spotlight on the political composition of majorities within it. We shall return to this central point in the next section.

Because of this immensely complex interweaving of political competencies and financial dependencies, Germany's system of federalism has traditionally been described as 'co-operative' or 'interlocking' (Scharpf *et al.*, 1976), in that it would simply not function if the various levels, as well as the individual actors within those levels, did not co-operate with each other (for examples of how this worked in the past, see Leonardy, 1991). This theme of co-operation, or more broadly speaking consensus, is one which runs through much of German politics.

One other function of federalism in the German political system needs to be mentioned: the recruitment of elites. It is very rare indeed for politicians to emerge on the national stage without first having worked their way up through the party organisation at local and *Land* level. Indeed, *Land* elections provide a perfect opportunity for aspiring chancellors to show their party that they are capable of winning elections. Accordingly, both chancellors and chancellor-candidates are frequently either ex- or serving *Land* minister-presidents, including Helmut Kohl and Gerhard Schröder, respectively, although Angela Merkel is a notable exception to this rule. The corollary to this is that all chancellors have to deal with powerful and confident minister-presidents, not only from the opposition but from their own party, who are often looking for a way to highlight themselves at the expense of the national leadership.

The dynamics of coalition politics

The second dimension to consider is that of coalition politics. Only once, following the 1957 election, has a single party (the CDU/CSU) been in a position to command a majority in parliament without a coalition partner, although even then it chose to form a coalition. The involvement of one of the smaller parties, in particular the liberal FDP, which is the only party to have formed alliances with both of the large parties, has over time served to produce what Manfred Schmidt (1987) has described as the 'policy of the middle way', in other words a broadly centrist public policy profile. This occurs in two ways. First, each coalition partner, irrespective of their size, has a full right of veto over any government policy proposal. Second, the principle of ministerial independence (the *Ressortprinzip*) means that incumbents are free to run their portfolios as they see fit. Especially if they come from the minor coalition partner, ministers are therefore effectively immune to political pressure from the Chancellor as head of the federal government. The dynamics of coalition government also hold true at *Land* level, although there are likely to be more coalition permutations, as well as more instances of single-party government (such as the CSU in Bavaria; see below and Chapter 5).

The Constitutional Court

The third dimension of fragmentation of power is the Constitutional Court. It too represents a direct response to Nazi dictatorship, during which the courts had no remit to challenge the dismantling of liberal democracy. Like the United States Supreme Court, the Constitutional Court has had a profound impact over the years on politics in Germany (see Kommers, 1997). Its importance is based on its wide-ranging powers of judicial review, which can focus on specific laws as well as individual norms of public policy. Furthermore, the Court acts as arbiter in disputes between other political institutions, most frequently between the federal and *Länder* levels. Judicially, it has handed down

Table 4.1 Federal governments and chancellors, 1949–2005

Election Year	Federal Government	Chancellor
1949	CDU/CSU–FDP, DP	Konrad Adenauer (CDU)
1953	CDU/CSU–FDP, DP, GB/BHE	Konrad Adenauer (CDU)
1957	CDU/CSU, DP	Konrad Adenauer (CDU)
1961	CDU/CSU–FDP	Konrad Adenauer (CDU); from 1963 Ludwig Erhard (CDU)
1965	CDU/CSU–FDP; from 1966 CDU/CSU–SPD	Ludwig Erhard (CDU); from 1966 Kurt-Georg Kiesinger (CDU)
1969	SPD–FDP	Willy Brandt (SPD)
1972	SPD–FDP	Willy Brandt (SPD); from 1974 Helmut Schmidt (SPD)
1976	SPD–FDP	Helmut Schmidt (SPD)
1980	SPD–FDP; from 1982 CDU/CSU–FDP	Helmut Schmidt (SPD); from 1982 Helmut Kohl (CDU)
1983	CDU/CSU–FDP	Helmut Kohl (CDU)
1987	CDU/CSU–FDP	Helmut Kohl (CDU)
1990	CDU/CSU–FDP	Helmut Kohl (CDU)
1994	CDU/CSU–FDP	Helmut Kohl (CDU)
1998	SPD–Greens	Gerhard Schröder (SPD)
2002	SPD–Greens	Gerhard Schröder (SPD)
2005	CDU/CSU–SPD	Angela Merkel (CDU)

Key: DP = Deutsche Partei; GB/BHE = Gesamtdeutscher Bloc/Bund der Heimatvertriebenen und Entrechteten

Note: This is a slightly simplified representation of the governments which have been in power in Germany since 1949. For a full breakdown, which includes full dates and transitional governments (for instance, in 1982), see Schmidt (2003b: 52–3).

rulings affecting practically all areas of life in Germany, including social and tax policy (for instance, in 2001), abortion (in 1975 and 1993), European integration (1994), the fiscal equalisation scheme between the *Länder* (1999), the deployment of German troops abroad (1994), asylum policy (1996) and repeatedly the public financing of parties (see Chapter 5). In terms of adjudicating disputes between institutions, it has occasionally been called upon to clarify the financial relationships within the community of *Länder*, as well as between individual *Länder* and the federation (of which more below). It was also asked to rule on whether the early dissolution of the *Bundestag* in 2005, which triggered federal elections later that summer, was constitutional.

Politically, the relevance of the Court for German politics should not be under-estimated. The fact that it has ruled so widely means that practically all areas of German politics and public policy are potentially subject to judicial scrutiny. Moreover, as cases can be referred to the Court for consideration not only by lower courts but by individual *Land* governments, the *Bundesrat* and one-third of the members of the *Bundestag*, the process of judicial review is also a powerful tool for opposition parties seeking to reverse a defeat in the formal legislative process. This is precisely what happened in 1993, when the Bavarian (and Catholic) CSU referred a cross-party compromise in the *Bundestag* over abortion to the Court, where the new ruling was struck down. In consequence, a veritable cottage industry of pundits has sprung up around the business of second-guessing the approach the Court will adopt to any given issue. It thus remains a highly important yet unpredictable player in German politics (Blankenburg, 1996).

Other elements in the German polity

The entire political process is overseen by the head of state, the Federal President (Table 4.2). As noted above, and in contrast to the Weimar Republic, his/her position is largely ceremonial, and although the choice and election of a president is often a highly partisan affair, the office is above party politics and thus enjoys considerable moral authority. However, in recent years, incumbents have fully exploited this moral authority to make strategic interventions in domestic politics. Thus, Richard von Weizsäcker criticised all the parties in Germany for what he saw as their obsession with power rather than making a difference, while Roman Herzog was one of the first public figures to call for a greatly accelerated pace of reform in 1997. Most recently, the current President, Horst Köhler, in 2006 refused to sign into law two bills which had already been passed by the two chambers of parliament. Certainly, the recent activism of presidents has had its critics; but, so far, successive incumbents have been insulated from such criticism by the high level of public respect their office enjoys.

Three other sets of domestic institutions need to be mentioned: political parties, parapublic institutions and interest groups (Katzenstein, 1987). As will be discussed in greater detail in Chapter 5, German political parties are unusual in that they are constitutionally recognised as political actors. Katzenstein (1987) classifies them, alongside parapublic institutions and federalism, as one of the three 'nodes' of the entire political system. Indeed, the degree to which state structures, and especially public appointments, have been penetrated by political parties has led some commentators to talk of Germany as a 'party state' (*Parteienstaat*) (see Chapter 5 and Schmidt, 2003b: 46–55). By contrast, parapublic institutions are formally state bodies, but they operate according to technocratic rather than political principles (see Katzenstein, 1987: 58–80; Busch, 2005b). Two key examples of parapublic institutions are the (now largely emasculated) *Deutsche Bundesbank*, which managed Germany's monetary policy until

Table 4.2 Federal presidents, 1949–2007

Years	President
1949–59	Theodor Heuss (FDP)
1959–69	Heinrich Lübke (CDU)
1969–74	Gustav Heinemann (SPD)
1974–79	Walter Scheel (FDP)
1979–84	Karl Carstens (CDU)
1984–94	Richard von Weizsäcker (CDU)
1994–99	Roman Herzog (CDU)
1999–2004	Johannes Rau (SPD)
2004–	Horst Köhler (CDU)

the introduction of the euro in 1999, and the Federal Labour Agency (*Bundesagentur für Arbeit*), which oversees unemployment and labour market programmes. Lastly, interest groups include not only the industry-based union movement and employers' organisations (see Chapter 7), but churches and sectoral organisations, such as farmers' and doctors' lobby groups. Often, parapublic institutions act as a nexus between government, employers and unions, and in contrast to the government, many interest groups are characterised by a high degree of centralisation (Katzenstein, 1987).

Crucially, in a further example of an institutional response to Nazi dictatorship, the state delegates the implementation of significant areas of its activities to both parapublic bodies and interest organisations. This is clearly visible in health policy, where the principle of self-governance is particularly well entrenched. Accordingly, significant elements of cost management and control are devolved to both parapublic institutions, in the form of the state health insurance administration (*Allgemeine Ortskrankenkassen*), and interest groups, in the form of the doctors' organisation which deals with the insurance companies over all billing matters (the *Kassenärztliche Vereinigung*).

One final dimension deserves consideration. Since 1957, Germany has been one of the key members of what has now become the European Union. As the competencies of the EU have increased, especially following the Single European Act in 1986, so the influence of the EU on national policy-making has risen: between 1998 and 2002 over one-third of all laws passed in Germany originally emanated from the supranational arena (Töller, cited in Schmidt and Zohlnhöfer, 2006: 24; see also Sturm and Pehle, 2005). In areas such as agriculture, of course, this proportion was even higher. Perhaps the most notable example of the impact of the EU in the German context is the entire transfer of monetary policy to the European Central Bank with the introduction of the euro in 1999. Chapters 7 and 9 discuss the impact of Germany on the EU, and vice versa, in greater detail.

Remarkably, the essentials of this institutional configuration, and especially the operation of federalism, remained relatively untouched by unification (Jeffery, 1995 and 2005: 85–6). Five *Länder* were re-established on the territory of the GDR and post-1990 the state of Berlin incorporated both the western and eastern halves of this formerly divided city. Most of the existing elements and structures of policy-making, including the parapublic institutions and the close involvement of sectoral interest groups in the delivery of policy, were transferred wholesale to the five new *Länder* plus Berlin (Jacoby, 2000). Only relatively minor structural changes were undertaken, such as the increase of the number of votes of the four largest western *Länder* from five to six to maintain their relative weight in the *Bundesrat*. Even though a government commission was set up to review the suitability of Germany's constitution in a post-unification environment, it concluded that only cosmetic amendments were necessary. But, in reality, unification has proved to be a significant challenge for the operation of the German polity, in particular the relations between the *Länder* and the functioning of the *Bundesrat* in federal politics (see below).

This complex web of institutions, and the range of interactions it produces, has famously been characterised by Katzenstein (1987) as a 'semi-sovereign' state (see also Green and Paterson, 2005). This term refers to the fact that power is highly fragmented both *within* the central (i.e., federal) government, due to coalition politics and the relatively limited direct power of the Chancellor, and *between* the federal government and the *Länder*, the Federal Constitutional Court, parapublic institutions and the key interest groups. Put differently, Germany is distinguished in international terms by an unusually large number of 'veto players': that is, 'an individual or collective actor whose agreement . . . is required for a change in policy' (Tsebelis, 1995: 301).

The result is that there is an institutional predisposition within the German political system towards only gradual policy evolution, or, as Katzenstein (1987) terms it, 'incremental policy change' (see also Green and Paterson, 2005). In turn, this institutional bias towards incremental policy change strengthens the dynamics of historical precedence, in that policy priorities, once agreed upon by the parties via the institutional process, become very difficult to change in their essence. Known in the political science literature as 'path dependence' (Peters, 1999: 63), this dynamic is visible in a range of domestic and foreign policy areas, from the issue of conscription (see Chapter 10) to the operation of the pension system (see Chapter 7). This predisposition is complemented by a normative emphasis on consensus between the main political parties wherever possible (Dyson, 1982). Again arising as a reaction to the sometimes polarised nature of politics in the Weimar Republic, there has historically been a palpable dislike of outright adversarial politics as sometimes found in Anglo-Saxon democracies. The result has been an inherent tendency within the German political system towards the 'politics of centrality' (Smith, 1976).

But, as Katzenstein (1987: 350) notes, incremental change does not per se equate with stagnation: 'It is easy to mistake incremental change for incapacity to change . . . There is a world of difference between incrementalism and immobilism.' Indeed, the period of the 'Grand Coalition' between 1966 and 1969, and perhaps especially the run-up to unification in 1989–90, showed that the German political system has been capable of reacting relatively rapidly when circumstances require.

Nonetheless, in recent years, there has been a sense within Germany that the political system is no longer delivering appropriate outputs. For over two decades, politicians and commentators have been debating Germany's economic position in a globalising world (the *Standortdebatte*), and what reforms to its welfare and economic system are necessary to maintain this position (to be discussed further in Chapters 7 and 8). This question has become especially acute in the context of the huge additional financial burden of unification (outlined in Chapter 3, pp. 47–8). Since the mid-1990s, this debate has become ever more anguished: in 1997, the word '*Reformstau*' ('reform blockage') came into vogue and President Roman Herzog made a public plea for greater purpose in tackling the challenges of social and economic reform. Since late 1998, when the SPD–Green government under Gerhard Schröder came to power, there has been a sense either that reforms have not been politically possible, or that where they have been attempted (as in healthcare), they have simply not been sufficient to address the extent of the problem. Perhaps a provisional climax in this question was reached after the 2005 federal election, when there was no majority for either of the two main party blocs (CDU/CSU–FDP and SPD–Greens). The following chapters will discuss the challenges and the solutions sought in a range of policy areas, but the task here is to examine the notion and dimensions of a blockaded system of government in greater detail.

Issues

Given the complexity of German federalism, it is probably not surprising that much of the debate over the ability of Germany's political institutions to deliver effective policy solutions has revolved around this particular issue. In essence, there have been four main topics discussed under this heading (see also Wachendorfer-Schmidt, 2005):

- the function of the *Bundesrat* as a veto player;
- the division of competencies between the federation and the *Länder*;
- the impact of European integration;
- the future financial relationship between the individual *Länder*.

The first question, concerning the *Bundesrat*'s function as a veto player in national politics, is perhaps the most visible in the public eye: as noted above, Germany's second chamber has been arguably the most powerful veto player, with around 60 per cent of all legislation, including most significant domestic policy initiatives, requiring its approval prior to 2006. Indeed, it was this dynamic which prompted Fritz Scharpf (1988) to characterise (West) German federalism as a 'joint decision trap', in which the potential for either actor to exercise a veto over the other's wishes necessarily produced outcomes at or around the lowest common denominator.

Furthermore, the party political relationship between the two chambers is highly complex. Even when the same coalition of parties have dominated both chambers, the *Bundesrat*'s approval could never be taken for granted, although this was obviously more likely than when the coalition of parties with at least a nominal majority differed between the two chambers. Yet a hostile *Bundesrat* majority did not necessarily lead to a blockade of the federal government's bills, due both to the high value placed on consensus politics and to the ability of the federal government to offer sweeteners to individual *Länder* and hence 'divide and rule' the *Bundesrat*. A prime example of this dynamic occurred during the vote on the 2000 tax reform, when the SPD–Green federal government secured the votes of *Länder* such as Bremen, which was governed by an SPD–CDU coalition at the time, by promising federal aid for local programmes (Jeffery, 2005: 92).

The key reason why the federal government has been able to divide and rule the *Länder* is because they, like many other areas of German society, are much less homogeneous now than they were prior to unification (Jeffery, 2005: 81–5). As Table 4.3 shows, the sixteen *Länder* vary very widely in terms of population, wealth, unemployment and public debt. In consequence, it has become much harder to develop joint positions among them; with each facing different political priorities depending mainly on whether they are large or small, rich or poor and in the east or west.

This heterogeneity among the *Länder* is reflected in the political composition of the sixteen *Land* governments. Before unification, there was a more-or-less clear divide between those states governed by parties in the federal coalition and those governed by the opposition: in other words, there were two clear blocs of votes in the *Bundesrat*. However, since unification, with ever-more parties competing successfully at *Land* level, the resulting composition of *Land* governments has also become more diverse (see Chapter 5). In particular, this has meant that coalitions which cut *across* the government–opposition divide in the *Bundestag* have become more common.

This matters because, for (all-important) consent legislation to pass the *Bundesrat*, thirty-five of the possible sixty-nine votes must be cast in favour. But in cases where a *Land* coalition does not reflect the government–opposition divide at federal level, it is usual for these *Länder* to abstain from contested *Bundesrat* votes. In turn, because of the requirement for an absolute majority of votes for consent bills to pass, abstentions effectively count as rejections. A by-product of this dynamic is that it becomes much easier for the main opposition party (at least to threaten) to blockade a government bill than it is for a federal government to pass it. Federal governments since unification have, as a rule, found it difficult to build and maintain a reliable majority in the *Bundesrat*. This

Table 4.3 Diversity among the sixteen *Länder* of Germany, 2005

Land	Population (millions)	GDP/capita (€)	Unemployment rate (%)	Public debt/ capita (€)	Horizontal equalisation transfers (€ billion)	Votes in Bundesrat	Composition of government (July 2007)
Baden-Württemberg	10.7	30,793	7.0	4,335	−2.2	6	CDU–FDP
Bavaria	12.5	32,378	7.8	3,133	−2.2	6	CSU
Berlin	3.4	23,433	19.0	15,907	+2.4	4	SPD–Left Party
Brandenburg	2.6	18,799	18.3	7,091	+0.6	4	SPD–CDU
Bremen	0.7	36,903	16.8	17,013	+0.4	3	SPD–Greens
Hamburg	1.7	45,866	11.3	11,721	−0.4	3	CDU
Hesse	6.1	32,451	9.7	6,093	−1.6	5	CDU
Lower Saxony	8.0	23,563	11.6	6,832	+0.4	6	CDU–FDP
Mecklenburg–Western Pomerania	1.7	18,327	20.3	7,149	+0.4	3	SPD–CDU
North Rhine–Westphalia	18.1	27,082	12.0	7,244	−0.5	6	CDU–FDP
Rhineland–Palatinate	4.1	24,015	8.8	6,894	+0.3	4	SPD
Saarland	1.1	26,162	10.7	7,804	+0.1	3	CDU
Saxony	4.3	17,729	18.3	4,043	+1.0	4	CDU–SPD
Saxony–Anhalt	2.5	19,454	20.3	8,522	+0.5	4	CDU–SPD
Schleswig–Holstein	2.8	24,356	11.6	7,792	+0.1	4	CDU–SPD
Thuringia	2.3	19,128	17.1	7,190	+0.6	4	CDU

Source: Statistisches Bundesamt; GDP/capita data taken from Schmidt, 2007: 200

was even the case under the Grand Coalition after 2005, when the federal government nominally enjoyed an overwhelming majority in both chambers of parliament. Then, especially, ambitious *Land* minister-presidents used the *Bundesrat* to parade on the national political stage at the federal government's expense. Furthermore, because of the system of staggered *Land* elections, federal governments have generally found it impossible to regain a *Bundesrat* majority once it has been lost (see Saalfeld, 2005: 64). The sole exception post-1961 was the CDU/CSU–FDP government under Helmut Kohl. Throughout the 1980s, it enjoyed a comfortable *Bundesrat* majority, but it lost this after the Lower Saxony election in spring 1990. It regained its majority through the extra-ordinary circumstances of unification in October 1990, when the five new, predominantly CDU–FDP-governed eastern *Länder* joined the Federal Republic. However, even this position was short-lived, and the federal government once again lost its majority in early 1991 following the Hesse and Rhineland–Palatinate elections.

The big political question arising out of Germany's intricate system of majorities is whether parties in opposition at federal level, once a federal government has lost its majority in the *Bundesrat*, can and do utilise their strong position in that chamber to obstruct the federal government's legislative agenda systematically. Certainly, the German political scientist Gerhard Lehmbruch (2002 [1976]) thought so in the 1970s, when the CDU/CSU opposition was clear about its intention to use its *Bundesrat* majority in order to hinder the SPD–FDP federal government's bills. But more recently, scholars such as Charlie Jeffery (2005: 91–2) have been more circumspect about making this claim (see also Lees, 2005: 116–24). They point out that only a small minority of bills is vetoed by the *Bundesrat* (see Rudzio, 2003: 330) and that *Länder* interests are a better indicator of voting intentions than the party political composition of their governments. As a result of these interests, as noted above, the federal government has, on rare but significant occasions, been able to 'buy off' individual, and often cash-strapped, *Länder*. Nonetheless, the threat of a potential veto by the *Bundesrat* can be as effective as wielding the veto itself. It is principally this requirement for a federal government to work with the federal opposition via the *Bundesrat*, especially when the two largest parties are not in government together, that has prompted Manfred Schmidt (2002) to characterise Germany as a permanent 'grand coalition state'.

While the ability of the *Bundesrat* to act as a veto player impacts primarily on federal politics, there has also been a growing discussion between the federal government and the *Länder* about the distribution of competencies, which culminated in the 2006 federalism reform (see below). In truth, such conflicts are arguably inherent in federal systems, and the Constitutional Court has been called upon on several occasions in the past to resolve them. But the concerns of the *Länder* have arisen out of the long-term trend for the federation to encroach on their competencies, primarily through the *Bundestag*'s rigorous exploitation of its right to legislate in 'concurrent' policy areas (Article 74 of the Basic Law). In essence, as noted above, this left the *Länder* with practically no possibility to conduct their own politics: it is no surprise that the minister-president of a *Land* is known, affectionately, as a *Landesvater*, a kind of avuncular figure whose primary role is to inaugurate public works projects and spread goodwill at events such as regional garden shows (the ubiquitous *Landesgartenschauen*).

The third issue to affect federalism is related to the previous point and constitutes perhaps an even more serious challenge to the competencies of the *Länder*: Germany's membership of the European Union and the resulting process of European integration (Bulmer *et al.*, 2000: 33–40; see also Chapter 9). Since the mid-1980s, and especially since the Single European Act of 1986, the *Länder* have collectively grown ever more concerned over what they have seen as the federal government's eagerness to transfer sovereignty to the EU in those areas which had traditionally been the *Länder*'s areas of competence. In consequence, the *Länder* have demanded more input into the EU's policy process, both in the form of their own representations in Brussels (Moore, 2006) and via their right to represent issues of direct concern to them in the Council of Ministers. Indeed, they famously threatened to veto the ratification of the 1992 Maastricht Treaty if progress was not made on their demands. Similarly, the *Länder* were the driving force behind the EU's decision at the 2000 Nice European Council meeting to set up the (ultimately ill-fated) constitutional convention.

Finally, the whole relationship between the individual *Länder* has begun to be challenged from within. In particular, the comparatively rich southern states of Hesse, Baden-Württemberg and Bavaria, the three main contributors to the horizontal fiscal equalisation scheme, have emerged as the leading critics of the current system and the way in which it binds together the *Länder*. In their view, the goal of equal living conditions appears to be ever more difficult to achieve, not least because of the significant economic differences between the old and new *Länder*. In place of the current arrangements, these three *Länder*, especially Bavaria, have argued for a much greater degree of autonomy, to include the 'repatriation' of competencies, especially from the EU level, as well as less scope for the fiscal equalisation system (Jeffery, 2005: 87–8). On this basis, they challenged the entire system of the *Länderfinanzausgleich* in the Constitutional Court in 1998. Although this resulted in a partial victory for the three plaintiff *Länder*, it ultimately translated into only a marginal reduction of their payments into the system.

Three poorer western *Länder*, Saarland, Bremen and Berlin, have argued at different times before the Constitutional Court for additional financial assistance not from the other *Länder* but from the federal government. As Table 4.3 shows, all three are small states suffering from structurally weak economies, with high levels of unemployment and public debt. In 1992, the Constitutional Court ruled that Saarland and Bremen were entitled to special grants from the federal government, on the basis that they were no longer in a position to recover from their parlous financial positions by themselves. By contrast, the state of Berlin was not so lucky. During the partition of Germany, West Berlin enjoyed lavish financial assistance from the federal government, reflecting its position as an outpost of the West deep inside the Iron Curtain. But after unification, these funds dried up, and, unusually for a capital city, Berlin remains desperately weak economically: half of its population is unemployed, living on income support or drawing pensions; its total public debt is almost €60 billion; and it is by far the largest beneficiary of horizontal transfers from the financial equalisation scheme, accounting by itself for over one-third of total receipts. The city's situation has not been helped by a notorious case of corruption surrounding the collapse in 2001 of a state-owned financial institution, the *Bankgesellschaft Berlin*, which saddled the city with a further €10 billion of debt. Berlin's current Mayor, Klaus Wowereit, displayed the city's typical black humour when he famously described it as 'poor, but sexy' ('*Arm, aber Sexy*'). The capital took the federal government to the Constitutional Court in 2003 arguing that, like Bremen and Saarland, it should benefit from additional federal support. But in October 2006 its claim was rejected by the Court, which argued that the problem was not so much one of revenue as one of expenditure. In a direct reference to Wowereit's much-quoted description, the presiding judge commented that perhaps Berlin was so sexy because it was not so poor after all.

Together, these three disputes illustrate how tensions between territorial units are developing. On the one hand, the richer states are less willing to subsidise their poorer neighbours; but, on the other hand, poorer states are finding it harder to improve their financial positions without assistance. At the same time, the other main player, the federal government, has, in light of its own fiscal pressures, been unwilling to step in. So far, such disputes have therefore tended to necessitate adjudication by the Constitutional Court.

Federalism has been perhaps the most visible area of debate over the question of whether Germany's institutional structure is a help or a hindrance in the pursuit of reform, but other elements of the political system are also coming under scrutiny. Periodically, there are suggestions to replace Germany's broadly proportional electoral system (see Chapter 5), which almost by definition produces coalition governments, with a majoritarian, first-past-the-post system. The role and power of the Constitutional Court is certainly discussed critically, too, although this tends to take place internationally rather than domestically (e.g., Stone Sweet, 2000): the Court regularly ranks among the top institutions in Germany for the level of trust it is accorded by the population. Perhaps most of all, organised interest groups have been blamed for Germany's economic problems (e.g., Streeck, 2005): even a casual observer of German politics will notice the degree to which the unions, churches and dispensing chemists, to name but three interest groups, manage to influence policy in the SPD, CDU/CSU and FDP, respectively.

Debates

Despite the complexity of the issues surrounding institutional reform in Germany, there have been a number of attempts in recent years to make real progress, especially over the question of the structure and content of federalism. In the aftermath of unification, there was a lively debate about the political and financial viability of sixteen independent *Länder*, each with a full-scale parliament, government ministries, senior administrative elite and often even its own broadcasting network. A number of proposals were made to merge the smallest *Länder* (in particular the city-states) with their larger neighbours (Sturm, 1992: 131–3). But, perhaps inevitably, such initiatives did not progress beyond an initial phase: there was never a realistic chance that states such as Lower Saxony and Rhineland–Palatinate, with their considerable fiscal challenges, would agree to take on the financial liabilities of the neighbouring states of Bremen and the Saarland, respectively, both of which were saddled with even worse debts per capita. Only in one case was a merger between two *Länder* attempted, between Berlin and Brandenburg in 1996. But this was defeated in a referendum in both *Länder*, and no further mergers have since been mooted.

Yet, against the odds, the German system of government has shown itself to be capable of reforming itself. In 2003, the SPD-led federal government and the sixteen *Länder* agreed to set up a joint commission charged with the 'modernisation' of Germany's federal system. Co-chaired by the SPD-leader, Franz Müntefering, and the CSU-leader and Bavarian Minister-President Edmund Stoiber, this represented an ideal example of the informal Grand Coalition State in action. Indeed, the protagonists (mainly the CDU/CSU and SPD) soon reached agreement on a range of issues, including the reduction of consent laws from 60 per cent of the total to about 35 per cent in return for a repatriation of some competencies to the *Länder*, such as the right to regulate themselves the pay and conditions for civil servants. Although the discussions temporarily collapsed in

December 2004 over the division of competencies in education policy, they were restarted under the Grand Coalition just one year later, following the 2005 election. In late 2006, a package of reforms to the federal structure almost identical to the 2004 deal prior to its collapse became law, and this has gone some way to disentangling the policy process at the federal level.

Despite such progress, the really controversial issue – the future of the horizontal and vertical fiscal equalisation schemes – was not even part on the agenda during this debate; instead, this was postponed to a second reform commission, which began its work in spring 2007. By summer 2007, its outcome was still open, which reflected the high stakes involved for all *Länder*, irrespective of the party political composition of their government. Indeed, the financial relationships between the *Länder* have generated some highly acrimonious disputes since unification. Because the five eastern *Länder* plus Berlin are all economically much weaker than even the poorest western state, the balance of the fiscal equalisation scheme has shifted eastwards since 1990: of the €6.9 billion distributed by the horizontal fiscal equalisation scheme in 2005, over 80 per cent went to the five eastern *Länder* plus Berlin, which in total accounted for just 20 per cent of the country's population. The imbalance was even greater among the vertical equalisation payments from the federal government, under which the same six *Länder* received over 90 per cent of payments, amounting to over €13.4 billion in 2005. Inevitably, this has created 'losers' in the west: the rich western states lose because they have to pay more, and the poor western states lose because they receive less. To make matters worse, there is so far no indication that the economic situation in eastern Germany will develop enough, even over the coming decades, to allow the six new *Länder* to become independent of the *Länderfinanzausgleich*. Thus, states like Bavaria are faced with having to support the poorer *Länder* for a very long time to come, which is obviously a source of political tension within that state's governing party, the CSU. At the same time, critics of the Bavarian position are quick to point out that Bavaria itself benefited for most of the period before 1990 from the same equalisation scheme.

So far, the issue has been dealt with by the federal government stepping in and shouldering most of the costs via the vertical equalisation scheme. In 1995, a first solidarity pact (*Solidarpakt I*) was negotiated between the *Länder* and the federal government. This was renewed in 2003, with the *Solidarpakt II* running until 2019. However, in both cases, the final deal depended on the willingness of the federal government to underwrite much of the additional expenditure that this involved (Sally and Webber, 1994; Jacoby, 2005: 39–44). In consequence, the *Solidarpakt II* continues to commit the federal government to long-term support of the *Länder*, as the €14.6 billion paid through the vertical support mechanism in 2005 (more than double the total generated by the horizontal mechanism) illustrates. But what this debate underlines most of all is that unification has brought out tensions in the organisation of German federalism which the existing structures have so far failed to resolve.

Conclusion

This chapter has provided a broad overview of the institutional configuration of Germany's political system. It has shown that its structure and consensual norms of operation clearly reflect the historical legacy of the Weimar Republic and the Third Reich. It has argued that the wide dispersal of power within the system, combined with a comparatively high number of 'veto points', has conditioned the political system to only gradual policy change. Significantly, even in times of rapid change, most notably the period leading up to unification in 1989 and 1990, there was little change in the institutions themselves, as the wholesale 'transfer' of structures, and especially of federalism, to the east illustrates.

In thinking about whether Germany has a blockaded political system, therefore, it is useful to distinguish between policy change and institutional change, as well as the links between these two factors. As many of the following chapters will go on to illustrate, policy change has indeed continued to demonstrate the incremental tendencies inherent in the political system. But, as this chapter has also shown, the institutional structures themselves have not changed much since unification: even after the 2006 reform, the most important characteristics of 'co-operative federalism', in particular its financial arrangements, remained in place, despite the fact that Germany's sixteen *Länder* are now a highly diverse range of entities with corresponding political priorities.

In turn, this heterogeneity of the *Länder*, which has translated into a lack of party political majorities in the *Bundesrat*, has frustrated the federal government's ability to make policy. Simultaneously, even the potential of a *Bundesrat* veto has made it possible for the main federal opposition party to act as a 'status preserver' for electoral reasons. Since the financial pressures created by unification mean that most political debates in Germany now revolve around cuts in provision rather than distribution of extra expenditure, it is difficult not to conclude that Germany's highly consensual political system makes it easy to fudge, if not block outright, the formulation of the painful measures most commentators agree are necessary to improve economic performance.

In other words, post-unification Germany's political institutions are faced with a challenge that they were simply not set up to manage. Therefore, it is difficult to deny that the political system in Germany, with its tendency towards the 'joint-decision trap', does not at least contribute to the ponderous public policy response to rapidly accelerating social and economic challenges. Yet, ironically, a full-scale revision of political structures towards a more majoritarian, 'Westminster' type of democracy is not necessary (Lijphart, 1999). Two relatively simple measures would probably suffice to break up the logjam. First, the requirement that consent laws attract an absolute majority of *Länder* votes could be inverted; in other words, the *Länder* would only be able to *block* consent legislation by an absolute majority. Second, by bundling *Land* elections around a set date in the calendar, mirroring, for instance, mid-term congressional elections in the United States, the phenomenon of constant electioneering, which has frustrated the ability of any government to make a sustained effort to solve difficult political problems, would also be reduced. Of course, the flip-side of this is that *Land* elections would become a de facto referendum on the federal government, whereas at present they reflect, at least to some extent, regional peculiarities (Jeffery and Hough, 2001). However, these remain nothing more than theoretical options at present.

Germany's political institutions remain locked in their pre-unification structures. The 2006 federalism reform has indicated that structural reform is possible, although notably only within the framework of a formal Grand Coalition. Crucially, the most fundamental reforms, in particular to the number of *Länder*, as well as to the financial arrangements between them, remain as elusive as ever.

Questions for discussion

1   **Who has power in German politics?**
2   **'The *Bundesrat* is the main reason for *Reformstau* in Germany'. Discuss.**
3   **How does the position of Chancellor compare to: a) the British Prime Minister; b) the French President; and c) the US President?**

Further reading

Conradt, D. (2004), *The German Polity* (London: Addison Wesley). Definitive analysis of the German political system.

Green, S. and Paterson, W. (2005), *Governance in Contemporary Germany: The Semisovereign State Revisited* (Cambridge: Cambridge University Press). A full-scale re-examination of Katzenstein's landmark semi-sovereignty thesis, covering a wide range of institutions and policy areas.

Schmidt, M. (2003), *Political Institutions in the Federal Republic of Germany* (Oxford: Oxford University Press). An outstanding and student-friendly examination of Germany's political system.

—— (2007), *Das Politische System Deutschlands* (Munich: Verlag C.H. Beck). The most recent and comprehensive book in German on the political system.

5 The party system and electoral behaviour

The path to stable instability?

Summary

The two-and-a-half-party system that characterised German politics for the majority of the post-war era is now a thing of the past. Two medium-sized (CDU/CSU and SPD) and three smaller (FDP, the Greens and the Left Party) parties now garner enough votes to make coalition formation – and consequently governing in general – a much more complex task than it used to be. Processes of dealignment (in western Germany) and partial alignment (in eastern Germany) ensure that voters have become more volatile and the traditional supporter bases of all the parties more fragile. Although unification did not spawn all of these developments, it has certainly exacerbated them and has contributed to the fragmentation of the party system and to an increasing diversity of electoral outcomes.

Introduction

Political parties play pivotal roles in all modern, Western democracies. They act as critical stabilising institutions in democratic systems of government. In more concrete terms, they bring people with similar political philosophies together and facilitate the selection of representatives to take up high office. They give voice to the interests of narrow groups within society – whether they be trade unions, environmental organisations, business associations or myriad sectional interests – and create policy packages that, if elected, politicians with executive power then seek to implement. Finally, political parties are vital mechanisms in simplifying the complex and messy business of day-to-day politics into messages that the wider population can understand and subsequently evaluate. Life in a democratic polity such as the Federal Republic is therefore unthinkable (for the vast majority of people) without the input of political parties.

Germany was long distinguished by a stable party system that rarely changed in basic structure from one election to the next. At the first federal election in 1949, ten parties managed to poll over 1 per cent of the vote, and all of them managed to gain some sort of representation in parliament. Through the 1950s, the German party system consolidated rapidly and political competition became highly structured. The centre-left Social Democratic Party and centre-right Christian Democratic Union (along with its Bavarian sister party, the Christian Social Union) grew to cover most of the moderate terrain in the political centre, accumulating the vast majority of the votes, with one of these parties subsequently forming governments with the smaller, liberal, Free Democratic Party. From 1957 to 1983 these were the only three parties in parliament, dividing political jobs between themselves, overseeing the flourishing German economy and helped to embed democracy. The rise of the Greens in the late 1970s and early 1980s – culminating in their entry into the *Bundestag* in 1983 – broke up the happy cartel, as party political life in Germany became more complicated (see Frankland and Schoonmaker, 1992). In 1993, the Greens merged with a range of eastern German civil rights groups to become Alliance 90/The Greens (*Bündnis 90/Die Grünen*), further stabilising itself as a serious centre-left actor with a long-term future. The unification of Germany in 1990 exacerbated this gradual process of party system diversification, as the successor party to the communist SED, the Party of Democratic Socialism (recently renamed the Left Party), entered the federal parliament not just in 1990, but in 1994 and 1998. A dip in support saw it all but leave the federal arena in 2002, but it returned triumphantly in 2005, polling 8.7 per cent of the popular vote (see Hough *et al.*, 2007).

This chapter examines these processes of consolidation, stabilisation and gradual fragmentation within the German party system in more detail. It begins by analysing the institutional setting of the parties before moving on to discuss the development of the two *Volksparteien* ('catch-all parties') and the other, smaller actors within the German party system. It analyses voters' views of the parties as well as their worries about an ever-increasing sense of disillusionment with their political representatives. The chapter then moves on to analyse some of the major challenges that face German parties – many of which were highlighted in clear and unflattering fashion in the 2005 federal election.

Background

Unlike in many other Western countries, German parties have been granted a privileged position within the constitutional order, and Germany is often referred to as a *Parteienstaat* (party state). This status grants parties not only particular rights and privileges, but responsibilities and obligations that go beyond those evident in most other democratic polities. Germany's constitutional forefathers were clear in their aim of forcing political parties actively to shape and mould political life within the country. They believed that structured competition between parties within a democratic system of governance would facilitate popular representation and ensure political accountability – things that had evidently been missing in the dismal Weimar Republic (1919–33) period of German history.

German parties are therefore granted legitimacy through the Basic Law. Article 21 stipulates that they are required to 'participate in forming the political will of the people' before stressing that they must be organised in an internally democratic way and must publicly account for all of the funds that they accrue (see Schmidt, 2003b: 20–1). The drafters of the constitution thought that parties should help define and shape public opinion rather than simply follow what they perceived to be the random and – at times – dangerous whims of the electorate. They were highly sceptical of direct democracy and subsequently limited referenda almost completely to the *Land* and local levels. The weakness of direct democracy at the federal level has subsequently enhanced the position of parties at the apex of political life (*ibid.*: 47). Furthermore, the *Parteienstaat* allows parties to monopolise political recruitment, as well as to enjoy extensive patronage rights. Regardless of the fact that appointments to public office are supposed to be made on merit alone, it is clear that posts in some parts of the judiciary, public administration, public broadcasting as well as some of the parapublic bodies are made with party interests firmly in mind (*ibid.*: 48). The apparent ubiquity of political parties has contributed to increasing disenchantment with them in recent times. Through the 1990s these feelings of what came to be known as *Parteienverdrossenheit* (disenchantment with parties) grew precisely because it appeared that they seemed rather more interested in looking after their own interests in this complex web of state regulation than those of the wider public at large.

Given this pivotal position, parties were given ample resource channels to fulfil their tasks as well as to educate the wider citizenry in political affairs, with the most prominent and well known of these channels being the political foundations that are linked to each of the parties that enter the *Bundestag*. Over 90 per cent of the funding for these organisations – the Konrad Adenauer and Friedrich Ebert foundations are affiliated to, albeit theoretically independent of, the CDU and SPD; while the Hanns Seidel, Friedrich Naumann, Heinrich Böll and Rosa Luxemburg foundations co-ordinate their activities with the CSU, FDP, Greens and Left Party, respectively – comes from the public purse, and they retain clear political profiles.

The prominent position of the political parties was further concretised in a 1967 'Law on Political Parties' which stipulated in more detail precisely what role they should play in the German polity. This law addressed such issues as how parties should be organised; it offered further direction on the rights and obligations of members of political parties; and it gave detailed advice on such issues as candidate selection and party finance. Despite the Federal Constitutional Court rejecting a newer, revised version of the law (passed in 1988) granting parties even more state support, German parties now gain roughly a third of their income from public sources – justified largely because of the pivotal role that they are seen to play in consolidating and protecting German democracy (Scarrow, 2006). We will return to the controversial nature of party funding later.

The party system

Although far from dominant in 1949, the two main parties – the SPD and the CDU/CSU – quickly expanded their voter bases to monopolise electoral competition. They thus became *Volksparteien*, an idea which was developed as an ideal type in the 1960s by Otto Kirchheimer. Although many authors have sought (with differing levels of success) to illustrate the flaws in Kirchheimer's argument, it has remained remarkably resilient. In essence, he posited that socio-structural change was in the process of altering the environment within which the mass membership parties of the post-war period existed, with Germany's major parties undergoing a particularly radical process of change themselves (Kirchheimer, 1966). The SPD and CDU/CSU no longer sought to integrate particular social groups and directly articulate relatively narrow interests; rather, the two *Volksparteien* grew to dominate the political process, maximising electoral potential over and above policy goals. In order to do this they broadened their ideological platforms and transcended traditional economic, religious and territorial divides. Furthermore, the experience of the Second World War and the close proximity of the Eastern Bloc fostered a strong aversion among political elites to parties of both the extreme right and the extreme left and encouraged a concentration of political competition in the centre. The ideologically driven development of catch-all parties, based loosely on two poles slightly to the right and slightly to the left of the centre, therefore became apparent in Germany before it did in other countries. This was complimented by a heady mixture of increased economic affluence and broad-based social consensus, progressively encouraging both the CDU/CSU and the SPD to move towards the political centre and garner support from an increasingly undifferentiated electorate (Padgett, 2001: 51–4).

The early leaders of the CDU, in particular, strove to create what in effect was Europe's first *Volkspartei*. During the Weimar Republic, political conservatism had been split by religion, with Catholics and Protestants generally voting for different parties, which in turn were unable to set aside their differences and unite against the rise of Hitler and the NSDAP. The CDU, which had not existed before 1945, therefore explicitly sought to incorporate both sides of the sectarian divide in a party which remained broadly conservative, broadly pro-Church and largely supportive of pro-business policies. Its aims were not to 're-Christianise' an increasingly secular Germany, but to apply a rather generalised set of Christian principles and values to practical politics. This involved a strong commitment to an organic model of society and a stress on integrating different social groupings into a unified, harmonious whole (Huntington and Bale, 2002: 45). The leaders of the CDU, and Konrad Adenauer in particular, were expressly keen to stress that the CDU was a *Volkspartei* of the centre, not of the right. Adenauer built a broad coalition based on anti-socialism and Christian values, without stressing the importance of ideology or class in the CDU's self-understanding. The CDU of the 1950s and 1960s therefore focused on social responsibility and a clear commitment to the social market economy, ensuring that the SPD was inevitably forced leftwards as the CDU came to epitomise many of the economic and social successes with which West Germans identified so closely. The CSU – the CDU's sister party which stands for election only in Bavaria (where, in turn, the CDU does not compete) – has traditionally been rather more conservative and yet also rather more 'social' in its orientation than its Christian Democratic partner. Consequently, it has developed a unique role as both a very successful Bavarian regional party and a nationally significant actor. Although they are separate political organisations, the CDU and CSU sit together in the federal parliament and have proven to be a potent electoral force. Together, they have embraced a broad alliance of voters as they prospered, in particular, in the *Bundestag* elections of the first three post-war decades.

It was not long, however, before the SPD – Germany's oldest party, dating from 1863 – realised that the CDU had created a clear recipe for success and attempted to follow suit. With the abandonment of the 1925 Heidelberg Programme, and subsequently its (at least symbolic) Marxist orientation, the SPD chose to dilute the importance of ideology and the class struggle in its own self-understanding. The programme that it adopted in Bad Godesberg in 1959 distanced the party from socialist doctrine and pleaded for a social market economy that also offered a safety net with which to support the less well off. The SPD attempted to broaden its profile rightwards and, most importantly, tried to remain competitive with the CDU. Electoral goals were overcoming ideological ones, even though the SPD undoubtedly remained a party whose members were still prone occasionally to indulge in electorally damaging programmatic disputes. Slowly, the party nevertheless realised that the class conflict it had espoused for most of its existence was not only outdated but was a major hindrance when competing in elections, and it gradually attempted to open itself up and win voters from all sectors of society. The SPD therefore became the model for the social-democratic *Volkspartei*.

The remoulding of the CDU and the SPD into genuine, broad-based, catch-all parties of the centre-right and centre-left, respectively, enabled them to expand and concretise their positions as dominant actors within the political process (see Figure 5.1). By the 1961 election, they were able to mobilise over 80 per cent of the popular vote, a figure

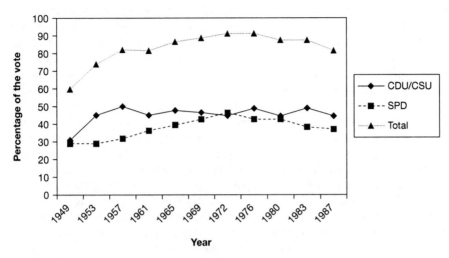

Figure 5.1 The proportion of the vote polled by the CDU/CSU and SPD in *Bundestag* elections, 1949–87

that they progressively expanded through the 1960s and into the 1970s. By 1976, over nine out of every ten voters were casting their second vote for one of the two *Volksparteien*, indicating the stranglehold that the CDU/CSU and the SPD had over the political process.

The only small party initially to forge a niche for itself was the FDP, developing away from its original national-liberal ethos and articulating both greater economic liberalism and a strong defence of civil liberties. The FDP's base is composed mainly of middle- and upper-class professionals and it has frequently been mocked as a party for those who earn above-average salaries (*Partei der Besserverdiener*). The FDP nonetheless developed into the king-maker, working first with the Christian Democrats (until 1966), then, after a brief three-year spell in opposition, swapping sides to form a coalition with the SPD (1969–82). Furthermore, as the wind went out of the sails of the social-liberal (SPD–FDP) coalition in the late 1970s, the FDP slowly became more interested in the advances of the CDU, and, in 1982, moved back to its traditional coalition partner by supporting a constructive vote of no-confidence in the *Bundestag*. Helmut Schmidt was defeated by Helmut Kohl, who now commanded majority support within the chamber and took over as Chancellor (see Box 4.1).

However, the position of the FDP has become much less comfortable in recent years. No longer is it simply the pivot party safely ensconced between the two *Volksparteien*, opting to work with whichever of the two larger parties fits its policy agenda. The rise of the Greens has pushed the FDP ever more into the arms of the CDU/CSU, as two blocs of parties have established themselves either side of the political centre. As was noted in Chapter 2 (p. 33), the Greens grew out of the social movements of the 1970s and 1980s, invoking a pacifist, environmentalist and libertarian agenda (Poguntke, 1993). Originally, they viewed themselves as an 'anti-party' party, stressing their opposition to conventional politics, claiming that post-industrial society was systematically abusing the planet, always liable to lurch towards militarism and dabbling with such dangerous projects as nuclear power. Early activists such as Rudi Dutschke and Petra Kelly subsequently sought a new society, claiming that they were 'neither left nor right but simply forward'. No matter what they claimed to be, the more right-wing parts of the party were unhappy with this agenda and broke away in 1982 (by which time the Greens were present in six western German *Land* legislatures) to form the Ecological Democratic Party. Those who chose to remain continued to stress their anti-military stance and their opposition to restrictions on immigration and on abortion, as well as their liberal policies on drugs and same-sex rights. They also displayed a penchant for overt political activism.

The 1982 split did not see the end of the Greens' internal feuding; on the contrary, high-profile arguments between so-called *Realos* (realists) and *Fundis* (fundamentalists) over party strategy shaped much debate in the party through the 1980s. The *Realos* adopted much more pragmatic approaches to everyday politics, seeing a role as a more constructive opposition and, ultimately, a party in government as being the best way to 'march through the institutions' of German democracy to help shape political outcomes. The more radical *Fundis* were committed to a fundamental restructuring of society and politics; they had little truck with power-sharing aims and rejected attempts to co-operate with all other parties. The ultimate victory of the *Realo* wing is critical in explaining how the SPD–Green coalition of 1998–2005 came about. Although to the left of the political centre, the Greens appeal to a slightly different 'new politics' electoral market than the more 'traditional left' SPD, and after testing out a number of red–green (the respective colours of the two parties) coalitions at the *Land* level, the Greens are now regarded as a political party much like any other.

The rise and stabilisation of the final party that is currently in the *Bundestag* – the Left Party – emphasises much that has changed in the German party system over the last few years (Hough *et al.*, 2007). The Left Party grew out of the primarily eastern German PDS – which itself grew out of the former ruling party of the GDR, the Socialist Unity Party – as it attempted to make its socialist platform more marketable in western Germany. It changed its name in mid-2005 in anticipation of its proposed merger with another left-wing protest party, the predominantly western German Electoral Alliance for Labour and Social Justice. The two parties finally joined forces in June 2007 under (another) new name *Die Linke* (Left Party). Although the Left Party is rarely perceived as possessing genuine policy competence, it has developed recognisable profiles in the areas of social justice, pacifism and particularly the articulation of eastern German interests (Hough, 2005). The successful candidature of former Finance Minister and SPD leader Oskar Lafontaine on a Left Party open list in 2005 enabled the party to poll 4.9 per cent of the vote in western Germany, and 25.3 per cent in the eastern states, thereby surpassing the Greens as the fourth-largest party in the *Bundestag*. This was followed up with a major success at the 2007 Bremen *Land* election, when the Left Party, which had hitherto been represented only in eastern *Land* legislatures, polled over 5 per cent in a western state (albeit an atypical one in terms of its size and social profile) for the first time.

Table 5.1 shows the federal election results for all five main parties since 1949.

Extremist and anti-establishment parties

The anti-totalitarian consensus that underpins German party democracy, the elaborate rules that were created to keep smaller (potentially extremist) parties out of the *Bundestag* (see below) and strong popular sensitivities against extremism have made the German party system much less open to new parties (of whatever colour) than is the case in other European states. The consolidation of the party system in the 1950s led to stable

Election	CDU/CSU	SPD	FDP	BÜNDNIS 90 DIE GRÜNEN	DIE LINKE.PDS	Others	Seats	CDU/CSU	SPD	FDP	BÜNDNIS 90 DIE GRÜNEN	DIE LINKE.PDS	Others
14.08.1949	31.0%	29.2%	11.9%	–	–	27.9%	402	139	131	52	–	–	80
06.09.1953	45.2%	28.8%	9.5%	–	–	10.0%	487	243	151	48	–	–	45
15.09.1957	50.2%	31.8%	7.7%	–	–	10.3%	497	270	169	41	–	–	17
17.09.1961	45.3%	36.2%	12.8%	–	–	5.7%	499	242	190	67	–	–	0
19.09.1963	47.6%	39.3%	9.5%	–	–	3.6%	496	245	202	49	–	–	0
28.09.1969	46.1%	42.7%	5.8%	–	–	5.4%	496	242	224	30	–	–	0
19.11.1972	44.9%	45.8%	8.4%	–	–	0.9%	496	225	230	41	–	–	0
03.10.1976	48.6%	42.6%	7.9%	–	–	0.9%	496	243	214	39	–	–	0
05.10.1980	44.5%	42.9%	10.6%	1.5%	–	1.5%	497	226	218	53	0	–	0
06.03.1983	48.8%	38.2%	7.0%	5.6%	–	0.4%	498	244	193	34	27	–	0
25.01.1987	44.3%	37.0%	9.1%	8.3%	–	1.3%	497	223	186	46	42	–	0
02.12.1990	43.8%	33.5%	11.0%	Green 3.8% B90/Gr 1.2%	2.4%	4.1%	662	319	239	79	Green 0 B90/Gr 8	17	0
16.10.1994	41.4%	36.4%	6.9%	7.3%	4.4%	3.6%	672	294	252	47	49	30	0
27.09.1998	35.1%	40.9%	6.2%	6.7%	5.1%	6.0%	669	245	298	43	47	36	0
22.09.2002	38.5%	38.5%	7.4%	8.6%	4.0%	3.2%	603	248	251	47	55	2	0
18.09.2005	35.2%	34.3%	9.8%	8.1%	8.7%	3.9%	613	225	222	61	54	51	0

Table 5.1 Bundestag election results, 1949–2005
Source: http://www.btwos.de

inter-party relationships and predictability in both party and voter behaviour. Smaller parties – with the exception of the FDP and, in later years, the Greens and the Left Party – were, for the most part, eased out of the electoral fight as the *Volksparteien* shaped political affairs. The number of parties in the 1953 *Bundestag* halved from twelve to six, while only four made it into the Bonn parliament in 1957. The Refugee Party (GB–BHE) managed to poll 5.3 per cent of the vote in 1953 but its interests were thereafter incorporated mainly into the CDU/CSU; the German Party (DP) experienced a similar fate, although it was not until 1961 that it left the federal political stage. The far-right National Democratic Party (NPD) enjoyed a number of successes in *Land* elections in the 1960s, but only once seriously threatened to enter the federal parliament – in 1969, when it polled 4.3 per cent of the vote. By contrast, the far left in the shape of the German Communist Party (KPD), which was banned by the Constitutional Court in 1956, only to reconstitute itself as the DKP in 1968, was unable to build on the 5.7 per cent it registered in 1949.

The unification of Germany in 1990 altered the rules of the game somewhat. Changes in the western states have been less pronounced than is the case in eastern Germany and four-party systems still tend to be the norm in western German *Land* politics. Occasional 'flash' parties do nonetheless make an appearance, particularly in the northern city-states. The most prominent of these was led by 'Judge Merciless', Ronald Schill, in Hamburg. Schill's Party of Law and Order (PRO) won 19.4 per cent in the *Land* election in Hamburg in 2001 and the former judge (who was dismissed from this position because of his excessively harsh judgements) took on the job of Home Affairs Minister. Schill's tenure was not a happy one and by December 2003 he had not only lost his ministerial job (amid, among other things, seedy allegations of cocaine abuse as well as numerous policy failings) but had been expelled by his own party. Schill's final dramatic act was to form a new party (Pro DM) with five former colleagues and threaten that if his party was not returned to the state parliament in the next election, he would leave the country for good. Pro DM polled a mere 3.1 per cent in the 2004 poll and Schill promptly decamped to South America, marking the end of a short but turbulent political career.

Other – less wacky – issue parties have also made an impact: the *Statt Partei* (literally, the Instead of Party) polled 5.6 per cent in Hamburg in 1993 and spent a number of years governing the state alongside the SPD and Greens; *Arbeit für Bremen* (Work for Bremen) – another group of disaffected former SPD members – did even better in Bremen in 1995, polling 10.7 per cent. The nature of small-party influence in areas such as Baden-Württemberg has tended to be that of the far right making an impact, and the periodic rise and fall of the *Republikaner* in Germany's south-west has been a regular facet of party competition there.

The introduction of seventeen million eastern Germans with (much) weaker ties to (the ostensibly western German) parties prompted, unsurprisingly, a more diversified form of political competition to take hold in their *Länder*. All eastern German *Land* parliaments, with the possible exception of Saxony (where the SPD is very weak), have three relevant parties – the CDU, the SPD and the Left Party – and each of these is of roughly comparable strength. The Greens and the FDP struggle, as a rule, to clear the 5 per cent hurdle (see below), but other ephemeral parties do periodically appear in eastern legislatures. As the Left Party has become ever more accepted as a political actor and its function as a genuine protest party has receded, parties of the far right have occasionally risen to fill the 'protest party' role. The right-wing populist German Peoples Union (DVU) was the first to make an impact, polling 12.9 per cent of the votes in a *Land* election in Saxony–Anhalt in 1998, and following up this success by entering the Brandenburg state parliament in 1999 (with 5.3 per cent of the vote). The DVU was founded by a Munich-based publisher, Gerhard Frey, as an informal association in 1971 and established as a party in 1987. Financially, it is dependent on Frey and he is the pivotal figure in directing its activities. The DVU managed to re-enter the Brandenburg parliament in 2004 with an increased share of the vote (6.1 per cent), but its success was soon overshadowed by a potentially more dangerous competitor as a rejuvenated NPD entered the Saxony parliament a few months later, having polled 9.2 per cent of the vote. Later, in September 2006, it entered Mecklenburg–Western Pomerania's state parliament after recording 7.3 per cent of the vote there.

The NPD is the largest, and frequently the most militant, of the far-right parties, and even before its recent breakthrough the federal government attempted to set a process in motion that would lead to it being banned on account of the anti-constitutional activities of some of its members. But the Federal Constitutional Court – the only institution that can take such a decision under the Basic Law – threw out the case when it was discovered that a large percentage of the party's leadership were in fact undercover agents sent in by the German secret services. The Court claimed that it was impossible to decide which moves by the party were based on genuine party decisions and which were dictated by the secret services in an attempt to secure the ban. In the context of this book's discussion, this episode is particularly important for highlighting the checks and balances imposed even on the Federal Republic's self-granted right to defend itself against threats to its existence (the idea of 'militant democracy' – see Chapter 2, p. 24).

The electoral system

The decision to regulate the activities of Germany's political parties reflects the lessons that the constitutional drafters wished to draw from the disastrous Weimar Republic period. And in the immediate post-1945 era such thoughts appeared well founded as a multiplicity of parties attempted to enter the *Bundestag*. The largest of these groups was the CDU/CSU (polling 31 per cent in the first election in 1949), closely followed by the SPD (29.2 per cent). The year 1949, however, proved to be the highpoint in terms of party system fragmentation for two reasons: first, the so-called 5 per cent clause – which permitted a party to enter parliament only if it managed to accrue 5 per cent of the vote in any one state – was expanded, ensuring that in order to qualify for parliamentary representation a party was required to register at least 5 per cent of the vote across *all* of the territory of the Federal Republic; and, second, the two strongest parties expanded their influence across the political spectrum, hoovering up most of their erstwhile opponents.

The electoral system used for all elections since 1949 is a variant of proportional representation known as the additional member (AMS) or mixed member proportional (MMP) system. Germans have two votes. The first is for a candidate in a single-member constituency, who is elected on a 'first-past-the-post' basis. In 1949 and 1953 there were 242 constituencies, while in 1957 and 1961 the number rose to 247. Post-1965 the number remained constant at 248, before jumping to 328 with unification in 1990. Post-2002, amid fears that the *Bundestag* was becoming too large, the number was reduced to 299. Much as is the case in the UK, the boundaries are drawn by an independent commission and are dependent on population size; currently, the industrial state of North Rhine–Westphalia has the most constituencies (sixty-four) while the small city-state of Bremen possesses the least (two). The second of the votes that Germans are asked to cast does not go towards electing an individual to represent them but to a party. Each party's strength in the federal legislature will match (or be as close as is mathematically possible to) its percentage of second votes. The second vote is therefore – in most normal circumstances – the more important of the two. The MdBs (*Mitglieder des Bundestages*, or Members of Parliament) that represent a party in Berlin will therefore be a combination of directly elected constituency MdBs and members of national party lists – selected from closed party lists in each of the sixteen states – who together ensure that the party's delegation matches the proportion of second votes that it receives.

This delicate mathematical balancing act can on occasion lead to the strange anomaly of a party gaining more directly elected candidates in a state than it should theoretically be allowed to send to the *Bundestag*. The SPD, for example, won every one of the thirteen constituency seats in Brandenburg in 2005 – yet, in terms of the proportion of second votes that it received, it should have been permitted to send only ten MdBs to the *Bundestag* from that state. When such anomalies occur – and they have occurred ever more frequently in recent years – the party simply keeps the extra seats that it is lucky enough to obtain. In 2005 the SPD won nine extra seats (*Überhangmandate*) in this way, while the CDU/CSU won seven, compared to four and one, respectively, in 2002. Significantly, at the 2002 election, when the CDU/CSU and SPD both polled 38.5 per cent of second votes, the three extra seats won by the SPD played a major role in giving the incumbent SPD–Green government a stable, albeit slim, majority in parliament.

In order to placate claims that the electoral laws disadvantaged smaller, regionally concentrated political parties – and mainly those representing national minorities such as the Danes in Schleswig-Holstein and the Sorbs in a number of eastern German states – a *Grundmandatsklausel* (direct mandate rule) was also introduced. This stipulates that if a party manages to win three (or more) constituencies outright, then it can forgo the need to poll 5 per cent of the vote to be eligible for distributed seats. Rarely do small parties achieve this. The Free Democrats have been represented in every *Bundestag*, but they have won only one constituency since 1957 – and that was in exceptional circumstances when former Foreign Minister Hans-Dietrich Genscher's huge popularity in his home town in eastern Germany, Halle, enabled the FDP candidate to poll a relative majority of the votes there in 1990. The Greens have managed to win seats directly only twice – when the charismatic Hans-Christian Ströbele won Friedrichshain-Kreuzberg in Berlin in 2002 and 2005. This rule was therefore a footnote in election rulebooks, as the smaller mainstream parties achieved 5 per cent of the vote (if sometimes barely) while concurrently never registering three directly elected MdBs. But this changed in 1994 when the eastern German PDS became the first modern party to break this trend. In 1994, it managed to register only 4.4 per cent of the vote nationwide, but it won four constituencies in its heartland of eastern Berlin. It therefore entered parliament with 30 MdBs, 26 of whom came from its party lists. Eight years later, the experience of the PDS illustrated how fine the line is between success and failure – it polled more or less the same number of second votes as it did in 1994 (4 per cent) but, crucially, won only two constituencies in eastern Berlin. The PDS was therefore represented in parliament solely by two MdBs as it had failed to gain that one, decisive, extra constituency which would have allowed that 4 per cent to be translated into MdBs.

Voter volatility

Elections in recent years have illustrated that German voters are now much more willing to change party allegiance than they used to be. Germany – like other Western democracies – has witnessed an increased willingness on the part of voters to 'dealign' themselves from the parties that they have 'traditionally' supported (Campbell *et al.*, 1960). Whereas once the cleavages of social class and religious orientation provided stable bases of support for both of the catch-all parties, the modern-day watchwords are 'floating voters', 'personalities', and 'issue-based politics'. This is not to say that voters are now devoid of ties to particular parties or that they are not influenced by their own social milieu; it is more a recognition that ever more voters are making ever later decisions over whom they choose to elect (Dalton, 1996).

Both of the main parties have subsequently seen their core electorates shrink. The electorate is ageing remarkably rapidly – in 2005 there were as many people over sixty as there were newly born children; and by 2050, Germany will have 4.5 million more over-sixty-fives than it does now (Statistisches Bundesamt, 2006b) – and a creeping conservatism aiming to preserve and defend pension levels, welfare benefits and social security spending is becoming evident (see Chapter 8). The SPD has witnessed a gradual but persistent decline in its core electorate – unionised workers. This is particularly important as traditionally social class has been seen as a key shaper of the vote. The shrinking number of people who see themselves as members of a particular class has inevitably led to a decline in what can be termed 'class voting' (Dalton, 2002). In 1957 – the zenith of class voting in Germany – the Social Democrats were receiving a clear majority of support from working-class electors (61 per cent), while middle-class voters were much more reluctant to support them (24 per cent). As Russell Dalton (2003: 63–4) argues, this is the type of divide one would normally associate with societies where class is the *primary* shaper of the vote, such as the UK. Over the next forty years this differential steadily eroded, hovering in the low-teens. The other pillar of German electoral behaviour – religion – has also declined in significance in recent years. The relationship between Catholics and Protestants has long played an important role in German political life, but the creation of the genuinely cross-denominational CDU/CSU took much of the energy out of their disagreements. Although religion rarely makes an overt impact on German politics now, it does shape voting behaviour in the western states. Catholics, particularly church-goers, are much more likely to support the CDU/CSU, as are – if to a lesser extent – active Protestants. The fact that there are – in quantitative terms – now far fewer regular church-goers than there once was therefore does nothing for the CDU/CSU's electoral prospects. A gap, however, still exists between the religious and the non-religious in terms of voting behaviour, with the SPD performing much better among agnostics, atheists and those who do not have any preference.

This picture becomes even more complicated if one looks solely at the eastern states: there, the centre-right CDU polled *better* among the working classes in both 1990 and 1994 as an inverse class–party relationship appeared to be developing. Although this has since changed, alignments remain weak and unstable, and evidence of genuine class voting is thin on the ground. Given that two-thirds of Easterners (compared to one-sixth of Westerners) say that they are non-religious, it is also not surprising to see that religion is much less significant in prompting voting preferences in the six eastern *Länder*. Short-term factors are therefore much more influential shapers of the vote than they are in western Germany.

The 2002 and 2005 elections illustrate some of these general tendencies well. Germans in both the east and the west – although the trend is certainly more evident in the former – take issues and candidate-perception ever more into account when casting their votes. The prodigious campaigning skills of Gerhard Schröder, for example, enabled him to turn around an apparently forlorn position in 2002 as he used issues surrounding the Iraq War and severe flooding in eastern Germany to pull off an unlikely Social Democratic victory (Paterson and Sloam, 2005). The SPD may not have won the election three years later in 2005, but – in a highly disadvantageous situation of high unemployment, low economic growth and general dissatisfaction with the government – it still managed to reduce a 20 per cent point gap to the CDU/CSU in the polls in June 2005 to a mere 1 per cent on polling day in September (Infratest Dimap, 2005a). Much of the reason for this lay in the lacklustre performance of Angela Merkel and the erratic behaviour of high-profile members of her 'competence team': namely, Edmund Stoiber's criticism of 'frustrated' eastern Germans and, more pressingly, the controversial tax plans of Merkel's prospective Finance Minister, Former Constitutional Court judge Paul Kirchoff.

An increasingly dealigned electorate is also much less willing to actively take part in party politics. Membership numbers have been dropping for decades, the only blip being the years around unification. Through the late 1990s and into the 2000s, the figures for all parties showed clear negative trends (see Table 5.2) and the era of mass-membership parties appears to be well and truly past. Coupled with lower turnout levels, this gives Germany's parties – like those in other Western European countries – plenty of food for thought as far as the strength of their links to the society they seek to represent is concerned.

Issues

Increasing party system fragmentation and voter dealignment need not necessarily be viewed negatively. Parties may have to fight harder to garner support, and rather than casting their vote as something akin to a reflex action, voters may conceivably be acting in more rational and logical ways that suit their own particular interests. Yet, reaching such a conclusion as a result of recent changes in both party system dynamics and voter perceptions in Germany would be misguided. Much has indeed changed and German politicians are faced with a number of issues that they need to confront if the stability of the 1950s, 1960s and 1970s is to be rekindled.

First and foremost, there is now the real threat that elections may not produce practicable government options. The steady two-and-a-half-party system of the pre-

Table 5.2 Party membership, 1995–2004

Year	SPD	CDU	CSU	FDP	Greens	PDS
1995	817,650	657,643	179,647	80,431	46,054	114,940
1996	793,797	645,852	178,573	75,038	48,034	105,029
1997	777,899	631,700	178,457	69,621	48,983	98,624
1998	775,036	626,342	178,755	67,897	51,812	94,627
1999	755,066	638,056	183,569	64,407	49,487	88,594
2000	734,693	616,722	181,021	62,721	46,631	83,475
2001	717,513	604,135	177,852	64,063	44,053	77,845
2002	693,894	594,391	177,705	66,560	43,795	70,805
2003	650,798	587,244	176,989	65,192	44,052	65,753
2004	605,807	579,484	172,892	64,146	44,322	61,385
Change, 1995–2004	−211,843	−78,159	−6,755	−16,285	−1,732	−53,555

Source: Scarrow (2006: 380)

unification era made coalition formation straightforward and essentially uncontroversial (Blondel, 1968). The disputes that followed the 2005 election result – when neither of the two blocs of red–green (SPD–Green) and black–yellow (CDU/CSU–FDP) managed to achieve a parliamentary majority – were both unseemly and unedifying, and the weeks of bickering between politicians illustrated some of the difficulties that are likely to recur when five parties sit in parliament and, in particular, when one of them (the Left Party) is not (yet) 'coalitionable'. Yet, at the *Land* level, there is plenty of evidence to suggest that creative coalition-making is both practical and possible. To illustrate this point, Table 5.3 shows the wide range of coalitions that were in existence in January 2005, just before the gradual collapse of the SPD–Green federal government (see Table 4.3, for *Land* governments in mid-2007). Only one state (North Rhine–Westphalia) had the same SPD–Green coalition that was in existence at the federal level, and the SPD in particular was more than happy to work with every other party in one way or another: with the CDU in Brandenburg and Bremen, with the FDP in Rhineland–Palatinate, and with the Left Party in Berlin and Mecklenburg–Western Pomerania (it governed alone in Schleswig-Holstein). Since unification, one can also add to this an SPD–Green minority govern-ment in Saxony–Anhalt that was tolerated for four years by the Left Party; coalitions of establishment parties with non-establishment protest groups in Hamburg (SPD–*Stattpartei*; CDU–FDP–PRO); and 'traffic light' (SPD–FDP–Green) coalitions in Brandenburg and Bremen. Diversity, therefore, is very much the order of the day in the Länder. Creative patterns of government formation may be possible at the federal level, too, before too long, if only the politicians dare to give them a chance.

Table 5.3 Coalition alignments in the *Länder*, January 2005

Land	Aligned with the federal government (SPD–Green)	Cross-cutting federal government and opposition	Aligned with the government federal opposition (CDU/CSU–FDP)
Baden-Württemberg			CDU–FDP
Bavaria			CSU
Berlin	SPD–Left Party		
Brandenburg		SPD–CDU	
Bremen		SPD–CDU	
Hamburg			CDU
Hesse			CDU
Lower Saxony			CDU
Mecklenburg–Western Pomerania	SPD–Left Party		
North Rhine–Westphalia	SPD–Green		
Rhineland–Palatinate		SPD–FDP	
Saarland			CDU
Saxony			CDU
Saxony–Anhalt			CDU–FDP
Schleswig-Holstein	SPD		
Thuringia			CDU

Source: Jeffery and Hough, 2006

The diversity within the party system has clearly taken on proportions unheard of in the post-war period. Essentially, Germany has three regional party systems:

- Eastern Germany (Mecklenburg–Western Pomerania, Brandenburg, Thuringia, Saxony, Saxony–Anhalt and Berlin). Three more-or-less similar-sized parties compete for votes. The SPD remains the 'pivot' party between the centre-right CDU and socialist Left Party. The FDP and Greens play little, if any, role.
- Southern Germany (Bavaria, Baden–Württemberg). The CDU in Baden–Württemberg and especially the CSU in Bavaria enjoy a structural majority in each of these states. The ability of the CSU to dominate Bavarian politics is particularly impressive and the party has been able to secure an absolute majority of seats in the *Land* parliament at every election since 1962. Because of the CSU's crushing dominance, politics in Bavaria is often said to work to a different time to the rest of the country ('*In Bayern gehen die Uhren anders*').
- Western and northern Germany (Schleswig–Holstein, North Rhine–Westphalia, Lower Saxony, Saarland, Rhineland–Palatinate, Bremen, Hamburg, Hesse). Although either the SPD or the CDU may have governed for long periods of time in the past, there now remains a more-or-less equal balance between centre-left and centre-right. Regular changes in *Land* governments are imaginable. Small parties are of some significance, particularly in northern Germany.

Regional party systems are the norm in many other European states, and the current period of diversification is perhaps simply a signal that Germany is continuing to normalise itself. Although this classification applies to the federal and the *Land* levels of party competition, it is clear that the permanent election campaigns that are fought by the parties on account of the staggering of *Land* election dates may prompt a degree of disillusionment among the electorate following the motto of 'so many elections, so little output'. The phenomenon of *Politikverdrossenheit* (disenchantment with politics) first appeared in the 1980s and quickly became *Parteienverdrossenheit* (disenchantment with parties), as ever more citizens became sceptical of the parties' abilities to solve contemporary problems in Germany. The hangover that followed the euphoric uniting of West and East Germany in 1990 quickly metamorphosed into disillusionment with politics and politicians, and – following a short period of hope when Gerhard Schröder took over the reins of power – descended further in the first years of the twenty-first century. The 2005 election will be remembered for the ineffectual and unattractive posturing by Schröder that dominated the newspapers in the weeks following it, lending further credence to claims that politicians have indeed lost appreciation of the needs of the 'man-on-the-street' and instead live in the small world of Berlin politics. Lower turnout levels – in all elections – are ample evidence of the loss of faith that German citizens have experienced towards their elected representatives, and it will take a concerted and systematic effort from all sides to re-establish positive links with the citizenry.

Long-running debates on the funding of political competition have not assisted politicians in their attempts to increase their standing within German society. Indeed, the thorny issue of who should fund party politics in Germany – and to what extent – remains one of the polity's perpetual sagas. Parties regularly claim that as their obligations as public actors expand in scope, their funding situation has grown ever more difficult. Many commentators, on the other hand, decry the black hole into which public money seems to be disappearing as parties suck in ever larger subsidies. Funding comes initially from membership contributions, donations from corporate sponsors and – since 1959 – public funds. Any party that gains 0.5 per cent of the vote in national elections is entitled to receive state funding. But the sum they receive has – much to the chagrin of critics –

increased steadily over time. Post-1967 they received the equivalent of €1.25 from the state for every vote cast in their favour at federal elections, but this rose to €1.75 and then, from January 1984, to €2.50 This was replicated for parties at the *Land* level in *Land* elections. Parties also receive free campaign advertising time on public television and radio, based on their performance in the previous election. However – in stark contrast to parties in countries such as the USA – they are not permitted to purchase any additional spots.

The relatively clear rules on financing parties did not prevent regular instances of abuse of the rules. Donations were sometimes made in highly creative ways – through completely fictitious firms or dummy bank accounts, for example – in order to facilitate tax scams. As was noted in Chapter 2 (p. 34), one of the most spectacular cases of illegal party funding came in the so-called Flick Scandal at the beginning of the 1980s when it was revealed that the Flick consortium had created a series of clandestine accounts for the purpose of 'cultivating the political landscape' – in layman's terms, bribing all of the parties (with the exception of the anti-establishment Green Party) to craft tax policies that suited Flick's interests. A national outcry and further efforts by the Constitutional Court in 1992 to clarify parties' financial affairs did not wipe out malpractice. Parties now received the equivalent of €0.50 per year for every valid vote they received in elections to the European Parliament, the *Bundestag* and each of the sixteen *Länder*. The only stipulation was that they still had to poll at least 0.5 per cent of the popular vote. Smaller parties – who had regularly claimed that the larger ones benefited from the previous system on account of their size and attractiveness to outside donors – were allowed to claim the equivalent of €0.65 for every vote up to five million votes. Furthermore, every party was permitted to claim matching funds from the state for the membership dues and donations they received from individuals (up to the equivalent of €3,000 per person), with the contributors permitted to write off their donations against tax. Box 5.1 gives a breakdown of the main parties' income in 2004.

The tightening of the rules gives the immediate impression that German parties now have little room to manoeuvre in terms of financing their activities. Strictly speaking, this is accurate, but – as a scandal in 2000 involving long-time CDU/CSU leader and Chancellor Helmut Kohl illustrates – parties remain adept at circumventing the rules.

BOX 5.1 POLITICAL PARTIES AND THEIR INCOMES, 2004

- SPD – €186.9 million, of which 27.1 per cent stems from membership contributions and 18.9 per cent from donations
- CDU – €154.3 million, of which 28.2 per cent stems from membership contributions and 29.9 per cent from donations
- CSU – €40.4 million, of which 25 per cent stems from membership contributions and 24.4 per cent from donations
- FDP – €36.9 million, of which 16.3 per cent stems from membership contributions and 27.4 per cent from donations
- Greens – €26.5 million, of which 20.4 per cent stems from membership contributions and 32.1 per cent from donations
- PDS – €32.2 million, of which 28.9 per cent stems from membership contributions and 10.2 per cent from donations

Source: Scarrow (2006: 383)

Kohl's ability to steamroller through this intricate legislative framework cost his party dear, and German politicians remain periodically susceptible to financial malpractice. Stories of other leading CDU politicians such as Wolfgang Schäuble accepting suitcases stuffed with banknotes from alleged arms dealers buttress the impression that while Kohl was at the centre of an illegal bank accounts affair, he was by no means the only person who was bending (or plain ignoring) the rules set out in the Party Law. In Bavaria, where the CSU's dominance has meant that the boundaries between party and state have often become blurred, political figures, and particularly its late leader Franz Josef Strauss, have periodically become embroiled in allegations of financial impropriety. SPD politicians, too, have been found guilty of collecting illegal contributions to party coffers, and Gerhard Glogowski, for example, was forced to resign as Minister-President of Lower Saxony after just thirteen months in office on account of his alleged involvement in dubious financial activities; in 2000, various SPD officials in Cologne were revealed to have had their 'hands in the till'. A steady trickle of similar affairs has sent confidence in the honesty and competence of the political classes plummeting.

Debates

Given that the German party system and party politics are faced with a multitude of challenges and tests, it is not surprising to find that currently there is a heated debate over where Germany's party democracy goes from here. There is clearly a need to restore faith in the political process. Interestingly, empirical evidence indicates that while Germans are generally disdainful of their political leaders, the situation is even worse in a number of other Western countries (Israel, Portugal, Slovakia and Poland, for example; see Infratest, 2005b: 1) and there is little evidence of any sort of widespread rejection of democratic principles. Be that as it may, there is – and has been for at least the last decade – a strong sense of *Politkverachtung* (literally, a contempt for politics) in German society. The 2005 election campaign, and particularly the unseemly battle for ministerial portfolios that followed it, did little to alleviate the impression that politicians remain both aloof from the citizens whom they claim to represent and, even worse, unable to pursue concerted policies of reform.

The Grand Coalition of the two largest groups in parliament under CDU leader Angela Merkel therefore has plenty to keep it busy. The 2006 federalism reform (Chapter 4, pp. 71–2) is likely to ease the institutional barriers to implementing a reform-orientated agenda, although quite how that will affect the constitutional standing of the political parties (if, indeed, it affects them at all) remains unclear. Talk of Merkel being a German Margaret Thatcher is misplaced in that the structural context within which she has to work – institutionally, socio-economically and culturally – remains very different from that which existed in the UK in 1979. The new Chancellor is certainly unlikely to change fundamentally the structural shape of German politics, even though her government has begun a process of institutional and policy regeneration.

While it is unlikely that debates on the financing of political activity will ever completely be resolved, there appears little likelihood that the fundamental tenets of the party finance infrastructure will substantially change. Parties in Germany – as elsewhere – are not only fighting many election campaigns (European, federal, regional, local) but are doing so in an environment that makes this an exceedingly costly exercise. Although the state provides considerable subsidies for the day-to-day activities of political parties, it is still clear that sophisticated marketing strategies, slick advertising techniques and modern campaign gimmicks drain party funds more drastically than was the case just a few years ago. Striking a balance between funding genuinely integral party activity and allowing parties to generate funds so that they can market themselves is no easy task, and – as the remarkable resilience of the parties in recent years illustrates – it is unlikely that future chancellors will seek any sort of wholesale reform of the web of financial incentives that currently exists.

One thing that *did* change with the 2005 election, obviously, was the gender of the Chancellor. Germany has, for the first time, a female head of government, and this has prompted much debate on the role of women in German society and within the political process. The proportion of women who are active in the upper echelons of German politics is at an all-time high (McKay, 2004). Most of the main parties realise the importance of breaking up the male-dominated, hierarchical structures that previously existed, and parties such as the Greens and the Left Party have not been scared to introduce quota systems to facilitate this. Indeed, in 2005, eight of the twelve members of the executive of the Left Party's parliamentary party were female, as were the two MdBs who represented it in the *Bundestag* between 2002 and 2005. Such quotas have nevertheless not engendered genuine equality just yet. Between 2002 and 2005, only 32.3 per cent of MdBs were female; even though this is well above the European average of 17.6 per cent, it is evidence that German parties – and particularly those of the centre-right – remain male-dominated organisations (McKay, 2004: 57). The CDU/CSU and FDP, in particular, are generally male parliamentary bodies, while the Left Party (which was 60 per cent female from 1998 and 2002, and 48 per cent female after the 2005 election) and Greens (regularly over 50 per cent female) possessed the most gender-balanced parliamentary parties. The quota system and attempts to feminise party political culture have not yet completely levelled the playing field. Silvana Koch-Mehrin – a young, high-flying MEP for the Free Democrats with a young family – epitomised the frustration that many women feel within German parties by famously responding to a journalist's question of how she juggles family and career by bluntly asking why she is constantly asked that question while her husband is not.

The rise of the NPD in parts of eastern Germany has prompted worries about the stability of Germany's democracy in the eastern states. Are Easterners still unconvinced of the democratic structures with which they have now lived for fifteen years? Given the desolate economic situation in the eastern states, are they prone to search for populist solutions to their apparently intractable problems? In light of Germany's troubled past, the rise of any right-wing party is treated with considerable alarm. The NPD's entry into two state parliaments in 2004 and 2006 was no different, particularly when it became clear that in Saxony's Holger Apfel the party had finally found a parliamentary leader with at least a modicum of political skill. Attempts to ban the party (discussed above) collapsed amid farcical scenes in 2003, and although it is not beyond the realms of possibility that Merkel's government may again attempt to go down this route, such a concerted effort appears unlikely at the moment. Should the rise of a right-wing extremist organisation be seen as a dangerous threat to Germany's (and particularly the east's) political culture, or is this yet another sign of the normalisation of political life in Europe's largest country? After all, Germany was one of few countries that *did not* – and in many ways still does not – have a strong right-wing party at the national level. These questions need to be articulated and addressed in the coming years.

However, the most significant debate – in many ways dwarfing all of those mentioned above – is much more straightforward: which way now with the process of socio-economic reform? As Chapter 7 will show, Gerhard Schröder's *Agenda 2010* package of reforms for modernising the labour market and Germany's extensive social support network was, in many ways, a radical departure from the consensus politics that had existed for decades. The old model of redistribution between the generations no longer appears to function as effectively as it once did, as Germans grow older and the state's finances become ever more precarious. Schröder's attempt to develop new strategies for providing for old-age pensions and public health nonetheless represent nothing more than a first step towards larger reforms of the welfare state and should therefore be seen only as a starting point for kick-starting the once fearsome German economic machine. The Grand Coalition of CDU/CSU and SPD may, some analysts argue, provide the sort of cross-party consensus that is needed to implement radical processes of reform. It will be easier to secure majorities in the *Bundesrat* and – providing internal one-upmanship does not take over – there is reason to believe that the government will continue, in some form, along the reforming path on which the SPD–Green coalition embarked in 2003.

But, a darker, more negative scenario is also feasible: the coming together of Germany's two catch-all parties leaves just the smaller parties in opposition. While the Greens and the FDP can be relied upon to oppose government policies in good spirit, there is also the worry that parties to the left and right may agitate on an overtly populist agenda – pulling votes away from the middle and towards the extremes. This scenario remains the less likely, but the CDU/CSU–SPD government needs to be aware of the responsibility that rests on its shoulders. For forty years through the Cold War era, the German party system and German democracy were beacons of stability. A consolidated party system, based on two and half parties, steered Germany through economically prosperous times, but things have clearly changed since 1990: partisan dealignment has increased and Germans are much more sceptical of the parties that represent them. Coming to terms with this disillusionment is something that the German political parties have yet to do effectively.

Questions for discussion

1 Is the German party state in need of fundamental reform? If so, in what way?
2 Are forces of increasing dealignment a challenge or an opportunity for German political parties?
3 How best should German party politics be funded?

Further reading

Lees, C. (2005), *Party Politics in Germany: A Comparative Politics Approach* (Basingstoke: Palgrave). A very thorough and systematic linking of theories of party competition and development to the practical realities of German politics

Padgett, S. (2001), 'The German *Volkspartei* and the Career of the Catch-All Concept', *German Politics* 10/2: 51–72. An excellent discussion of the electoral performance of Germany's two most significant parties, the SPD and the CDU/CSU.

Useful websites

<http://www.wahlrecht.de/english.htm> provides full election results for *Land*, federal and European elections.
<http://www.wahl-o-mat.de/> provides an interactive voting recommendation based on the parties' programmes at respective elections (in German only).

6 Citizenship and demographics

A country of immigration?

Summary

This chapter considers two changes – one current and the other future – to the composition of Germany's population. First, Germany has been one of the main destinations for immigration in the European Union; and second, Germans themselves are living longer and having fewer children. The combination of these factors has created a number of difficult political challenges surrounding issues such as Germany's identity, immigrant integration and the future of the welfare state, many of which have now been on the political agenda for more than twenty-five years. At the same time, it has not been easy to develop new solutions to some of these challenges because of Germany's long-established self-perception as a 'non-immigration country'.

Introduction

Over the past fifty years, immigration has transformed many Western European countries into ethnically and culturally diverse societies. While such inflows have affected a range of countries, including France, the UK, Austria and the Netherlands, by far the most significant destination for immigration in the European Union has been Germany. For example, Germany has by far the largest foreign population in absolute (although not relative) terms. In particular, it has a very large and well-settled Turkish population, consisting of 1.7 million people in 2006. In that year, around one-quarter of all foreign residents of Berlin were Turkish nationals, giving the city the largest Turkish community outside Turkey itself.

Inevitably, Germany's Nazi history makes its response to immigration particularly sensitive. Incidents of racially motivated violence, although common throughout EU member-states, are usually reported particularly thoroughly in the foreign press when they occur in Germany. For historical reasons, politicians in Germany have until recently felt unable to articulate an assertive definition of political values to which they expect immigrants to adhere, in contrast to the way that French republicanism always did (and still does). Furthermore, and precisely because of Nazi persecution during the 1930s, political asylum is imbued with a moral significance in Germany which is unparalleled anywhere else in the EU.

Against this background, this chapter discusses the reasons for, the implications of and the political responses to the challenge of immigration. Alongside this, it also sketches out the contours of one of the most fundamental challenges the country faces over the next fifty years: demographic changes in Germany's population size and structure, as well as skills shortages in key sectors of the economy. The scale and nature of the demographic challenge first and foremost affects Germany's welfare state, which is why this issue features correspondingly strongly in Chapter 8. However, it is outlined here because immigration is one of the principal options, and arguably the only short-term solution available to governments in their attempts to address both demographic and skills shortages.

Background

As in most other European countries, the history of immigration to Germany is predominantly a post-1945 story. Indeed, from the late nineteenth century to the end of the Second World War, Germany was primarily a country of emigration, with millions of its citizens leaving for such countries as the United States. It was only after the war that this balance shifted and Germany became one of the main destinations for immigration in the developed world. Initially, such immigration was focused on ethnic German refugees, who had been expelled from the former German territories of East Prussia, Silesia and Pomerania in the immediate aftermath of Nazi Germany's defeat. In addition, large numbers of Sudeten Germans from Czechoslovakia were expelled by the Benes government. All told, between 1945 and 1949, some twelve million refugees arrived in the Allied zones of occupation; around two-thirds of them ended up in West Germany, principally in the *Länder* of Bavaria, Lower Saxony and Schleswig-Holstein.

Although these immigrants were, technically speaking, German citizens, their successful integration into mainstream society could by no means be taken for granted: many towns, especially in northern Germany, saw their populations double in the aftermath of the Second World War as a result of the arrival of refugees, which unsurprisingly generated considerable social tension. However, the refugees quickly organised themselves politically, and their party, the GB/BHE, scored 5.3 per cent in the 1953 federal election, enough to make the CDU/CSU-led government under Konrad Adenauer sit up and take note. In response, the government passed a range of laws providing generous levels of assistance for this objectively disadvantaged group in society. These measures took the sting out of their political tail, and by the late 1950s the GB/BHE had been subsumed mainly into the CDU/CSU (see Chapter 5, pp. 63 and 82).

By then, the first of four new sources of immigration had emerged. As a result of the 'economic miracle' of the early and mid-1950s, West German industry and agriculture were desperately short of labour. The situation was compounded after 1955 by the reintroduction of conscription with the re-establishment of the West German armed forces. The labour shortages were most pronounced in manual and high-risk jobs, which Germans became increasingly reluctant to fill. The government's answer to this problem was to organise the recruitment of unskilled labour on a temporary basis from Mediterranean countries, principally Italy, Spain, Greece, Yugoslavia and, in particular, Turkey. This quickly became a popular option for employers and government alike: the recruited temporary workers, or *Gastarbeiter* (guest workers), were willing to perform the more unsavoury tasks in factories, while their temporary residence incurred few social costs for the government. The system of recruitment began in 1955 with agricultural workers from Italy, but was rapidly expanded in early 1960s. By the time that the impending first oil shock forced the SPD–FDP government under Willy Brandt to end recruitment in 1973, it was estimated that some fourteen million *Gastarbeiter* had come to West Germany, of whom eleven million had already returned home (Bade, 1994: 54). At the end of 1973, there were around four million non-Germans living in West Germany, comprising 5.7 per cent of the population (the figures do not quite tally with those given above for *Gastarbeiter* because one million immigrants were not classified as guest workers).

Contrary to the expectations of the main political parties, the end of recruitment in 1973 did not mean the end of immigration, as the remaining *Gastarbeiter* realised that any departure from West Germany would, by definition, rule out the possibility of return. It was for this reason that their residential perspective changed from a short-term episode in West Germany to a more permanent settlement (Rist, 1978). In practice, this change of perspective had long been encouraged by industry, which found the costs of retraining guest workers afresh every couple of years prohibitively high and therefore increasingly sought *unlimited* work permits for its foreign employees. This in turn generated the next main phase of immigration to Germany – family migration – as a result of which the overall number of non-nationals living in West Germany did not fall, as expected, but rose slightly between 1973 and 1979. Initially, this consisted of spouses and children of the (mainly male) guest workers already living in Germany. But as subsequent generations of immigrants grew up in Germany, they too started to look to their home countries for spouses, and family migration continues to represent one of the main sources of immigration into Germany today. In this respect, the development in Germany has been very similar to that of other European immigration countries, such as the UK, France and the Netherlands.

By the late 1970s, the third main source of immigration to Germany today was emerging. In a direct response to the persecution of the Nazi era, West Germany had included a particularly generous asylum provision in the Basic Law, which technically went beyond the provisions of the main component of international law in this area, the 1951 Geneva Convention. Throughout the 1950s and 1960s, West Germany had experienced only small numbers of annual applications, but during the late 1970s they increased rapidly to reach a provisional high of 107,000 in 1980. In response, new procedural restrictions were hastily put in place, and while these served to reduce new applications during the mid-1980s, the number rose again in the latter years of that decade to reach 121,000 in 1989. Even though West Germany adopted a comparatively restrictive interpretation of what constituted political persecution, which meant that the vast majority of applications were not recognised, it still proved possible for many (failed) asylum-seekers to secure the right to remain in the country on humanitarian grounds.

The number of asylum-seekers reached crisis levels following the end of the Cold War and the lifting of travel restrictions between Eastern and Western Europe. With united Germany lying at the heart of Europe, it continued to receive by far the greatest number of asylum-seekers in the European Union, with over 1.2 million applications between 1990 and 1993. In the latter year, after an emotional political and public dispute, and against the background of anti-foreigner violence and rising support for extremist parties, the constitutional right to asylum was restricted in a cross-party compromise. In the following years, the number of asylum applications dropped sharply, and by 2006 it had fallen to just 30,000.

The end of the physical division of Europe also helped to bring about the fourth main source of immigration to Germany. Although large numbers of war refugees had arrived in both Germanies prior to 1949, millions of ethnic Germans remained in Poland, Romania and the Soviet Union. For the most part, these were the descendants of emigrants who had left Germany centuries earlier, but their maintenance of German culture meant that most endured widespread persecution by the communist authorities both during and after the war. From 1953, West Germany had offered these Germans by ethnicity, albeit not by citizenship, a right of return. Although the communist governments allowed only small numbers to emigrate (and in the case of Romania during the 1980s, only in return for hard-currency payments), a steady flow of immigrants was able to come to West Germany, where they could claim German citizenship directly, as well as generous welfare support. But, as with political asylum, the end of the Cold War meant that, suddenly, large numbers of people were now able to avail themselves of this opportunity: between 1989 and 1993, over 1.4 million ethnic Germans emigrated to Germany. Here, too, changes in the law made in 1990 and 1993 introduced procedural restrictions, including a language test, and instituted the gradual phasing out of ethnic German immigration over the coming decades. By 2006, the number of new immigrants, most of whom by now came from the countries of what was once the Soviet Union, had declined to a trickle of just 8,000. Crucially, here too, family migration has become a factor: of new ethnic German immigrants, only around 25 per cent are of German origin; the remainder are dependants, in the form of spouses and children.

In addition, two other forms of migration need to be mentioned. First, not only has the number of German nationals *emigrating* been rising, reaching 150,000 in 2004, but the incidence of return immigration by German nationals has been on the increase, numbering 128,000 in the same year. In that context, by far the largest migration movements by nationality, both in terms of immigration and emigration, are by German citizens. Second, between 1993 and 2005, Germany received a total of almost 200,000 Jewish immigrants from countries that used to be in the Soviet Union.

Overall, the picture in 2006 was that Germany had a large, settled and stable immigrant population (see Box 6.1); in this respect, Germany has been very similar to other European immigration countries. But there has also been a crucial difference: whereas countries such as the UK and France have had relatively liberal citizenship laws, Germany's citizenship provisions have been highly restrictive, not only in terms of naturalisation as an adult but at birth. The principal reason for this is again historical: imperial Germany's first full citizenship law, from 1913, had a broadly ethnic definition of nationhood (Brubaker, 1992). In itself, this was not unusual for that era, but what is significant is that the 1913 law survived the Weimar Republic and Nazi Germany to form, in conjunction with Article 116 of the Basic Law, the essence of post-war citizenship in West Germany (Green, 2004: 30–1). In particular, this definition of citizenship explicitly included the GDR, which West Germany never formally recognised as a legitimate state: even the 1972 *Grundlagenvertrag* (see Chapter 2, p. 31) was a recognition in practice only, not in law. For this reason, the political consensus was that the 1913 law could not be changed as long as the partition of Germany persisted. Indeed, it was only in 2000 that a replacement citizenship law came into force.

Because the 1913 law relied solely on the principle of descent (*ius sanguinis*) for the ascription of citizenship at birth, Germany until 2000 had no provision for the children of foreigners born within its territory to gain citizenship automatically at birth (the so-called territorial principle, or *ius soli*). For this reason, the descendants of immigrants,

BOX 6.1 IMMIGRATION AND THE NON-NATIONAL POPULATION IN GERMANY, 2000–6 (IN THOUSANDS)

	2000	*2001*	*2002*	*2003*	*2004*	*2005*	*2006*
Non-national population	7,297	7,319	7,336	7,335	6,717*	6,756*	6,751*
New asylum applications	118	118	91	68	50	43	30
Ethnic German immigrants	95	97	91	72	59	35	8
Dependant visas issues	76	83	85	76	66	53	n/a
Naturalisations of non-ethnic Germans	187	178	155	141	127	117	125

* From 2004, the basis of establishing the number of resident non-nationals changed, as a result of which the total number of non-nationals in that year fell to 6.7 million. However, these figures are not comparable with those for 2003.

Other key facts (2006 unless otherwise stated)

- The 2005 *Mikrozensus* found that almost one-fifth of the total population (over fifteen million persons) had 'migrant background': i.e., they, their parents or their grandparents had immigrated into Germany.
- 20 per cent of the non-German population was born in Germany.
- Main nationalities: Turkey (1.7 million), Italy (535,000), other EU member-states in total (2.2 million).
- Over 95 per cent of non-nationals lived in the ten old *Länder* plus Berlin. Key cities: Frankfurt/Main (30 per cent foreign population), Cologne, Stuttgart.
- Germany's non-national population is extremely well settled. Over two-thirds of foreigners had more than eight years', over one-third more than twenty years' and over one-fifth more than thirty years' residence.
- Yet, in 2005, only 60 per cent of foreigners (excluding EU nationals) had permanent-residence status, which is normally available after five years.
- The average residence period was 17.3 years (1980: 9.0 years).
- The unemployment rate of non-Germans is generally around double that for the entire population: 20.3 per cent compared to 11.7 per cent in 2004.
- Educational attainments are also low: in 2003, 10.2 per cent on non-national school-leavers achieved university entrance qualifications, compared to 26 per cent of Germans; 19.2 per cent of non-national school-leavers left with no qualifications at all (7.9 per cent of Germans).
- Despite historically high numbers of applications, it is not easy to obtain asylum in Germany. Of 547,000 decisions taken between 2000 and 2005, just 8.8 per cent were initially recognised; 30 per cent were rejected on formal grounds.
  Sources: Statistisches Bundesamt; *Bundesamt für Migration und Flüchtlinge*; www.bamf.de; authors' calculations

some now in their third generation (i.e., the grandchildren of original immigrants), have tended to remain foreigners unless they choose to undergo a lengthy, complicated and expensive naturalisation process as adults. In consequence, take-up of German citizenship by immigrants has been consistently low over the past decades. Because of this, in the German context, the correct terminology is not to talk not of 'immigrants', but of 'non-nationals'.

Politically, the issue of immigration has, from the outset, been considered almost exclusively from the perspective of prevention, rather than management. This position has been epitomised by the statement 'Germany is not a country of immigration' (*Deutschland ist kein Einwanderungsland*), which was a staple of practically every government policy statement on immigration until 1998, when the new SPD–Green government brought a more nuanced tone to the debate. In addition to these two parties' instinctively less inhibited approach to immigration, a key factor behind this shift in policy was Germany's looming demographic and skills crisis. In fact, this represents one of the most fundamental challenges facing the country today (Box 6.2). As in other developed countries, life expectancy in Germany has steadily risen over the past decades, and in 2005 it stood at seventy-six and eighty-two years for men and women, respectively. However, and again as in other European countries, the number of deaths in the population has exceeded the number of live births since the early 1970s. In statistical terms, Germany's fertility rate (which measures the number of children born per woman) has long been far below the notional level of 2.1 needed for any given population to maintain its size. Indeed, at 1.3, Germany's fertility rate in 2005 was one of the lowest in the EU. What is more, unification initially served to worsen the situation considerably, as the fertility rate in the new *Länder* fell to just 0.8 in 1994, although it has since then recovered to approach typical Western levels.

The combined effect of these two trends of low fertility and rising life expectancy has been a 'double whammy': Germany's population has been ageing and it is about to shrink significantly. This has huge implications for Germany's welfare system (see Chapter 8), as the healthcare and pension needs of ever-rising numbers of longer-living over-sixty-fives have to be met by what is projected to be a smaller population in wage-earning employment (*sozialversicherungspflichtige Beschäftigung*).

As Box 6.2 shows, the next fifty years are likely to see see far-reaching changes in Germany's population structure. Moreover, and *despite* projected net immigration, Germany's population is likely to decline. This will not only affect potential economic output (the lower the population, the lower the economic output in absolute terms), but more importantly will have seismic implications for the affordability of the country's welfare provision.

To make matters worse, and despite persistently high levels of unemployment of almost 4.8 million (or 11.7 per cent of the labour force) in 2005, the German economy has suffered from severe shortages in several employment areas, including key high-skilled sectors, such as information technology, pharmaceuticals and engineering, and lower-skilled branches, such as the hotel trade and agriculture (Green, 2007; Reinberg and Hummel, 2004). An initial response to this longer-term trend was provided by Chancellor Schröder in 2000, when he announced the introduction of a limited work-permit scheme for highly skilled migrants in information technology (Kolb, 2005). Although German business organisations welcomed this move, they also emphasised the need to make the programme available in a much wider range of sectors.

BOX 6.2 GERMANY'S LOOMING DEMOGRAPHIC CRISIS

- Life expectancy is projected to rise between 2006 and 2050: from 76 to 84 (men) and 82 to 88 (women).
- Assuming constant fertility rates of 1.4 and net immigration of 200,000 persons per annum, the total population of Germany is projected to fall from 82.4 million in 2005 to 74 million in 2050.
- The proportion of over-65s in the population will rise from 19 per cent (2005) to 32 per cent (2050).
- In 2000, the United Nations Population Division published projections of how these general trends would affect population sizes and structures. It calculated that the Potential Support Ratio (PSR), which measures the ratio of 15–64-year-olds to those aged 65 and older, will halve from 4.4 in 1995 to just over 2 in 2050.
- In order to keep the size of the working population constant, Germany would need 458,000 immigrants each year to 2050, leading to a total population of 92 million.
- In order to keep the PSR at 1995 levels, Germany would need 3.4 million immigrants each year, leading to a total population of 299 million in 2050.

Sources: Statistisches Bundesamt (2006b);
United Nations Population Division (2000)

While the primary policy implications of the demographic changes concern social welfare and family policy (which will be discussed in detail in Chapter 8), the central problem is that immigration is practically the only option available to address this issue in the short term (although not in the long term – immigrants age too). In combination with the emerging skills shortages in the German economy, these developments therefore served to bring labour migration back on to the policy agenda. While there is widespread agreement among the parties that Germany must be in a position to recruit the 'brightest and best' to work in its companies, there has been much less consensus over the extent to which lower-skilled immigration should be permitted, not least because the national average unemployment rate is usually double that among non-nationals (see Box 6.1, above). Certainly, the notion that population shortages can be made up through immigration is difficult to maintain in practice. As the 2000 United Nations report on population developments showed, the number of immigrants needed annually just to keep the size of the working population constant by 2050 (which would still entail a severe reduction in the Potential Support Ratio) is far above any level which is practically or politically sustainable. On the other hand, even when other (long-term) measures such as lower pension levels and longer working lives are taken into consideration, it is difficult to see how immigration will not be needed to play at least some role in addressing this problem.

Issues

With such a diverse range of immigrants, it is not surprising that the range of issues facing German policy-makers is equally wide. Yet, in reality, these issues can be summarised in one question: is Germany a country of immigration?

On the surface, the answer seems obvious: with continuing permanent migration by asylum-seekers, ethnic Germans and the dependants of both, Germany is already a country of immigration and will continue to be so in the coming decades. Certainly, any visitor to cities such as Berlin and Cologne cannot fail to notice the impact of immigration on them. Indeed, just as chicken tikka massala is considered to have replaced fish and chips as Britain's national dish, so the *Döner Kebap* is held to have usurped the *Currywurst* as Germany's favourite fast-food snack.

But there is more to this question than first meets the eye. Right until 1998, leading figures from the CDU/CSU, including successive interior ministers, argued that Germany was not a country of immigration, because it had never sought actively to recruit permanent migrants to settle in the country, in the way that countries such as the United States and Canada had done in the past. Strictly speaking, of course, this has been, and remains, true: as their label implied, the guest workers who came to work in West Germany in the 1960s and early 1970s were not expected to remain in the country permanently. Asylum-seekers and dependants are permitted entry because of Germany's international commitments; ethnic Germans are, of course, considered as Germans without a passport. None of these groups is, or has been, allowed entry to Germany because of an active immigration policy. Even after the change of government in 1998, there was no suggestion that Germany should adopt an 'open-door' policy in immigration and asylum, although the Greens have traditionally argued for a much more liberal refugee policy.

Even so, the SPD–Green federal government after 1998 did explicitly distance itself from this old maxim, a position which was accepted, albeit grudgingly, by the CDU/CSU once the scale of skills shortages became clear in 2000 and 2001. But, in turn, this raised two new and potentially more important questions. If Germany *was* now a country of immigration, *what kind* of country of immigration could and should it be? And what would this mean for German society?

The first of these questions can be broken down into a number of elements. The most important of these concerns the issues of how Germany should relate to the wide range of different ethnicities, cultures and religions (especially the largely Muslim Turkish population) which have now established themselves as significant minorities in its large cities. Should Germany aspire to be a multicultural society, which tolerates and even celebrates a wide range of different cultural practices? Or, at the other extreme, should it require its immigrants to adopt German culture without exception? In other words, should immigrants and non-nationals be expected to assimilate themselves into German society? On this crucial question, the political parties initially adopted a wide range of positions in the 1980s, although there has been considerable convergence around the middle ground between these two extremes since then. On the one hand, the Greens, coming from a radical left-wing perspective (see Chapter 2, p. 33 and Chapter 5, p. 79), originally favoured equal rights for all residents of Germany, irrespective and independently of their nationality (Murray, 1994); however, by the mid-1990s, this had been replaced by a simpler policy of increasing access to German nationality. On the other hand, the CDU/CSU's policy was based on what Rogers Brubaker (1992) has defined as an 'ethnocultural' understanding of nationhood, which emphasised the ethnic and cultural homogeneity of membership in the German citizenry. By the 1990s, this position too had mellowed, to focus instead on requiring non-nationals to adhere to the principles of the Basic Law and on learning the German language. The SPD and FDP have taken positions to the right and left of the Greens and CDU/CSU, respectively.

Of course, even conservative politicians have usually shied away from explicitly demanding 'assimilation', because of its connotations with Nazi racial policy, generally preferring the more neutral (and substantively quite flexible) notion of 'integration'. Although, notably in summer 2002, during the federal election campaign, the SPD Interior Minister Otto Schily, no doubt in a nod to conservative voters, declared in a newspaper interview that 'the best form of integration is assimilation' (*Süddeutsche Zeitung*, 27 June 2002). Integration describes a process by which both immigrants, who are themselves a highly diverse group, and host societies come to tolerate and respect each other. Inevitably, how much each side should be expected to tolerate the other is open to interpretation, and a glimpse of conservative opinion on the issue was given by Friedrich Merz, the CDU/CSU *Fraktionsvorsitzender* in the *Bundestag* in 2000, when he suggested that immigrants and non-nationals should adapt to Germany's leading culture (*Leitkultur*) (for a critique of this term, see Klusmeyer, 2001). Needless to say, this idea provoked great controversy, not just among the left but within Merz's own party.

Policy approaches to integration in Germany have therefore been defined by a funda-mental tension. On the one hand, immigrants and non-nationals are (tacitly) *expected* to assimilate, but on the other they cannot be *required* to do so for historical reasons. As a result, the underlying expectation of policy-makers has been that immigrants and non-nationals should *choose* to become Germans, both in terms of their nationality and by inner conviction. For this reason, German citizenship policy traditionally, and especially before 2000, has been based on the assumption that non-nationals must be integrated before obtaining German nationality, which cannot therefore be considered as a stepping-stone to integration. Similarly, Germany remains one of the world's clearest opponents of dual nationality: for, as conservative politicians argue, how can someone have achieved integration into German society while still retaining a formal identification with another country (Green, 2005)?

Germany's approach to integration has therefore been characterised by abstract notions such as loyalty, commitment and identification – terms which have little meaning in everyday life, where concrete issues such as unemployment and racial discrimination are more likely to impact on the lives of non-national and migrant residents. Yet, by focusing on such notions (and by being in the past perhaps a little too conscious of history in preferring not to spell out what Germany requires of its non-nationals), the problems of integration in practice have not received the attention they deserve. For, despite a growing number of individual success stories – for instance, the growing number of immigrant entrepreneurs – non-nationals as a whole suffer from poorer education and higher unemployment levels than Germans (see Box 6.1). Often this is complicated further by inadequate language skills, without which it is difficult for individuals to improve their situation, thereby creating a vicious circle of social marginalisation. In this respect, too, Germany is no different from many other European countries.

Interestingly, these problems have affected not just Turkish immigrant communities, the largest and thereby most visible national grouping. Other nationalities and, perhaps most remarkably, ethnic German immigrants must also overcome similar difficulties in their integration. Crucially, this situation has created fears among some Germans of 'parallel societies', in which non-nationals and immigrants co-exist alongside German local communities, but with the migrant community essentially self-sufficient in language, media, employment opportunities and even value systems. A particular focus in this latter context has been arranged and forced marriages within the Turkish community and the periodic occurrence of so-called 'honour killings' of young Turkish women (on this topic, see the controversial book by Kelek, 2005).

Needless to say, it is a moot point whether the deficiencies in integration of non-nationals in Germany can be put down to their unwillingness (or, worse, inability) to adapt, or to the reluctance of Germans to accept immigrants as equals in society, as illustrated by the low residential status of many foreigners (see Box 6.1), by Germany's restrictive citizenship laws and by the absence prior to 2006 of any explicit anti-discrimination legislation. The important point is that political parties across the spectrum now accept that a more active integration policy, to include formal language and citizenship classes, the successful completion of which is linked to the individual's residence status, is indispensable.

At the same time, a related challenge is the question of how to increase levels of naturalisation. As Box 6.1 showed, the number of naturalisations declined in every year between 2000, the year when citizenship policy was liberalised to include a limited form of *ius soli*, and 2005. This long-term trend of comparatively low naturalisation figures, especially when calculated as a percentage of the non-national population resident in any one year, has helped sustain the marginalised position of non-nationals: put bluntly, without the right to vote in national elections, political parties have little incentive to devote much attention to the concerns of immigrants. However, it should be noted that EU nationals *do* have the right to vote in local and European elections in Germany. Moreover, most jobs in the civil service (*Beamtentum*) are open only to German nationals. In consequence, there are still relatively few migrant employees to be found in public service, whether in schools, the police, local authorities, central government or the judiciary.

The federal government recognised as early as 1984 that naturalisations would need to increase in order to avoid a long-term crisis of political legitimacy. The problem is that in the twenty-plus years since, not much action has been taken, not least because the logic of choice in Germany's integration policy (see above) dictates that a high level of integration must be proven (not just achieved) before naturalisation is possible. For this reason, but also in light of persistent integration deficits, German naturalisation policy has gradually raised the bar for the acquisition of citizenship. Thus, Germany already requires generally higher periods of residence than other countries (eight years since 2000). In addition, its continued opposition to dual nationality is a major disincentive to naturalisation (Green, 2005). Since 2005, all applications for naturalisation have been referred to the internal security service for vetting. And in 2006, formal language and naturalisation tests were introduced as part of the naturalisation process. Becoming German as a foreigner has therefore become more demanding over recent years. But the material benefits of nationality are minimal: social citizenship rights (i.e., unemployment, health and pension rights) are organised on an insurance basis (see Chapter 8) and access to these is hence defined by contribution levels, not nationality. Indeed, the general availability of social citizenship rights is such that some authors (notably Soysal, 1994) have described Germany as a 'post-national citizenship'. So non-nationals have little direct incentive to become Germans, other than to gain the vote and benefit from having an EU passport when travelling. Not surprisingly, this has not been enough to encourage the two-thirds of foreigners who meet at least the eight-year residential requirement for citizenship to undergo the long-winded and expensive process of becoming a German and consequently giving up their former nationality.

In many ways, the debate about integration is one about the future of German cultural identity in the light of large-scale immigration. Among the CDU/CSU, the notion that immigration constitutes a threat to Germany's identity is well established. It is perhaps inevitable that Islam is considered to be the primary form of this threat, given that most of the largest non-national minority is predominantly Muslim, and given the explicitly Christian nature of German conservatives. Indeed, many conservative politicians, especially from the CSU, responded to the *Leitkultur* debate by framing this notion in the context of Germany's 'Christian–occidental heritage'. By contrast, the SPD, FDP and Greens, as well as sections of the CDU/CSU, place the emphasis firmly on the need for all inhabitants to respect Germany's constitutional values and the rule of law.

Although integration, in its various guises, is arguably the most important issue facing Germany in this area, there are six other facets of the debate over whether Germany is a country of immigration which merit attention. The first of these concerns labour migration. While there is now much public awareness of Germany's parlous demographic development, Germany's fertility rate remains stuck at its current low level of around 1.3; in other words, the negative trends which have developed over the past thirty years are continuing, and their cumulative effect will therefore intensify. But even if Germany manages its changed demographic situation with only some new migration, the challenge is to recruit highly skilled migrants. This is not as straightforward as it seems, for in this aim Germany is competing with other developed countries, especially the United States. The 'Green Card' programme of 2000 represented a tentative first step in this direction, but the take up, at only around two-thirds of the available 20,000 permits, was quite low. This indicates that Germany's problem is not managing demand for work and residence permits, but persuading the 'brightest and best' that Germany is a desirable place to go and build their careers.

A second, and related, issue concerns family reunification: without the prospect of uncomplicated residence for their families, few highly skilled workers are likely to be prepared to settle in Germany. But for years, policy in Germany in this area remains defined by the late 1970s, when immigrants were perceived to be circumventing the 1973 recruitment ban by means of family reunification. Indeed, in 2007, the regularities for family reunification were tightened, with the introduction of the requirement that non-German spouses should have acquired a basic knowledge of the German language *before* being granted entry. A particularly contentious issue has been that of the maximum age for children to immigrate to join their parents (*Kindernachzug*). In most EU countries, this is set at eighteen, but the limit in Germany has been sixteen since 1981. However, over the years, the CDU/CSU has persistently argued that this needs to be reduced even further, to at least ten, but ideally six, the school starting age in Germany. The logic behind this is that minors who immigrate at sixteen will have no language skills, will be too old to gain these skills, will therefore gain no qualifications and thus will be consigned to a life on welfare benefits, which is in the interests of neither the immigrants nor German society. Although the CDU/CSU has never been able to translate its demands into legislation, this remains a latent issue in the politics of immigration in Germany.

Third, Germany's asylum system continues to pose recurrent challenges to policy-makers. Despite a sharp drop in the numbers of applications, Germany remains a popular destination for asylum-seekers within the EU, not least because its existing immigrant communities act as a 'pull' for new migrants, and because of its geographical location at the heart of Europe. Much of this immigration is illegal, and people smugglers favour the long, unfortified borders Germany shares with Poland and the Czech Republic. As in many other European countries, the perception in Germany is that many, if not most, asylum-seekers are economic rather than political refugees, and critics point to the consistently low recognition rates for them (see Box 6.1). In reality, of course, it is notoriously difficult to distinguish accurately between so-called 'genuine' and 'bogus' asylum-seekers; one indication of how this balance is struck in Germany might be the fact that over one-third of asylum applications are rejected solely on procedural grounds, including factors such as failing to return the necessary forms on time. Until 2005, Germany also pursued a particularly narrow interpretation of so-called 'agents of persecution', which it assumed could only be agencies of the state. Political persecution by militias or rebels, therefore, automatically disqualified applicants for asylum. Overall, asylum policy remains an emotive subject, with the CDU/CSU keen to explore ways of reducing numbers of applicants still further, and the Greens and the Left Party insistent on the inviolability of the constitutional principle of asylum.

The fourth main element of the debate concerns the question of security, the profile of which has become increasingly important ever since the terrorist attacks on the United States on 11 September 2001. In the aftermath, it was revealed that some of the perpetrators had lived, quite legally, in Hamburg in the years leading up to the attacks. In July 2006, two suitcase bombs failed to explode on trains in Dortmund and Koblenz; had they done so, they would have caused significant casualties. Together, events such as these have inevitably given the security dimension of immigration a greater urgency, and have confirmed the fears of those politicians, mainly among the CDU/CSU, who have viewed Islam as a threat not only to German cultural identity but to physical security. In the 2004 Immigration Law (*Zuwanderungsgesetz* – see below), the security services were given new powers and the deportation of suspected terrorists was made possible without their conviction.

Fifth, ethnic German immigration remains contentious. Although the 1993 law (see above) began the gradual reduction of this form of immigration, as well as limiting it to countries that were once in the Soviet Union, immigration by ethnic Germans and their dependants is set to continue, albeit at a much reduced level, for the foreseeable future. But in a difficult employment climate, the challenge of integration is effectively as great for this group as it is for non-nationals.

Lastly, the perceptions of immigration among the public can have a direct impact on the electoral performance of extreme right-wing parties. Whenever asylum is perceived to become a significant problem, as was the case in the early 1990s, extremist parties such as the *Republikaner*, NPD and DVU can make headway at *Land*, if not at national elections (see Chapter 5, pp. 82–3). In recent years, as Chapter 5 pointed out, the focus has been more on the new *Länder*, where extremist parties have scored successes in Saxony–Anhalt, Brandenburg and Saxony. Frequently, the success of such parties has been accompanied by anti-foreigner violence: the early 1990s saw a number of horrific incidents in both east and west, including several deaths, and the new *Länder* remain particularly sensitive places to look different. This is despite the fact that fewer than 5 per cent of non-nationals live in the east. Given the historical sensitivity of extreme right-wing parties, the mainstream parties are constantly exhorting each other to deal with the issue of immigration and integration in a responsible manner. At the same time, the temptation to politicise this issue for the purposes of mobilising one's own electorate has, on occasion, been difficult for the CDU/CSU and SPD to resist.

Policy responses

Like the debates outlined above, Germany's policy responses have, until recently, been defined by the political notion that Germany was not a country of immigration. While other countries have easily passed immigration laws, successive federal governments, especially those led by the CDU/CSU in the 1980s and 1990s, refused to do so, for the simple reason that, as Germany was not a country of immigration, such a law would send out the wrong signals. But the corollary of this approach was that Germany did not develop an integrated framework for immigration and integration which allowed it to define policy goals according to its own interests. Instead, the history of immigration policy in Germany is one of *reactive* policy-making, in which the results have usually trailed far behind the reality in Germany's cities.

Thus, even though the recruitment of guest workers began in 1955, it was only ten years later that the first law governing the residence of non-nationals was passed (the *Ausländergesetz*); prior to then, the only piece of legislation to cover this area had been a Nazi police decree of 1938! The new law was heralded as a significant improvement, although it quickly came under intense criticism from interest groups on account of its highly restrictive approach to granting permanent-residence permits – the logical response to guest-worker immigration, and entirely in keeping with the non-immigration country dogma.

Despite small numbers of non-nationals settling permanently prior to the end of recruitment in 1973, it was not until 1977 that the government began to give some thought to structuring the long-term residence of non-nationals. A joint federation–*Länder* commission that year confirmed that Germany was not a country of immigration and established three aims of what was henceforward called 'foreigners' policy' (*Ausländerpolitik*): first, that no new immigration should be permitted; second, that existing foreigners should be encouraged to return home; and third, that those non-nationals remaining should be integrated into German society. Notwithstanding the clear contradiction between the second and third aims, these were to constitute the essence of Germany's approach to immigration and integration for the next twenty-five years, although the second element lost prominence after the mid-1980s. In other words, immigration and citizenship policy is a classic example of 'path dependency' dynamics in German policy-making, where initial policy decisions determine the decisions that can be taken in the future (Green, 2004).

Another example of this path dependency dynamic can be seen in citizenship policy, where a set of guidelines was agreed in 1977 to flesh out the otherwise imprecise criteria laid down in the still valid citizenship law from 1913. In these guidelines, naturalisation as an adult was made subject to long residence periods, high fees and the avoidance of dual nationality. Here again, the non-immigration country ideal was invoked: given this, so the guidelines argued, naturalisation could only ever be an exceptional act. The guidelines therefore helped condition the restrictive approach to naturalisation which was to become an issue in later years.

By 1982, the SPD–FDP government under Helmut Schmidt had been persuaded, albeit somewhat grudgingly, that a more proactive approach to legal integration was needed.

However, later that year, it was replaced by the CDU/CSU–FDP coalition under Helmut Kohl, whose stated priority was to *reduce* the number of non-nationals living in Germany. In 1983, the Interior Minister Friedrich Zimmermann (of the CSU) therefore introduced financial incentives to encourage foreigners to return to their countries of origin. It also attempted to reduce the maximum age for dependent children to come to Germany with their parents from the level of sixteen (established in 1981) to six. In the former case, the incentives proved to be largely ineffectual (Herbert, 2001: 255); in the latter, the CDU/CSU ran into strong opposition from the churches, who pointed to the constitutionally enshrined duty of government to safeguard the family (Article 6 of the Basic Law) and from the FDP, its coalition partner. In 1988, Zimmermann tried to use the political pressure for a reform of the 1965 *Ausländergesetz* to impose a draconian system of residence permits, but that too failed, largely due to pressure from within the government.

Soon afterwards, he was sacked as Interior Minister, and his successor, Wolfgang Schäuble, quickly managed to build a majority for a new *Ausländergesetz*, which was passed in 1990. Although this fell well short of the expectations of the opposition, it did lay down clear criteria under which a permanent residence permit had to be issued, formalised in law the conditions for family reunification and introduced a 'simplified naturalisation procedure'. This applied to non-nationals with over fifteen years' residence or aged between sixteen and twenty-three, and was available at a heavily discounted fee over 'normal' naturalisations.

As noted above, unification did help to change Germany's migration situation fundamentally, and, in the early 1990s, very large numbers of asylum-seekers and ethnic Germans arrived in the country. Against the background of anti-foreigner violence and resurgent extreme right-wing parties, the opposition SPD finally gave in to the CDU/CSU–FDP government's demands for an amendment to the constitutional right to asylum, which it had pushed for ever since numbers started to rise again in the mid-1980s. In December 1992, the three parties therefore agreed a wide-ranging compromise on immigration, to include the gradual phasing out of ethnic German immigration discussed above, as well as a further slight liberalisation of naturalisation requirements. On asylum, the reforms included the introduction of a list of so-called 'safe countries of origin', from which asylum applications would automatically be rejected, and of so-called 'safe third countries'. All EU member-states and all countries bordering Germany were declared 'safe third countries', with the assumption that any asylum-seeker passing through these countries to reach Germany could be returned there, as he or she could safely have sought refuge in them.

After the 1994 federal election, the issue of citizenship and naturalisation returned to the agenda. Even though the reforms of the early 1990s were showing results, the starting point was so low (only around 14,000 naturalisations annually in the late 1980s, or 0.3 per cent of the non-national population) that their overall effect was still limited. Moreover, with over 100,000 non-nationals being born in Germany every year, parts of the CDU began to agree with the opposition SPD and Greens in arguing for *ius soli*. However, the majority in the CDU/CSU staunchly opposed this, on the basis that it simply did not require a foreigner to display any level of commitment to German society and because it would lead inevitably to a proliferation of dual nationality (one of the key sources of dual nationality is when children are born in a *ius soli* country to non-national parents; they therefore gain the nationality of their country of birth as well as that, or those, of their parents). Ultimately, they were able to block any attempts towards liberalisation in this area.

However, when the SPD–Green coalition under Gerhard Schröder won the 1998 election, it put a reform of the existing citizenship law from 1913 at the top of its agenda, both because this was an area in which the two parties largely agreed, and because it laid down a clear marker of the new government's modernising credentials. Its bill, published in early 1999, included unlimited dual citizenship, a form of *ius soli* and reduced residential requirements, although it also demanded language skills as a requirement for naturalisation. But the government totally underestimated the degree to which public opinion opposed the notion of dual nationality, and following a unique petition campaign in early 1999, which led to the defeat of the SPD–Green government in the crucial Hesse state election that February, the government was forced to compromise. The revised law, in force since 2000, includes a modified form of *ius soli*, but requires that its beneficiaries choose between their German nationality and that of their parents by the age of twenty-three. At the same time, the principle of dual nationality remains rejected in policy.

Although the Federal Interior Minister Otto Schily (of the SPD) initially showed no desire to add a full-scale immigration law to the reform of citizenship, the positive reception of the Green Card project during 2000 and pressure from business encouraged Chancellor Schröder to push ahead with this project before the 2002 federal election. After a long and tortuous process, spanning a total of four years and involving the Constitutional Court and a conciliation committee (*Vermittlungsausschuss*) between the *Bundestag* and *Bundesrat* (see Green, 2004), Germany's first full-scale immigration law (2004) came into force in 2005. It lays down a comprehensive structure for the management of migration, to include compulsory integration courses not just for non-nationals but for ethnic Germans (Box 6.3).

Conclusion

This chapter has outlined the variety of pressures which currently define immigration and integration policy. It has argued that policy-makers and political parties have wrestled for decades with the question of whether Germany is a country of immigration and what that implies for policy and German identity more broadly. In the context of this book, the three themes of reconciliation, consensus and transformation are clearly visible. Germany's asylum and citizenship policies clearly bear the hallmark of history, albeit in different ways. Although this is now a highly politicised area of public policy, there is also broad consensus between the main parties over the general thrust of immigration and integration policy; visible disputes tend to be limited to symbolic totems such as dual citizenship and aspects of asylum policy. In terms of transformative pressures, Germany's demographic development can be singled out as a challenge of seismic implications, not only for immigration but for the welfare state, which is the subject of Chapter 8.

What can be said about the overall development of policy? Although the coming into force of the Immigration Law in January 2005 marks a significant turning point in German immigration policy, it would clearly be wrong to conclude that an adequate policy response now exists. In keeping with established patterns of German public policy, policy-making in this sector has over decades been 'incremental' (Green, 2004). Yet the demands of business for migrant labour and migrant communities themselves have evolved at a much faster rate, leaving government policy to play a more-or-less perpetual game of catch-up. Thus, the effectiveness of the Green Card programme has been

---

BOX 6.3 PRINCIPAL FEATURES OF THE 2004 IMMIGRATION LAW

- No new labour migration other than highly skilled individuals.
- Residence permits merged with work permit.
- Reduction of residence titles from six to two: (temporary) residence permit and (permanent) settlement permit. Settlement permit to be available after five years' residence, subject to employment and five years' pension contributions.
- Terrorist suspects can be deported on the basis of an 'evidence-based threat prognosis' (*tatsachengestützte Gefahrenprognose*) – i.e., before criminal conviction in a court of law.
- Age by which children may subsequently join their parents in Germany kept at sixteen.
- Recognition of non-state agents of persecution for asylum-seekers. Improvement of residence status, but recognition of refugee status may be withdrawn if circumstances in the country of origin have changed after three years.
- Temporary residence status for rejected asylum-seekers (*Duldung* – suspends deportation for humanitarian reasons) scrapped. In 2000, 260,000 people held a *Duldung*, one-quarter of which had first been issued in 1997 or earlier. However, existing holders of this status remain stuck on it.
- Introduction of integration courses for immigrants and ethnic Germans, to consist of roughly 600 hours' language classes and 30 hours' tuition on German history, culture and law.
- Compulsory attendance at courses for immigrants with low knowledge of German. Failure to attend may impact on renewal of residence permit.
- Creation of new *Bundesamt für Migration und Flüchtlinge* to manage labour migration, integration courses and asylum process.

---

severely compromised by the bureaucracy's engrained restrictive approach to any new labour migration, no matter how highly skilled it is. It was only in 2006 that Germany finally implemented the EU's Race Equality Directive from 2000 into national law (Green, 2007). Although such a law clearly cannot constitute a universal remedy to the problem of discrimination, it lays down an important marker that all persons, regardless of their ethnic origin, have a right to expect equal treatment in society.

Germany's second major problem lies in the question of access to citizenship. Despite a number of reforms over the decades, progress towards enfranchising migrant communities, many of whom now have very long periods of residence, has been painfully slow. Indeed, the number of naturalisations has been falling since the new citizenship law came into force in 2000. And, while around 50 per cent of children born to non-national parents now gain German citizenship via *ius soli*, they are faced with the possibility of losing it again once they reach the age of twenty-three. Perhaps more than anything, the fact that the average residence period of non-nationals is rising, which indicates that increasing numbers of non-nationals are living in Germany for very long periods without naturalising, underlines that citizenship policy still has a long way to go before it fulfils its 1984 goal of achieving much higher levels of naturalisation.

Certainly, a range of other factors might be identified for this low level of take-up of citizenship. Clearly, many non-nationals do not see much advantage in becoming German: after all, they already possess all the main rights of citizenship, except voting. At the same time, the government could probably do more by simply advertising the possibility of naturalisation more widely. But perhaps the most important factor has been Germany's long-standing opposition to dual nationality: the process of securing release from one's citizenship is both time-consuming and can be very expensive. For better or worse, many non-nationals in Germany are evidently unwilling to give up their citizenship of birth. By simply accepting dual nationality, both in naturalisations and *ius soli*, Germany would immediately make naturalisation much more attractive, not least because it would become much less complicated. Ironically, Germany's citizenship policy lists a wide range of cases where dual nationality must be tolerated by the authorities. These exceptions are so extensive that around 40 per cent of all annual naturalisations since 2000 have tolerated dual nationality.

Nonetheless, a change may be on the horizon. Although naturalisations on a year-on-year basis have been low, their cumulative effect has been significant: since unification in 1990, some 1.6 million non-nationals have become Germans. Crucially, these people vote overwhelmingly for the SPD and the Greens (Wüst, 2004), which in future elections will force both parties to pay more explicit heed to their interests.

While there is clear pressure on public policy to evolve more rapidly, events of recent years have shown that many voters are deeply suspicious of any policy liberalisation. German immigration and citizenship policy is thus caught between, on the one hand, the need to attract more high-skilled labour and to manage what is effectively cultural pluralism, and, on the other hand, the political imperative for parties to emphasise their restrictionist credentials to the electorate. For many voters, immigration is a clear economic, cultural and, in the light of 9/11, security threat. The decision of Germany, along with Austria, to impose seven-year restrictions on the free movement of workers from the eight new Central and Eastern European member-states of the EU from 2004 must be seen in precisely this context, as must the subsequent public concern over the realisation that Polish and Czech meat-packers and builders could legally circumvent this restriction by declaring themselves to be self-employed (see Chapter 7, p. 128).

Indeed, the EU is already a major source of policy content in this area. The inclusion of the recognition of non-state agents of persecution was included in the 2004 Immigration Law as a result of European-level negotiations, although the agreement of the relevant directive was delayed by Germany while its domestic debates over immigration continued. Even though the trend towards greater Europeanisation is likely to continue over the coming years (see Chapter 9), Germany may not be as supportive of this agenda as it once was. When EU-level co-operation in immigration and asylum was formalised in the 1992 Maastricht Treaty, Germany was a major driving force behind this initiative, as Chancellor Kohl hoped to 'export' the asylum issue, which at that stage was dominating domestic politics, to the EU (Henson and Malhan, 1995). However, by the time the Amsterdam Treaty, which brought immigration and asylum under the so-called 'first pillar', came into force in 1999, German support for a full Europeanisation of this policy area had dropped in temperature from red-hot to decidedly lukewarm (Hellmann, 2006). The reason for this lay in the fact that, by then, Germany had instituted its own measures to restrict asylum under the 1993 reforms. Yet, at European level, German negotiators were now being confronted by countries adopting positions which were frequently more liberal than Germany's, especially in asylum and family reunification policy. Germany's concerns that its own standards, which it perceives as rigorous, could be 'hollowed out' has made it reluctant to support the full harmonisation of policy necessary to make this policy area work at EU level. Instead, it has preferred measures which involve the setting of minimum standards (as in the 2003 Family Reunification Directive) or mutual recognition of standards (as in the Directive on the Status of Long-Term Resident Third Country Nationals) (Green, 2007). Of course, this approach makes something of a mockery of the notion of a harmonised EU policy.

Germany is therefore faced with several critical challenges in the fields of immigration, citizenship and demographics. For decades, it was not possible to address these issues head-on politically. Although this situation has now changed, the main political parties have struggled to develop adequate responses to any of these challenges, so immigration and integration are set to remain high on the agenda of German politics over the coming years.

Questions for discussion

1 **Is Germany a 'country of immigration'?**
2 **To what extent does Germany need new immigration?**
3 **'It is Germany's moral duty to maintain a liberal asylum policy'. Discuss.**

Further reading

Boswell, C. (2003), *European Migration Policies in Flux: Changing Patterns of Inclusion and Exclusion* (Oxford and London: Blackwell/RIIA). Ideal comparative introduction to the issues of immigration policy in Europe.

Green, S. (2004), *The Politics of Exclusion: Institutions and Immigration Policy in Contemporary Germany* (Manchester: Manchester University Press). Comprehensive discussion of over forty years of immigration policy in Germany.

Herbert, U. (2001), *Geschichte der Ausländerpolitik in Deutschland* (Munich: C.H. Beck). Excellent historical analysis of immigration to Germany.

Useful websites

<http://www.bamf.de> – website of the Federal Office for Migration and Refugees, with comprehensive statistics (in German only).

<http://www.integration-in-deutschland.de/cln_011/nn_285106/SubSites/Integration/EN/00_Home/home-node.html?__nnn=true> – English-language portal aimed at immigrants covering all aspects of their integration.

<http://www.migration-info.de> – regular newsletter reporting recent developments in migration policy in Germany and elsewhere (in German only).

7 Economic management

The end of the 'German Model'?

Summary

For much of the post-war period, the so-called 'German Model' of economic management was hailed as a great success, not only in terms of reconstruction after 1945 and the development of Germany into a major economic power but for the consensual nature of industrial relations. This chapter outlines the main characteristics of the German Model and examines pressures on the institutional framework of economic management in post-unification Germany, focusing on industrial relations, corporate governance and European integration. In sum, it asks to what extent the German Model remains 'fit for purpose' in the twenty-first century.

Introduction

Germany possesses one of the world's most successful economies. In absolute terms, it is the third-largest economy globally and regularly vies with the United States and Japan for the title of the world's largest exporter of goods. In terms of wealth, as measured by Gross Domestic Product (GDP) per person at purchasing power parity (i.e., taking into account variation in price levels), Germany is also one of the twenty richest countries in the world. German workers enjoy high levels of welfare, relatively short working weeks and some of the most generous holiday entitlements anywhere. In fact, so successful has the German economy been, especially given the degree to which it suffered during the Second World War, that it has become common to talk of the 'German Model' of economic management. This chapter explores what makes it so special. It also surveys the range of pressures, both external and internal, which have combined to place the German Model 'under stress' (Padgett, 2003).

Background

Germany's status as one of the world's leading economies is all the more remarkable in light of its roller-coaster historical development. Germany only really began to industrialise after unification in 1871 under the leadership of Bismarck. However, once begun, this process was extremely rapid, to the extent that, by 1914, Germany had already joined the UK, France and the United States as one of the world's great industrial powers. Of course, like other countries, the First World War almost bankrupted Germany as a nation, and this, when combined with the heavy reparations imposed at the 1919 Treaty of Versailles, left Weimar Germany economically vulnerable. But worse was to come. As was discussed in Chapter 2, the 1920s saw Germany afflicted by gradually worsening hyperinflation, the effects of which were devastating, effectively destroying any remaining wealth not already lost in the ravages of the First World War (see Feldman, 1997).

The state of the economy certainly contributed to Hitler's rise to power in 1933, although the Nazis were conversely also able to benefit politically from the general improvement in economic conditions from 1933 onwards. Many German businesses, especially those linked to armaments production, thrived under National Socialism. The boom even continued into the Second World War itself, due not least to the widespread use of slave labour in industry, for instance by the notorious IG Farben conglomerate: production levels rose until as late as 1944, after which increased bombing and shortages in raw materials led to a rapid collapse by around two-thirds by the time of *Stunde Null* in May 1945 (on the economy under Hitler, see Tooze, 2006).

The late 1940s proved to be another era of economic hardship for Germans. At least initially, a German economic revival was not a priority for the Allies. In the British and especially the Soviet zones of occupation, entire factories were dismantled and shipped to the victorious occupiers as reparations. To make matters worse, the winter of 1946–7 was one of the coldest on record and led to severe food shortages and starvation. The entire economy in the Western zones remained tightly controlled by the Allies, as a result of which the black market flourished: in many German cities, the cigarette became the preferred currency.

Two main factors contributed to the Allies' decision to reverse their policy of keeping their zones of occupation economically weak. First, there was the question of sheer cost: the UK especially was simply in no position to support the German economy financially. But, even more importantly, relations between the Western Allies and the Soviet Union broke down in 1946, heralding the start of the Cold War. On 1 January 1947, the British and US occupation zones were merged economically, marking the first formal steps on the road to a West German state. Now, economic reconstruction became a priority, and on 21 June 1948 the old (worthless) *Reichsmark* was replaced by the new *Deutsche Mark* and all restrictions on the availability of goods were lifted simultaneously (see Katzenstein, 1987: 84–9). This audacious move was the brainchild of Ludwig Erhard, an instinctive economic liberal who went on to become the first Economics Minister of the Federal Republic and is widely acknowledged as being the father of West Germany's so-called social market economy (*soziale Marktwirtschaft*). His prescription for recon-struction was a model of 'ordo-liberalism', which had been developed in the so-called 'Freiburg School' of pre-war German economists. In practice this meant that the state focused on providing clear rules of the economic game within which free competition could flourish. Ordo-liberalism thus constitutes an alternative both to full free-market capitalism along US lines and the pure command economy which was the hallmark of Marxist–Leninist states such as the Soviet Union.

The currency reform was a stroke of genius which helped West Germany's economy to expand rapidly in subsequent years: between 1950 and 1960, average annual real GDP growth rates (i.e., allowing for inflation) were 8.2 per cent; to reflect this, the term 'economic miracle' (*Wirtschaftswunder*) was coined. But other factors combined with the currency reform to make this miracle possible. Despite the war damage, West Germany's industrial infrastructure had survived largely intact, and it was therefore well placed to benefit from the strong market forces unleashed by the currency reform. Moreover, West Germany received around $1.4 billion (at 1940s prices) in aid from the United States through the Marshall Plan, although it was by no means the main beneficiary country. Perhaps most of all, West Germany benefited from an undervalued currency vis-à-vis its main competitors, which made its exports comparatively cheap; indeed, exports have traditionally been the driving force of economic growth in Germany. The remarkable growth of the economy also served a vital political function: as Chapter 2 noted, the *Wirtschaftswunder* famously legitimised parliamentary democracy to an otherwise sceptical population (see Almond and Verba, 1963).

Between 1961 and 1969, average real growth rates slowed markedly to 4.4 per cent annually, including a first minor recession in 1966–7, but they still remained above the European average. By now, West Germany had also begun to expand the social foundations of its market economy, in which strong economic performance was matched by generous welfare benefits (see Chapter 8). But Erhard's legacy of liberalism was by no means politically uncontested. Under the first Grand Coalition, between 1966 and 1969, the Economics Ministry was headed by a brilliant academic, Karl Schiller (of the SPD). Schiller, a Keynesian economist, believed that the government, rather than staying out of the economy wherever possible, should have a co-ordinating and guiding role. Under his leadership, West Germany passed the 1967 Stability Law, which required federal governments to pursue four goals concurrently: price stability, high levels of employment, steady economic growth and the ability to withstand external economic shocks. Collectively, these four goals were known as the 'magic quadrilateral' (*magisches Viereck*), because in real life it is practically impossible to meet all four goals simultaneously. Schiller also established a regular forum for macroeconomic co-ordination, consisting of employers, employees, academics and politicians. Known as the 'Concerted Action' (*Konzertierte Aktion*), this body met between 1967 and 1977, and represented the high point of West German tripartite macroeconomic management, otherwise known as 'neo-corporatism' (see Schmitter and Lehmbruch, 1979).

As in other European countries, West Germany's golden era of post-war growth came to an end in the early 1970s, sparked by the collapse of the Bretton–Woods exchange rate system in 1971 and the first 'oil shock' in 1973, when oil prices quadrupled in the space of a year. But despite a further drop in average real growth rates between 1971 and 1980 to 2.8 per cent per annum, West Germany's economy weathered the resulting storm comparatively well, to the extent that the SPD–FDP government coined the phrase 'German Model' (*Modell Deutschland*) during the 1976 federal election campaign. During the 1980s, average annual real growth rates declined once more, to 2.6 per cent, although the economy picked up strongly at the end of that decade.

Despite this slowdown in growth, the overall success of the West German economy, both given its historical context and compared to other developed countries, has attracted considerable scholarly attention (notably Shonfield, 1965; Katzenstein, 1987; Hall and Soskice, 2001; see also Busch, 2005a), as well as more popular contributions which have extolled the apparent superiority of the German Model over its more liberal Anglo-Saxon counterpart (e.g., Albert, 1992; Hutton, 1996). Such contributions have coined their own terms to capture the nature of capitalism in Germany, such as 'Rhineland capitalism' (Albert, 1992) and the 'co-ordinated market economy' (Hall and Soskice, 2001).

But what is *Modell Deutschland* in practice and how does it work? Essentially, this label refers to a particular constellation of institutional structures, workplace practices and normative values in the management of Germany's economy and industrial relations. As in any other mixed economy, its main actors are employers (*Arbeitgeber*), employees (*Arbeitnehmer*) and the state. The principal institutional dimensions of the German Model are outlined in Box 7.1 below.

BOX 7.1 THE INSTITUTIONAL STRUCTURE OF THE 'GERMAN MODEL'

The role of the state

- The state provides overall stability, including in fiscal policy, and a clear legal framework for competition ('ordo-liberalism').
- The central bank (*Bundesbank*, and from 1999, the European Central Bank), not the government, is responsible for setting interest rates (monetary policy) without political interference.
- Other regulatory responsibilities are devolved to parapublic institutions, such as the Federal Cartel Office (competition law), the *Kreditanstalt für Wiederaufbau* (KfW) (which originally distributed funds from the Marshall Plan) and the Federal Labour Agency (*Bundesagentur für Arbeit*) (which manages labour policy in Germany).
- The government is provided with independent economic advice by a further parapublic institution, the Council of Economic Advisers (*Sachverständigenrat*).

Labour representation

- German unions (*Gewerkschaften*) are organised on an industry-wide and not trade basis. They are traditionally large and powerful actors in their own right. Formally politically neutral, they have nonetheless traditionally been close to the SPD.
- The two largest unions are the metalworkers' union (IG Metall), covering most manufacturing, and the service-sector union (Ver.di), each with 2.3 million members in 2006. They are thus also two of the world's largest labour organisations.
- IG Metall and Ver.di dominate the German Federation of Unions (*Deutscher Gewerkschaftsbund*, DGB), in which they account for 70 per cent of the members. Six smaller unions are also affiliated to the DGB.
- In addition, civil servants have their own union (*Deutscher Beamtenbund*, DBB), in which a further 1.3 million members are organised; there are also a number of other smaller unions not in the DGB.

Employers' organisations

- Although many large German companies are household names, the backbone of the economy consists of small and medium-sized enterprises (the *Mittelstand*), which are often family-owned businesses. In 2003, they accounted for over 99 per cent of all companies, generating over 42 per cent of all revenues.

There are three main employers' organisations:

a) the *Bundesverband der Deutschen Industrie* (BDI) represents the political interests of industry in Germany;
b) the *Bundesvereinigung der Deutschen Arbeitgeberverbände* (BDA) comprises the employers' wage-negotiating bodies;
c) the *Deutscher Industrie- und Handelskammertag* (DIHK) accredits trades- and craftsmen and supervises apprenticeship training programmes.

The system of corporate governance

- Public limited companies (*Aktiengesellschaften*) have a board of directors (*Vorstand*) and a supervisory board (*Aufsichtsrat*).
- Traditionally, only the very largest German companies sought to raise capital through stock markets. The majority of firms relied instead on long-term relationships with individual banks (*Hausbanken*) for funding, or raised their funds privately.
- Even today, some of the best-known German names, such as Aldi, Bosch and Bertelsmann, are privately owned companies and not listed on any stock exchange.
- Until the mid-1990s, it was usual for financial institutions, principally banks and insurance companies, to hold seats on the *Aufsichtsrat* of any given public limited company. Indeed, banks and insurance companies often even owned substantial shareholdings in these companies.
- Large industrial companies in turn held shares in the main banks, thereby creating a network of cross-ownership which made it almost impossible for foreign companies to take over large German businesses.

Industrial relations in Germany

- Germany has traditionally enjoyed harmonious industrial relations, with relatively few working days lost through strikes in international comparison.
- Wage negotiations are usually conducted collectively on an industry-wide level between the relevant union and its counterpart in the BDA. For instance, the employers' organisation in manufacturing is *Gesamtmetall*, which normally negotiates a collective wage deal (*Tarifvertrag*) for all its members with IG Metall. The government is not allowed to interfere with wage negotiations, for instance via a wages policy (the principle of *Tarifautonomie*). For this reason, and in contrast to France and the UK, Germany so far has not had a national minimum wage.
- In all but the smallest companies, employees are also represented in a works council (*Betriebsrat*), which is required by law to be consulted in key decisions the company makes.
- Moreover, for companies with over 2,000 staff, employees' representatives hold half the seats in the *Aufsichtstrat*, with the chair having the casting vote. This is known as co-determination (*Mitbestimmung*).

Together, this institutional set-up embodies Katzenstein's model of semi-sovereignty in West Germany (Katzenstein, 1987; see also Chapter 4, pp. 65–6). The state has relatively little direct influence in economic governance, and devolves significant responsibilities to powerful, centralised societal actors (especially in wage bargaining), as well as to parapublic institutions, for instance in the form of the *Bundesbank*/European Central Bank and the Federal Labour Agency. This structure certainly bears the mark of history: thus, the enshrined independence of the *Bundesbank* in setting interest rates to control inflation constitutes a direct response to the harrowing memory of hyperinflation in the 1920s. Similarly, the strength and independence of both the employers' organisations and unions reflect the desire to prevent a repetition of their marginalisation under the Nazi regime's *Gleichschaltung* (see Chapter 1, p. 12). The constitutionally guaranteed independence of the collective wage-bargaining process and the establishment of works councils can be seen in the same context.

But the essence of the German Model goes beyond mere institutions and four further dimensions are important in this context. First, the significance of consensus, a key element of the social market economy, must not be underestimated. Traditionally, employees and employers have worked hand-in-hand for the benefit of their company, rather than in a confrontational fashion. This spirit of co-operation is epitomised by the fact that union leaders regularly sit on the supervisory boards of major companies, as well as by the fact that union membership extends far beyond the political realm of the SPD: most famously, the Federal Minister for Social Affairs between 1982 and 1998, Norbert Blüm, was a member of one of Germany's main unions, IG Metall, despite coming from the centre-right CDU. Similarly, the chief executive of Daimler-Benz between 1987 and 1995, Edzard Reuter, was a member of the SPD. Thus, unions were prepared to forgo large wage increases in times of difficulty, while employers were happy to share the success of the company with their workers in times of plenty. The *Konzertierte Aktion* between employers, unions and the government between 1967 and 1977 is a further expression of the high value attached to co-operation and consensus in the German Model.

Of course, such a system of mutual trust was predicated on employers taking a long-term view of business and profit, and this constitutes the second key normative dimension to the German Model. Because they were traditionally not financed via the stock market, German companies have in the past not been forced to concentrate exclusively on maximising returns for shareholders; instead, their priority has been *stakeholder* value, which has institutionally included employees. Indeed, proponents of the German Model such as Will Hutton (1996) have singled out this aspect as a critical reason for the apparent superiority of Rhineland capitalism.

Third, and linked to the previous two issues, labour in West Germany has traditionally been highly productive, which in turn is a central determinant of wage levels: put simply, the higher the productivity of a workforce, the higher the level of wages that an employer is able to pay. One reason commonly put forward for this productivity is the system of apprenticeships, under which training is given in companies and educational establishments (*duales Ausbildungssystem*). This has helped to create a highly skilled workforce, making Germany an ideal location for manufacturing high value-added items, such as cars. Here, *Mittelstand* companies also play an indispensable role: two-thirds of all apprenticeships are completed in small and medium-sized enterprises.

Fourth, the welfare dimension of the social market economy should not be underestimated. Chapter 8 discusses the nature of, and trends in, Germany's welfare state in greater detail, but suffice it to say in this context that the federal government has taken advantage of West Germany's strong economy to expand welfare state provision considerably at critical junctures. Two such junctures can be identified. First, in 1957, the CDU/CSU-led federal government instituted a reform to pensions which linked future payments to gross wage increases; henceforth, the cost of state pensions would soar, as a historical analysis of contribution rates shows (Streeck and Trampusch, 2005: 177). Second, the SPD–FDP government under Willy Brandt presided over a large-scale expansion of federal expenditure, which grew annually by an average of around 12 per cent between 1970 and 1974 (Sarrazin, cited in Zohlnhöfer, 2006: 294). Most of this extra expenditure went on welfare, education and transport.

That said, the German Model is something of an ideal type, to which reality did not always conform perfectly. There have been a number of very significant industrial disputes in West German history, notably over co-determination in the early 1950s and over the thirty-five-hour working week in the mid-1980s. In particular, after almost two decades of moderate wage growth, there were a number of unofficial strikes by IG Metall members in 1969 (see Streeck, 2005). The union responded with high wage demands in the subsequent wage negotiation rounds. In consequence, wages rose on average by 12.5 per cent annually between 1969 and 1974 (Borchardt, cited in Zohlnhöfer, 2006: 293); not only were these increases very high, but they had knock-on effects for the financing of the pensions system. In addition, the relationship between the *Bundesbank* and the federal government has, on occasion, been strained. During the 1970s, and as a result of the increases in wages and public expenditure outlined above, the *Bundesbank* pursued a strict policy of inflation control, which was contrary to the SPD–FDP federal government's preference. In 1990, the president of the *Bundesbank*, Karl-Otto Pöhl, was highly critical of the 1:1 exchange rate proposed by Chancellor Kohl for the currency union between West and East Germany.

For its part, the federal government has not always limited itself to setting an ordo-liberal framework, but has sometimes displayed quite interventionist tendencies. Thus, until the late 1980s, the German state, whether at federal or *Land* level, owned significant shares in major German companies, including the national airline Lufthansa and the energy company VEBA; even in 2007, Lower Saxony owned around 20 per cent of the stock of Volkswagen, Germany's largest car manufacturer. Elsewhere, the government continues to pay substantial subsidies to support various sectors of the economy, with the coal industry being a prime example. Even though the sums involved have been gradually decreasing, the federal government alone granted €6 billion in direct state aid and a further €14.4 billion in tax breaks in 2006 (*Deutscher Bundestag*, 2006). Nor has the federal government been above intervening directly in companies: in 1999, the SPD–Green government under Gerhard Schröder saved, at least temporarily, around 60,000 jobs at Holzmann, a major construction company. Above all, the government has created one of the most highly regulated labour markets in Europe, with strong levels of protection for employees, and has set requirements for trades which have effectively protected certain professions. One of the best-known cases of the latter is chimney-sweeps, who enjoy a legally enshrined monopoly in Germany.

But overall, the German Model can be characterised by the high-skilled production of high-value goods, with consensual industrial relations, in which companies are not required to maximise short-term profits. Incremental policy changes in the context of semi-sovereignty helped generate high levels of wealth and welfare, as well as social peace more generally (Katzenstein, 1987). Recently, though, this model has been under considerable strain. The following section outlines the principal pressures, some of which are linked to unification, others pre-date it.

Issues

For all its strengths, the German Model has been under challenge for some time. As has been the case in welfare policy (Chapter 8), too, several of these challenges originated in the 1970s, rather than as a result of unification, although the latter has contributed some very significant challenges to the German economy. In the 1980s, there was already a lively discussion between the government, BDI and unions over the viability of (West) Germany as a location for production (*Standortdebatte*), with the focus on whether labour costs were unjustifiably high. During the 1990s, the notion of 'globalisation' helped to define the environment in which the *Modell Deutschland* operated. Although this is a notoriously vague term, it generally refers to the patterns of economic inter-dependence between advanced industrial democracies in the context of global competition, which appear to have accelerated since the collapse of communism and the end of the Cold War (see Hay and Marsh, 2001). Thus, the volume of global trade has risen markedly since 1990, promoted not least by factors such as the gradual emergence of Central and Eastern European economies from communism, as well as the accession of China to the World Trade Organisation in 2001. Moreover, China, India and the countries of Central and Eastern Europe, all of which have much lower wage levels than Germany, are emerging as more attractive locations for industrial production. Germany was therefore never going to be able to insulate itself against the negative forces of globalisation; indeed, as one of the world's principal trading nations, its economy has benefited from this dynamic, too.

This section now outlines four further, and often interlinked, challenges to the German Model: unification; changes in patterns of corporate governance; changes in employment and industrial relations; and the impact of the EU.

Unification

Although unification has also helped transform the structures of *Modell Deutschland* (see below), its main significance is as a very real, albeit unique, external shock to economic performance. The economic challenge of regenerating the east has been enormous and, as Chapter 3 showed (pp. 47–9), the original expectation that unification would essentially pay for itself proved to be acutely mistaken. Instead, the new *Länder* turned out to be in need of much more investment than was initially expected, requiring astronomical sums of money. While growth in the west has continued to be respectable, it simply stagnated in the east (see Table 3.1). On a national basis, Germany's real GDP growth rates have been some of the lowest in the EU; indeed, there was scarcely *any* real growth between 2001 and 2005.

Perhaps the most telling trend in Germany's post-unification economic performance is that unemployment has been a persistently heavy blight. Again, there is a clear split between east and west, with formal rates in the former almost double those in the latter. In reality, they are likely to be even higher, once people on work-creation schemes and similar programmes are taken into account. But equally, it would be wrong to view unemployment as a purely 'eastern' problem: there are significant pockets of it in western Germany too, either in such economically peripheral areas as the ports of Wilhelmshaven and Bremerhaven or in the old industrial heartlands of North Rhine–Westphalia. Crucially, the German Model was simply not designed to cope with such persistent and large-scale unemployment. As Chapter 8 will go on to show in more detail, the viability of the welfare state depends on a high number of people in so-called wage-earning employment (*sozialversicherungspflichtige Beschäftigung*). However, the higher the unemployment rate, the greater the strain on the welfare state, both via payments from the unemployment insurance scheme and through early retirement into the statutory pension scheme. Thus, not only do employees and employers finance a significant element of the costs of unemployment through their payments into the statutory insurance schemes, but over time this creates a major incentive for employers to restructure their workforces in favour of more capital-intensive production. This point will be returned to later.

Changes in patterns of corporate governance

The structure and culture of corporate governance has experienced far-reaching change since 1990 (Beyer and Höpner, 2003). As Box 7.1 shows, German companies have traditionally enjoyed a strong and arguably cocooned relationship with their banks, leaving them able to concentrate on long-term success, rather than on delivering the type of short-term shareholder value that is usually associated with more aggressive Anglo-Saxon capitalism. Indeed, as was noted, this was seen as a particular strength of the German Model. However, from the mid-1990s onwards, major German companies began to disengage from this very close interrelationship with other firms; henceforth, shareholder value became king. Edzard Reuter's successor as chief executive of Daimler Benz, Jürgen Schremmp, was one of the pioneers of this trend by vigorously promoting a more Anglo-Saxon business culture. Interestingly, the trigger for this was not an external crisis, but the decision of key banks to focus in the future on their core business, rather than bear responsibility for much of German corporate life. Whereas, as late as 1996, the chairs of the supervisory boards in twenty-nine of the hundred largest companies came from Deutsche Bank, this had reduced to zero just five years later (Beyer and Höpner, 2003: 184). In parallel, share ownership, which had never previously been a popular form of individual saving, took off hugely in the late 1990s, sparked in part by high-profile privatisations such as Deutsche Telekom, the state-owned telecommunications giant, in 1996. This was just one of several divestments by the federal government, which between 1994 and 2000 generated the equivalent of almost €19 billion in revenue. This process was accompanied by a range of political reforms of the framework of corporate governance, notably the 1998 Control and Transparency in Enterprises Law, which simplified the rules on stock voting rights to increase shareholder democracy (see Deeg, 2005).

By the late 1990s, even hostile takeovers, which were hitherto unheard of in Germany, were starting to occur. The most spectacular example was the takeover of the engineering and communications company Mannesmann by the British company Vodafone in 2000, which at the time constituted the largest corporate takeover in history (Garrett, 2001). The fact that a household name in Germany could simply be subsumed into another company, and a foreign one at that, provoked widespread debate. The affair gained more popular notoriety when it emerged that the main board had been awarded some €60 million in bonuses by the supervisory board immediately before the takeover was completed. In its aftermath several key figures on the Mannesmann supervisory board, including the chief executive of Deutsche Bank, Josef Ackermann, were charged with fraud. This resulted in one of the most high-profile white-collar trials in German history, which ultimately ended only in late 2006 when the defendants agreed to pay substantial fines in return for charges being dropped. Of importance for this discussion is that Ackermann never denied making the payments, but he justified them as entirely normal practice for rewarding success in a modern corporate environment. This gives some indication of how far corporate governance in Germany has evolved in the space of just a few years.

Changes in employment and industrial relations

As well as changes in corporate governance, the nature of employment and the labour force have also evolved. Like many other EU member-states, Germany has undergone a process of de-industrialisation, as traditional industries, such as heavy engineering, steel and coal, have struggled to compete against developing-world competitors. The old industrial heartland of Germany, the *Ruhrgebiet*, has changed beyond recognition as steel mills and factories have closed. Germany has, however, been slow to develop a diverse and dynamic service sector, especially at the low-paid end, and this has undoubtedly contributed to the persistence of long-term unemployment.

A key indicator of this changing nature of work has been the structure of employment. Traditionally, *Modell Deutschland* assumed that the default employment status of individuals was wage-earning employment. Crucially, this status includes full contributions, on an equal basis between employers and employees, to the various statutory insurance schemes. The importance of this assumption should not be underestimated, as the financial structure of Germany's expansive welfare state was essentially predicated on these contributions, which are used to meet existing liabilities (for instance, for pensions) rather than building up individual entitlements for the future. The implications of this 'pay-as-you-go' system of financing welfare are discussed further in Chapter 8. However, the total number of people in wage-earning employment decreased steadily from 29.33 million to 26.18 million between 1992 and 2005. In its place, other forms of employment have increased, and total employment levels have thus remained more-or-less equal. These alternative forms of employment include self-employment as well as part-time, low-paid jobs with upper income limits (so-called 'mini-jobs' and 'midi-jobs') (Czada, 2005). The key point is that none of these forms of employment generates equivalent levels of revenue for the statutory insurance schemes: the self-employed are responsible for making their own provisions for welfare, and the contribution rates for mini- and midi-jobs are greatly reduced. With current income in the insurances meeting current, not future, liabilities, the net result of this has been that the rising cost of financing Germany's welfare state has, over the past decade, fallen on ever fewer shoulders.

Partly as a result of this, the institutions of organised industrial relations are also undergoing fundamental change (Streeck and Hassel, 2003; Menz, 2005). On the employees' side, union membership has been falling: while the DGB unions still had a total of 9.8 million members in 1994, this had dropped by one-third to 6.6 million in 2006. Membership of the two largest unions, IG Metall and Ver.di, has dropped by a similar proportion over the same period. The proportion of union members among all employees (the union density) fell from 27 per cent in 1980 to around 17 per cent in 2000 (Streeck and Hassel, 2003: 109). As Chapter 5 showed (p. 85), these changes have also been reflected electorally in the reduction over time in the absolute size of the SPD's core electorate of unionised workers.

On the employers' side, the number of companies in employers' sectoral organisations such as *Gesamtmetall* has also been dropping, from almost 60 per cent in 1980 to 32 per cent in 1998 (Menz, 2005: 201). This 'crumbling' of the 'pillars of social partnership' (Streeck and Hassel, 2003) also extends into the structures of collective wage bargaining. The proportion of workers covered by collective wage agreements (*Tarifverträge*) has declined, while the number of 'opening clauses' (*Öffnungsklauseln*), which allow companies to withdraw from wage agreements in times of economic difficulty, has risen dramatically. All these trends are particularly pronounced among the non-traditional service sectors of the economy, and most especially geographically in the east (figures in Menz, 2005: 201; also Streeck and Hassel, 2003; Deeg, 2005). In that sense, the accession of five new *Länder* and Berlin to the Federal Republic has not only had a significant impact on economic performance but has helped to transform the very structures of the German Model.

Europeanisation

The fourth area to have challenged the German Model is Germany's membership of the European Union, and the resulting process of 'Europeanisation'. This term is discussed in greater detail in Chapter 9, but for the purposes of understanding changes in the German Model, it can be defined as the impact of EU legislation on national structures of policy. And in the area of economic management, the impact of the EU has been considerable (Dyson, 2003; Dyson and Goetz, 2004).

First, and perhaps foremost, Germany exported its model of an independent central bank directly to the EU, in the form of the European Central Bank, which took over the management of monetary policy upon the introduction of the euro on 1 January 1999. The ECB thus replaced the *Bundesbank* as the institution with sole control over interest rates in Germany, as well as in all other 'Eurozone' countries. While at the time this was seen as a clear victory for German interests and influence (Bulmer *et al.*, 2000), it has turned out to be a double-edged sword for the German economy. For whereas the *Bundesbank* set interest rates solely according to German needs, the ECB has to control inflation in all other Eurozone states as well. And because inflation has been higher in other member-states than in Germany, the ECB has had to keep interest rates at a level which is unnecessarily high for Germany's economic-well-being, thereby restricting investment and growth (Deeg, 2005: 348).

Second, the EU's Stability and Growth Pact, which was adopted by member-states at Germany's explicit behest in 1996, has also proved to be a mixed blessing. In the context of monetary union and the adoption of the euro, the Pact was intended to stop individual member-states from offloading the destabilising effects of large budget deficits on to the other countries in the Eurozone by limiting normal annual government deficits to 3 per cent of GDP, with the prospect of fines against persistent infringers. At the time of its formulation, there was little doubt about the targets of this Pact, namely such perceived profligate, high-debt countries as Italy. Yet, embarrassingly, the crisis in its public finances meant that Germany itself broke the Pact each year between 2002 and 2005 (see Table 3.1). Indeed, the Council of Finance Ministers suspended proceedings against Germany and France, which was in a similar position, only after massive political pressure was exerted by the two countries. This episode did Germany great harm among its partners in the European Union.

Third, the EU's single-market programme, while providing enormous benefits for some German companies, has also shone a stark spotlight on those elements of *Modell Deutschland* that did not quite conform to the standard of ordo-liberalism. Thus, cherished elements of the German Model have fallen foul of the European Commission on competition grounds, be it preferential conditions for public savings banks (*Sparkassen*), Germany's still closed market for energy provision or the so-called 'VW Law', which prevented any individual shareholder in Volkswagen from exercising more than 20 per cent of votes, regardless of how many shares that individual or organisation holds. Where necessary, the federal government has in fact lobbied quite hard to defend such exemptions; thus, it took a ruling by the European Court of Justice in autumn 2007 finally to overturn the VW Law.

Fourth, the eastern enlargement of the EU in May 2004, which saw eight Central and Eastern European countries plus Malta and Cyprus become full members, has posed a challenge to the German economy. Unlike previous enlargements, which had largely been to richer European countries, the differences in incomes and wages between existing and new member-states were particularly large. Faced with the possible free movement of labour, one of the core benefits of EU membership, Germany, along with most other member-states, feared large-scale labour migration from the countries bordering it to the east: Poland and the Czech Republic. In consequence, the federal government insisted that the free movement of labour be postponed for seven years, until 2011. Nonetheless, soon after enlargement, Germany was facing large numbers of eastern European tile-layers and abattoir workers, who worked on a formally self-employed basis in order to circumvent the restrictions. They were simply much cheaper for companies to employ than indigenous labour, so thousands of German workers lost their jobs. Moreover, with the 2011 deadline drawing nearer, a new influx of cheaper labour may yet cost many more German workers their jobs. This indicates just how vulnerable the German economy has become to external pressures.

Debates

Collectively, the German political system has so far failed to get to grips with these challenges; indeed, the continued underperformance of the German economy is seen as one of the main symptoms of the notion of *Reformstau* (see Chapter 4, p. 66). However, after several years of indifferent growth, there has been a modest economic recovery: real GDP growth reached 2.7 per cent in 2006, the highest level for six years; that year unemployment fell too, although it remained stuck above four million. But debate has continued over what should be Germany's response to the challenges outlined above.

First and foremost, the two main parties have so far failed to develop a convincing answer to the question of whether Germany, in principle, should retrench or liberalise, with all that this entails for the economy and the welfare state. The problem is that there is little real difference between the CDU/CSU and the SPD on this issue: both are committed to the social market economy, albeit with a slightly more liberal emphasis in the CDU/CSU and a slightly more interventionist emphasis in the SPD. Electorally, both are competing for the political centre ground, which in turn remains instinctively suspicious of Anglo-Saxon-style capitalism. One of the curiosities of this debate is that the term 'neo-liberal' has become something of an insult in discussions, especially among the centre-left. In consequence, neither party has so far had any great incentive to embrace economic and social reform.

In substantive terms, one durable element of the debate over economic management has been the question of whether labour costs are so high as to discourage production in Germany (this was previously a feature of the *Standortdebatte* of the 1980s). Ironically, thanks not least to a series of very moderate collective wage bargains agreed by the unions after 2000, real wage costs (i.e., allowing for inflation) have essentially remained static over recent years, to the extent that German companies in 2005 had some of the EU's lowest labour costs per unit produced in the EU. Indeed, the fact that real wages have been constant for so long has itself impacted negatively on the economy: consumer spending on Germany's high streets has shown little growth since 2000. Another indicator of the lack of spending power in consumers' pockets has been the strong growth of the discount supermarkets Aldi and Lidl, which are now two of Germany's top ten food retailers.

The absence of real wage growth in recent years can also be explained by the growing burden of taxation. Remarkably, salaries now account for a diminishing share of the total costs of employment, down from 57 per cent in 1991 to 53 per cent in 2004. Instead, the costs of taxation and especially total contributions to statutory insurance schemes have risen, thereby not only soaking up any increases in wages which were negotiated by the unions and employers, but raising the total cost of employment for companies. In order to reduce this, the welfare state or its financial basis would require reform, and in consequence the discussion over the future of the German Model usually goes hand-in-hand with debates over welfare reform (these are discussed in more detail in Chapter 8).

A second element of the overall debate has been how the German Model can and should respond to external pressures, and in particular Europeanisation. For it is from the EU that some of the most direct challenges, in the form of liberalisations, to economic management in Germany have emanated. In consequence, Germany has found itself, at least initially, opposing the 2004 Takeover Directive and the 2006 Services Directive, and, like many other member-states, has been lukewarm about implementing the goals of the 2000 Lisbon Agenda, the aim of which is to make the EU the most competitive economy in the world by 2010. This shift in perspective on European integration in practice has coincided with a more interest-orientated approach in EU policy-making (an issue to which we shall return in Chapter 9).

So far, the main parties, whether in government or opposition, have all struggled to cope with these challenges. Part of the problem has undoubtedly been the semi-sovereign nature of the German state, with the government unable to involve itself in the wage-bargaining process. But whereas in the past, the German Model was characterised by consensus-orientated negotiation to everyone's mutual benefit, the changing structure of employment outlined above has fundamentally altered the positions of both unions and employers. Now, in industrial relations, short-term, narrowly defined interests tend to predominate on both sides, thereby presenting a classic collective action problem (see Streeck, 2005). Moreover, even when deals are struck, the decreasing organisational density of both unions and employers makes it difficult to legitimise these in the wider economic environment.

In response, the federal government has tried to revive the spirit of tripartite, neo-corporatist negotiation of the *Konzertierte Aktion*. In the last years of the Kohl government, an Alliance for Jobs (*Bündnis für Arbeit*) was formed to bring together the federal government, employers and unions in a concerted effort to reduce unemployment – without success. When the SPD–Green government came to power in 1998, Chancellor Schröder, who prided himself on his business credentials and revelled in the label 'Comrade of the Bosses' (*Genosse der Bosse*), tried to revive the Alliance and extend it to include international benchmarking programmes, such as the ill-fated 'Third Way' with the UK's Labour government. However, this too ultimately collapsed without any positive results. In what Kenneth Dyson (2005b) has described as a 'tipping point' for economic management, Schröder then took the initiative himself in the form of *Agenda 2010* on labour market and welfare reform, which he introduced in 2003. Henceforth, the SPD–Green government relied increasingly on expert commissions to produce policy recommendations on all the most controversial issues, including the labour market and pensions (Dyson, 2005a).

Politically, these challenges to the German Model have left many Germans deeply disillusioned. For historical reasons, the notion of consensus and shared responsibility resonates particularly strongly among voters, and the fact that large companies' exhortations about increased shareholder value have often gone hand-in-hand with almost exponential increases in salaries for senior board members has angered many of those in more lowly positions. Significantly, notions of equity and solidarity are particularly strong in the east, as Chapter 5 noted.

The situation is complicated by the fact that the number of welfare recipients now exceeds those in wage-earning employment (see Chapter 8), which means that there is a very large number of voters who potentially stand to lose from economic and welfare reform. Therefore, normative concerns about equality within German society have allied with naked self-interest to create a powerful force in electoral terms. Its effects can be viewed in elections throughout the past ten years. In 1998 and 2002, the SPD put justice (*Gerechtigkeit*) at the heart of its federal election campaign and won both; conversely, when Schröder launched *Agenda 2010* and the associated cuts in welfare, he precipitated a major electoral backlash, culminating in the SPD's defeat at the crucial 2005 North Rhine–Westphalian *Land* election, which itself prompted the early federal election later that year. In early 2005, disaffected SPD members founded the Electoral Alliance for Labour and Social Justice, which, in alliance with the ex-communist PDS, went on to score a major success in that year's federal election (see Chapter 5, p. 80). Nor has the CDU/CSU been spared the voters' ire: in the 2005 election, its leader, Angela Merkel, ran an unusually reform-orientated campaign, only to be rewarded with one of the worst results in the party's history. So far, therefore, voters in Germany have shown little appetite for extensive economic reform.

Conclusion

Its sheer size alone ensures that the German economy is highly complex and diverse, and in the context of a textbook such as this only an overview of key trends can be provided. Nonetheless, the secret of the success of the German economy is clearly visible. This chapter has highlighted how the decentralised state, a powerful central bank, consensual industrial relations and a skills-focused system of production have consistently combined to provide Germany's population with one of the highest standards of living in the world. Given the totality of Nazi Germany's defeat in 1945, that is no mean feat.

At the same time, this chapter has shown where Germany's system of economic management is currently under stress from various transformative pressures. Unification has been a major factor, by imposing unprecedented demands on the economy, both in terms of dealing with unemployment and in generating enough tax revenue to finance the enormous transfers that have been necessary. But unification has also exacerbated longer-term trends in German society, in which the traditional pillars of social partnership, unions and employers' organisations are losing relevance. To be sure, this trend is reflected in other areas of German society, notably the party system, where a similar process of dealignment has taken place (see Chapter 5, pp. 84–6). Membership of the European Union, for all its benefits, has at times been uncomfortable for Germany, as the idiosyncrasies of its system of economic management have come under the spotlight.

Yet, to borrow from Mark Twain, the reports of the death of *Modell Deutschland* may have been exaggerated. Indeed, as a growing number of authors (often writing from a non-German perspective) are finding, the German economy retains many intrinsic strengths, which will mean that when it does bounce back, it will be fitter and leaner (Deeg, 2005; Harding, 2007). More broadly, the contributors to Hall and Soskice's (2001) collection find no reason to suppose that there will be an inevitable convergence of varieties of capitalism around a rapacious Anglo-Saxon model with only minimal social provisions. There is no question that German companies are competitive internationally; in fact, many, such as the software company SAP, are enjoying ongoing and considerable financial success as market leaders in their respective sectors. Nor is the notion of co-operation *passé*: IG Metall played a major role in developing BMW's innovative system of four nine-hour shifts to maximise the capacities of its Bavarian plants (Whittall, 2005).

Arguably, the future viability of the German Model depends principally on one factor: the reform of the welfare state. As it stands, this imposes growing costs on both employees and employers, strangling domestic consumer demand and providing employers with an irresistible incentive to restructure their workforces further away from wage-earning employment. Achieving welfare reform without alienating the millions of voters who are likely to lose from such a reform is the squaring of the circle that has so far eluded successive governments. The effects of the various attempts undertaken so far will be the subject in the following chapter.

Questions for discussion

1   Is the German Model superior to other forms of managed capitalism?
2   Why has the structure of employment changed so much in Germany?
3   Is the German Model doomed to become Anglo-Saxon?

Further reading

Dyson, K. and S. Padgett (eds) (2006), *The Politics of Economic Reform in Germany: Global, Rhineland or Hybrid Capitalism* (London: Routledge); special issue of *German Politics* 14/2. The best recent collection of high-quality analyses of the German Model.

Katzenstein, P. (1987), *Policy and Politics in West Germany: The Growth of a Semisovereign State* (Philadelphia, Penn.: Temple University Press). Covers key aspects of economic management and industrial relations in West Germany

Useful website

<http://www.destatis.de/e_home.htm> – the Federal Statistical Office's website has comprehensive economic data available on a dedicated English-language site.

8   The reform of the welfare state?

Summary

Traditionally, West Germany enjoyed the reputation of having a particularly generous welfare system. Indeed, the comparatively high level of benefits was seen as an integral element of the social market economy and *Modell Deutschland*. However, for a range of reasons, but mainly cost, pressure on this system has been building since the 1970s, and especially since unification. But the political challenge of reforming Germany's welfare provisions has proved extremely difficult to manage, as political parties have had to impose unpalatable cuts on an electorate accustomed to generous unemployment benefits, comfortable pensions and comprehensive health insurance. The resulting political disputes have not only been some of the most contentious of recent years, but are set to define much of German politics in the future.

Introduction

When seen from the outside, especially from Anglo-Saxon countries, Germany is often regarded as the classic example of a high-welfare state, with perceived generous unemployment benefits, comfortable pensions and comprehensive health insurance. Indeed, welfare provision, which is by far the single largest element of public expenditure, was considered integral to the German social market economy as well as, more broadly, the 'Rhineland' style of managed capitalism (see Albert, 1992; Hall and Soskice, 2001; see also Chapter 7). And, indeed, this characterisation is generally accurate for the period up to the mid-1970s, which Bleses and Seeleib-Kaiser (2004: 27–8) describe as the 'golden era' of German welfare policy. But since then, both the structure and extent of welfare have come under increasing challenge. Collectively, these challenges have necessitated a retreat from a number of established policy positions. Even though this process of retrenchment has been quite gradual and from a comparatively high level, welfare state reform has been possibly the single most contested policy issue in post-unification Germany. This is an area of enormous complexity, and within the limited confines of this chapter it is impossible to provide more than an overview of the principal structures and a flavour of the ongoing debate. Nevertheless, this chapter aims to generate an understanding of why reform of the welfare state is such a central element of German politics today.

Background

First, though, Germany's image as a welfare paradise needs to be put into context. Above all, Germany never found itself at the upper end of welfare expenditure in the EU: that accolade consistently went to the Scandinavian countries. Rather, West Germany pursued a policy of the 'middle way' (Schmidt, 1987), which saw it fall between the extremes of Anglo-Saxon 'market' and Scandinavian 'welfare' capitalism. And while welfare expenditure in Germany certainly rose after unification (see below), this was also the case in other countries, such as France, in the same period. Germany thus continues to occupy the middle ground in terms of comparative welfare expenditure (Schmidt, 2001).

In addition to the level of welfare expenditure, its delivery needs to be contextualised. For (West) Germany most closely represented the ideal type of a 'conservative welfare state regime' identified by Esping-Andersen (1990), in which comprehensive social insurance programmes guarantee the existing income status, usually of the male, in the case of sickness, unemployment or old age; dependants, such as spouses, derive welfare benefits only from the status of the (male) breadwinner. This conservative welfare state model stood in contrast to 'social democratic' welfare states (in which the state provides and delivers universal benefits) as well as to 'liberal' welfare states (in which the state is limited to providing means-tested benefits to the poorest in society). The aim of Germany's welfare state was therefore never to achieve large-scale redistribution from rich to poor, but rather to sustain existing standards of living for its beneficiaries. This dynamic has also contributed to the relatively low levels of social mobility in Germany, which were revealed by the OECD's 2000 Programme for International Student Assessment (PISA). From a feminist perspective, Jane Lewis (1992) has argued that Germany squarely fits into the 'strong male breadwinner' model of social policy, which highlights the role of women as homemakers and supporters of the economically active male. Indeed, the female employment rate in Germany has tended to be relatively low, certainly in comparison with other Northern European countries, and stood at just 59 per cent in 2003 (Statistisches Bundesamt, 2006a).

Yet, Germany was one of the first industrialised countries to provide any form of organised welfare policy: as early as 1884, imperial Germany under Bismarck introduced a sickness insurance scheme, and most of its social insurance schemes date from this time; for this reason, it is still common to talk of the 'Bismarckian' welfare state. When, after the 1949 federal election, the new CDU/CSU-led government under Konrad Adenauer began to bolster the welfare state in the context of the social market economy, it therefore drew on well-established principles of German social policy. Of course, West Germany's welfare provision cannot be seen in isolation from the Cold War: given the existence of the communist German Democratic Republic, West Germany simply had to be seen to be delivering higher levels of welfare to its citizens.

How does the German welfare state work? In essence, and despite the pressures outlined below, provision continues to be organised around five statutory social insurance schemes, covering pensions, health, unemployment, accidents and long-term nursing care. In the standard case, wage-earning employees (*sozialversicherungsplichtige Beschäftigte*) pay a percentage of their gross salary into these funds up to a threshold level, after which contributions remain constant. Significantly, the principle of solidarity plays a central role in Germany's welfare state in two key ways: first, personal premiums are based on ability to pay and not on personal risk; second, there is solidarity between employees and employers, as the percentage of gross salary paid by the former is matched by the latter. The combined sum is used by the insurance provider, normally a public authority or private company (but, notably, not the government), to meet existing commitments. Thus, contributions into, say, pension funds are not invested, but rather spent immediately on existing liabilities towards current pensioners. This is known as a 'pay-as-you-go' system (*Umlagefinanzierung*) and is the standard model for statutory social insurance in Germany. It effectively constitutes an unwritten contract between the generations (*Generationenvertrag*), in which the young, who are in work, pay to support the elderly, who are not.

At the same time, there are a number of significant exceptions to this basic principle. For instance, the self-employed are excluded from the statutory systems altogether and make private provision for their welfare; high-wage earners above the threshold can opt-out of the statutory health insurance and take out private insurance, which usually offers better levels of coverage than do the statutory schemes and is itself not run on a 'pay-as-you-go' basis; and civil servants (*Beamte*) make a partial financial contribution to their healthcare only – their pension needs, as well as the remainder of their healthcare costs, are financed out of current *Länder* and federal government budgets (as *Beamte* cannot be sacked, no unemployment insurance is necessary). At the other end of the spectrum, around 6.5 million holders of so-called 'mini-jobs' are generally not subject to statutory contributions, and their employers make only a flat-rate contribution of 25 per cent of gross wages to the combined statutory funds. Insurance providers, too, are highly fragmented and based often on a combination of provision by vocation and location. Many, but by no means all, are privately owned; nonetheless, they provide services both to statutory-insured workers and private individuals. While not all of the possible permutations for social insurance can be listed here, the point is that there are numerous deviations from the default configuration of a wage-earning employee paying into the statutory insurance system. In sum, this creates a highly complex mosaic of welfare provision in Germany (see Czada, 2005: 165–7). Boxes 8.1 and 8.2 provide an overview of the main characteristics of this system and of expenditure patterns, respectively.

While this system of welfare insurance has been very successful in terms of preserving the social and income status of its beneficiaries, it has one crucial structural side-effect: the financing of welfare, largely shared as it is between employers and employees, constitutes a direct tax on employment. Put very simply, this has meant that increases in welfare expenditure have inextricably led to increases of non-wage labour costs, which, depending on the measure used, are already comparatively high in Germany: employers have seen their contributions to the four main statutory insurance schemes rise from just over 15 per cent of gross wages in 1975 to 21 per cent in 2003 (Bleses and Seeleib-Kaiser, 2004: 44). Crucially, this has created significant incentives for employers to change the structure of their employment, for instance by shedding surplus labour through unemployment or early retirement, by employing 'mini-jobbers' instead of full-time wage earners, or by outsourcing their labour force abroad altogether. Yet, in turn, this leads to higher demands for welfare expenditure which again leads to further increases in the employers' contribution rates to statutory insurances – ultimately creating a classic vicious circle (see Streeck and Trampusch, 2005: 175).

Issues

Ever since the mid-1970s, when social welfare expenditure reached its zenith under the SPD–FDP government, there has been one overriding issue in social welfare: cost. The containment of total welfare expenditure was relatively successful during the 1980s, but

---

BOX 8.1 THE SOCIAL INSURANCE SYSTEM IN GERMANY

Germany's statutory social insurance system for wage earners rests on five pillars.

1 Pensions insurance (*Gesetzliche Rentenversicherung*)
   In 2006, contributions stood at 19.5 per cent of gross salary, paid equally between employers and employees. In 2004, the pensions level was 70 per cent of net salary (i.e., after tax) for a standard pensioner with 45 years' contributions. Pension increases are linked to gross wages, not inflation. Average pensions in 2005 were about €1,000 and €500 per month for men and women, respectively. Over time, the general trend in contributions to pensions insurance has been a gradual rise upwards – rates rose to 19.9 per cent in 2007.

2 Health insurance (*Gesetzliche Krankenversicherung*)
   The exact premium varies between insurance providers, but on average stood at 13.3 per cent of gross salary in 2006. This is also split equally between employers and employees, although since 2005 employees have paid an additional 0.9 per cent of gross salary by themselves. The general trend in health insurance contributions has been upwards. Statutory health insurance schemes have about 70 million members; a further 8 million persons are members of private health insurances.

3 Unemployment insurance (*Gesetzliche Arbeitslosenversicherung*)
   In 2006, unemployment insurance accounted for 6.5 per cent of gross salary, split equally between employers and employees. Originally, this paid almost 70 per cent of former net earnings for 12 months, followed by support for an indefinite period at around 55 per cent of former earnings. Until 2001, there was no requirement for recipients to take on new jobs at a lower level of pay than their previous employment. However, since 2006, insurance benefits are paid for 12 months only (*Arbeitslosengeld I*), previously 32 months, after which individuals transfer on to the tax-financed *Arbeitslosengeld II* (otherwise known as *Hartz IV*), which is the equivalent (much lower) level of income support (*Sozialhilfe*). In 2007, contributions to unemployment insurance fell to 4.2 per cent of gross salary, financed in part by an increase in Value Added Tax.

4 Long-term nursing care insurance (*Pflegeversicherung*)
   Introduced in 1995 to finance long-term care in old age, the premium consists of 1.7 per cent of gross salary, split equally between employers and employees. Up to 2007, contributions to this scheme have remained broadly constant.

5 Accident insurance (*Unfallversicherung*)
   Paid by employers only. Contribution rates vary according to the profession concerned.

---

it has been subjected to massive new pressures since unification in 1990. As Chapter 7 showed total wage-earning employment has fallen steadily during the 1990s and beyond, and successive governments have grappled with the challenge of escaping the vicious circle this has created for welfare expenditure and employment. However, unification is by no means the only challenge to Germany's welfare state, and this section will discuss some of the other key developments to impact on its structure.

BOX 8.2   KEY INDICATORS OF SOCIAL WELFARE EXPENDITURE IN GERMANY

- In 2006, the combined total contributions by employers and employees to statutory insurance schemes were around 42 per cent of gross salary. This represents a rise from 35.5 per cent in 1990 and 26.5 per cent in 1970 (Streeck and Trampusch, 2005: 177).
- In 2004, €563 billion (57 per cent of total public expenditure) was spent on welfare.
- In 1975, welfare expenditure accounted for 32 per cent of Gross Domestic Product. This had fallen to 28 per cent by 1990, but has since increased again to 31 per cent in 2005. In the new *Länder*, this level stands at almost 50 per cent of GDP.
- Between 1995 and 2005, expenditure on pensions accounted for about 12 per cent of GDP annually; over the same period, spending on healthcare accounted for a further 10 per cent.
- As well as contributions from employers and employees, the pensions system receives additional funding from the federal government to the tune of around €80 billion annually. This now represents one-third of the entire federal budget, a rise from around 12 per cent in the early 1980s.
- Total expenditure on health in 2002 was around €234 billion, of which almost €140 billion was spent by the statutory health insurance system. As a percentage of GDP, Germany in 2004 had the highest health expenditure of the fifteen EU member-states. However, in terms of indicators of health, Germany shows no significant overall difference from other industrialised countries.
- Since 1996, the number of welfare recipients has exceeded the number of persons in wage-earning employment (*sozialversicherungspflichtige Beschäftigung*) (Czada, 2005: 169)

Sources: Statistisches Bundesamt; BMAS (2006)

First and foremost, the challenge to Germany's welfare state cannot be separated from the country's demographic development (see Chapter 6). Here, the limitations of the 'pay-as-you-go' system, especially in financing the pensions system, become clearly visible. In essence, as long as enough children are born, there is no real problem in financing pensions under this system. However, over the past forty years, Germany has experienced both increasing life expectancy, which increases the number of years that individuals draw their pensions, and fewer births, which reduces the number of people who will be working to finance these rising demands for pensions. Accordingly, whereas in 1970 there were fifty beneficiaries for every hundred contributors into the pensions insurance, that figure had risen to sixty-nine by the beginning of the millennium. Over the same period of time, the average duration of an individual's pension rose from 11.1 to 16.8 years (cited in Sesselmeier, 2006: 25–6). This trend is likely to worsen as the proportion of the population of retirement age increases over the coming decades. Indeed, as Box 6.2 showed, the United Nations Population Division has projected a further halving in Germany's Potential Support Ratio by 2050 from its 1995 rate. Unsurprisingly, this has created significant cost pressures. These have had to be met both by rising contribution rates, which of course increase the total costs of employment, and principally by a growing subsidy of pension expenditure from general federal taxation, which reached the staggering sum of almost €80 billion in 2005 (Box 8.2) – equivalent to the total expenditure at all levels (federal, *Länd* and municipal) on education (see Schmidt, 2003a).

The state itself has also fallen victim to this trend. Like the rest of the population, its civil servants (*Beamte*) are living to greater ages and therefore require longer pensions. But *Beamte* do not pay pension contributions and the financing of their retirement is entirely a matter for governments, in particular at *Land* level, where the vast majority of civil servants are employed. So great is the number of former officials from the *Land* administrations that by 2020 around 10 per cent of total *Land* tax revenue will need to be spent solely on meeting the pension needs of the *Länder*'s former employees (*Der Spiegel*, 19 March 2007). In response, the *Länder* made the devolution of pay and conditions of civil servants to regional level a central element of the 2006 federalism reform (see Chapter 4, pp. 71–2). Most have now increased the working hours of public servants and cut benefits such as Christmas bonuses.

Similar and persistent upward cost pressures have emerged in health insurance. In part, these can also be explained by demographic changes – like the pensions system, the statutory health insurance system (although notably not private health insurance) is financed by a 'pay-as-you-go' system. But a range of other factors are significant here, too. Already the size of the overall sector, at €234 billion in 2002, means that the health industry wields significant financial clout. Thus, entire towns in Germany live off the provision of health spa cures (*Kuren*), in which patients can spend up to six weeks on sick leave, paid for mainly by the health insurer, for many ailments, including stress. Any attempt to cut such expenditure inevitably is met with staunch resistance from regional politicians who fear for local economies which may already suffer from high unemployment.

Elsewhere, as already noted in Chapter 4 (p. 65), a key actor in the financial management of statutory healthcare delivery is the medical profession, which, outside of hospitals, generally comprises individual private providers. This creates significant incentives for the duplication of provision and treatment, because individual providers, as entrepreneurs, are in principle responsible for determining the amount they demand from insurance companies. Moreover, doctors treating patients in statutory insurance schemes do not bill insurance companies directly but collectively, via the so-called *Kassenärztliche Vereinigungen*, which act as clearing houses. In consequence, for statutory insurance schemes, there is practically no transparency in the relationship between cost and the medical service provided by an individual doctor.

Spa cures and the *Kassenärztliche Vereinigungen* are just two examples of how Germany's immensely diverse structure of health provision operates. Yet, as successive federal health ministers have discovered over the years, the system has proved remarkably resilient to reform from the outside. A key reason for this is no doubt that the principle of self-regulation, a feature of many areas of German politics, is particularly prevalent in healthcare, which has made it almost impossible to introduce change against the will of the sector's various producer interests. Moreover, these healthcare providers, including doctors, pharmacies, pharmaceutical companies and the owners of hospitals (such as universities, churches and municipalities as well as private businesses), collectively constitute one of the best-organised and most powerful interest lobbies in German politics (Bandelow, 2007). Over the years, each individual interest group in this field has been extremely successful in defending its constituency's financial position, which has meant that most political efforts towards cost containment have been unsuccessful. However, far from all actors in this sector benefit equally: for instance, hospital doctors in Germany have on average some of the lowest wages for their profession in the developed world (see figures in *Der Spiegel*, 3 July 2006).

Persistent high levels of unemployment in Germany have also created major cost pressures for the statutory unemployment insurance scheme. This too operates on a 'pay-as-you-go' basis, and in the context of high unemployment has therefore also been hit by the 'double whammy' of higher demand matched by lower contributions. Indeed, the federal government's annual subsidy to the Federal Labour Agency (*Bundesagentur für Arbeit*), which manages the statutory unemployment scheme, is, at around €30 billion, now the third-largest item in the federal budget (after pensions and debt servicing).

A further challenge to the cost structure of the welfare state, and especially to its ability to finance pensions, is the growth in early retirement (Czada, 2005: 168). From the late 1970s onwards, this was used actively by companies, and in co-operation with both government and unions, to transfer surplus workers out of the labour market and into the welfare system. Notably, in order to provide an incentive to individuals to take this option, early retirement was generally available without a significant loss of benefits; the additional costs incurred were simply loaded on to the pension funds' liabilities (Streeck, 2005). When combined with the fact that, once military service and the length of a university education are taken into account, many German graduates do not start full-time employment until their late twenties, the total time in (taxpaying) employment often falls well short of the notional forty-five years needed to secure a full pension entitlement. This, too, has a double impact on the pensions system: not only are individuals paying into the system for shorter periods, but they are drawing on it for longer periods. One should be clear, however, that this is a simplified picture; it does not always reflect individual choices. In reality, it is extremely difficult for the over-fifty-fives to find work: in 2005, just 45.4 per cent of those aged between fifty-five and sixty-four were in employment, compared to an overall employment rate of 65.4 per cent (see also Wink, 2002). In cases of people in their late fifties who become unemployed, the standard solution has been to allow them to draw unemployment benefit for a number of years, after which they are moved more-or-less directly into early retirement, with all its cost implications. This is also one of the main reasons for the relatively low average pension level (see Box 8.1). So, raising the participation rate for older workers could potentially have a positive impact on the viability of the pensions system: in principle, although not always in practice, more employment means more contributors to the statutory insurance schemes. However, raising the participation rate is rather difficult to achieve in an environment where both unemployment generally and long-term unemployment in particular are already high.

An issue with a similar resonance, although different in focus, is the employment rate of women. Historically, and in comparison with other countries, the female employment rate in Germany has been low, and its rise since unification is at least in part due to the fact that the rate is much higher in the new *Länder*, almost at the same levels as for males. This is because, in the GDR, most women were simply expected by the state to go out to work. Here, too, the potential to increase the number of contributors nationally to the statutory insurance schemes has therefore not been fully exploited. But, more broadly, the employment situation of women also feeds into the broader demographic discussion of why the fertility rate in Germany is so low, despite relatively generous maternity provision and financial support, for instance in the form of tax concessions. Instead, the structures of the conservative welfare state model (Esping-Andersen, 1990; Lewis, 1992), in which women were traditionally expected to act as primary carers in families, are clearly visible. Thus, there is practically no state-run nursery education available for children under the age of three in the old western *Länder* as a whole, but especially outside the cities; by contrast, coverage in the east is much better, again largely as a remnant of GDR policy (Bleses and Seeleib-Kaiser, 2004: 85). Even for children over the age of three, who have a legal right to a place in kindergarten, coverage is by no means universal. And the situation for mothers wishing to return to work does not improve even once children start school: although the number of all-day schools is increasing, the standard model remains that children are home in time for lunch. Culturally, too, there is a widespread expectation that mothers should stop working completely for at least three years *per child*, which is reflected in the positions of both conservative politicians and in Roman Catholic circles. Interestingly, the pejorative German term *Rabenmutter*, used to signify a mother who leaves her children to fend for themselves, has no equivalent in English.

Together, this means that couples in general, but working women in particular, are faced with a particularly stark choice when it comes to starting a family. With combining work and parenthood effectively impossible, prospective mothers either have to give up their existing careers altogether or have no children at all. But the opportunity cost of giving up a career rises with the level of educational qualifications obtained; accordingly, the rate of childlessness among women university graduates is estimated to be particularly high, at anything up to 40 per cent. Equally unsurprisingly, women in Germany, as in many other European countries, are delaying both marriage and motherhood: in 2004, the average age of first-time mothers exceeded thirty for the first time. Thus, family policy, itself an element of the welfare state, is growing in importance as the challenges of Germany's demographic development for welfare provision become ever clearer.

Despite these long-term factors, all of which pre-date 1990 in their origins, the impact of unification must not be underestimated. As Roland Czada (2005) shows, thanks to reforms during the 1980s to compensate for future demographic changes, the statutory insurance funds, especially the pensions system, were in remarkably good financial health in 1989. Moreover, the pensions system in (the more populous) western part of Germany is projected to maintain large-scale surpluses over the next ten years; it is only because these surpluses are almost entirely swallowed by the pensions *deficit* in the (less populous) east that the system as a whole is barely breaking even (Czada, 2005: 179). The main effect of unification has therefore been to put enormous and sudden pressure on welfare expenditure. Correspondingly, welfare expenditure rose rapidly from its low of 27.8 per cent of GDP in 1990 to 32.1 per cent in 1996. There were two key reasons for this. First, very high and long-term levels of unemployment, especially in the east, have necessitated high overall levels of payments. Second, unification helped increase the number of pensioners; if they came from the east, they had of course not paid into the West German system. But this trend was magnified further by the propensity of the German system simply to move older and long-term-unemployed members of the labour force into early retirement. During the mid-1990s, large numbers of what had effectively become unemployable members of the labour force in the new *Länder* were moved into this status (figures in Bleses and Seeleib-Kaiser, 2004: 72).

The final pressure to be considered comprises the legal and political implications of the above. Certainly, the challenges of welfare reform are acknowledged across the political spectrum. That said, the short-term incentive to implement change is minimal. For one thing, policy reform in this area is only ever likely to be effective in the long term, in other words far beyond the next parliamentary election. Of course, this is partly because of the nature of the issue: demographic changes, for instance, are by definition long term. But significantly and for historical reasons, changes in public policy are also subject to the legally enforceable principles of *Verhältnismäßigkeit* and *Vertrauensschutz*. Respectively, this means that policy changes must be proportionate to their purpose and they must not change citizens' legitimate expectations of outputs which have built up over time. Together, and crucially, these make any kind of sweeping reform, for instance an overnight and across-the-board cut in benefits, impossible.

Debates

Most of the challenges outlined above have revolved principally around cost, so it is this that has helped define many of the political debates and the policy responses over recent years. In essence, the political choice has been whether cost increases should be borne by the providers, for instance by demanding increased efficiency in the health system; by individual citizens, for instance through introducing quarterly charges for medical consultations; or by society, for instance by increasingly financing welfare from general government taxation as opposed to via social insurance schemes (Streeck and Trampusch, 2005: 175–6; see also Streeck, forthcoming).

In reality, this has by no means been an easy balance for successive federal governments since 1990 to strike. Taking providers in health policy to task, for instance, has rarely delivered anything more than minor changes, due principally to the sector's well-established principle of self-regulation (see Chapter 4, p. 65), but also to the exceptionally effective operation of their interest groups. Increasing the contribution of general taxation to the welfare system has the advantage of not raising further the level of non-wage labour costs for employers, but it is extremely difficult in a time when the state's fiscal position as a whole is precarious (see Chapter 3, pp. 47–8). Lastly, shifting the burden on to individual citizens, in other words privatising the responsibility for welfare provision, has also worked only at the margins, as this has proved highly unpopular with voters: this very point was a key factor in the SPD–Green government's decline in popularity between 2002 and 2005. Crucially, with the number of welfare recipients exceeding those in wage-earning employment since the mid-1990s, it is becoming increasingly difficult to build the necessary electoral coalitions for undertaking more far-reaching welfare reforms: put bluntly, there are too many voters with too much to lose from any serious privatisation of welfare provision. This is a particular problem for the two main parties in Germany, the CDU/CSU and the SPD, both of which explicitly define themselves as 'socially responsible'. What is more, the people most likely to lose out under such welfare reform are by definition the socio-economically weaker sections of the population; for historical reasons, this too runs contrary to much of the population's understanding of equality and solidarity.

The limitations on any federal government to manoeuvre in this issue are most graphically illustrated in the quest to satisfy increasing demands on the pensions system. One the one hand, contribution levels could be raised, although this would further raise the cost of wage-earning employment in Germany. It would also be politically damaging for any government to allow contributions to exceed the sensitive 20 per cent mark of gross wages. On the other hand, the federal government could increase its subsidy from general taxation, but this is already the single largest item of expenditure; if anything, with the overall tax level already at an historic high, the pressure is on the federal government to *reduce* its pensions subsidy. Alternatively, pensioners themselves can and have been required to bear the cost, for instance through imposing freezes on the annual round of pensions increases. But this too is highly risky in electoral terms: one of the largest interest groups in Germany, with some 1.4 million members, is the *Sozialverband VdK Deutschland*, which represents in particular the disabled and pensioners. More broadly, and with their high levels of mobilisation, the over-sixties are growing in importance as an electoral force (see Chapter 5, p. 65), and political parties therefore ignore the interests of the 'grey vote' at their peril.

How, then, have federal governments sought to deal with the challenges in individual elements of the statutory schemes? The remainder of this section will examine this question by outlining responses in pensions, healthcare, unemployment insurance and family policy, before turning to the broader question of where the political fault-lines lie.

In pensions, as noted above, the main task has been to deal with the demographic challenge of growing numbers of pensioners supported by ever-smaller numbers of wage earners. The structural problems of the pensions system date right back to its inception in its current form in 1957, when the CDU-led government under Konrad Adenauer linked future rises in pensions to gross wage increases (more than average earnings and far more than inflation), in what was effectively a blatant sop to pensioners in the run-up to that year's federal election. While this tactic reaped handsome rewards at the polls that year, in the form of the only absolute majority for a political party at any federal election, it did sow the seeds for the current problems that the system faces, as the value of pensions (and, with them, contribution rates) grew at a very rapid rate during the 1960s and 1970s. Indeed, Alber (cited in Bleses and Seeleib-Kaiser, 2004: 68) calculates that, had this trend continued unchecked, the value of pensions would have risen from 70 per cent of average net earnings in the mid-1970s to 90 per cent by 1997. More importantly, the system's inherent assumption that fertility rates would continue to be high, which would guarantee its long-term financial viability, turned out to be misplaced.

Traditionally, the politics of pension reform has been marked by a strong emphasis on cross-party consensus, leading generally to only incremental amendments to the system. But after the mid-1990s, the extent of the looming financial crisis meant that pensions began to be highly politicised between the SPD and the CDU/CSU (Czada, 2005), with both parties stylising themselves as advocates for the weakest in society. Still, over the years, a number of reforms have been undertaken to address rising costs as a result of unification as well as demographic developments (details in Bleses and Seeleib-Kaiser, 2004: 67–79; Streeck and Trampusch, 2005: 179–83; see also Czada, 2005: 178–82). The most important elements of these reforms have focused on four issues. First, under the 2005 pensions reform, the level of pensions is set to fall gradually from currently 70 per cent of average net earnings to 67 per cent in 2040 and 64 per cent by 2050. Second, since 2001, individuals have been encouraged to make greater private provision for pensions. Although the scope of this reform was itself decidedly modest, it potentially represents a major change, as it constitutes a first step towards the privatisation of responsibility for pension provision – a significant shift given the drop in pension levels over the coming decades. Third, various measures have been introduced to rein in the extensive possibilities of early retirement. Finally, the pensionable age has been increased gradually. Initially, such reforms were limited to brining the retirement age of women in line with that of men, but in 2007, the Grand Coalition also agreed to raise the pensionable age for everyone from sixty-five to sixty-seven by 2029.

Individually, none of the measures undertaken can be considered a wholesale reform. But, cumulatively, their effect is considerable: in 2003, a government commission calculated that 'the average pension benefits in 2030 will be 40 per cent lower than they would have been under the pre-1989 rules' (Czada, 2005: 181). Nonetheless, the effect on pension levels of the huge annual subsidy from the federal budget must not be underestimated: were this ever to be cut, never mind removed altogether, far more drastic action would become immediately necessary. Of course, the principle of *Vertrauensschutz* makes this almost impossible, meaning that, to all intents and purposes, the federal government is condemned to continue to subsidise pensions at a high level indefinitely.

As in pensions policy, the challenge of cost containment has dominated governmental responses in health policy (see details in Bandelow, 2007). But any real attempt to reform the system since unification came up against formidable opposition from the established interest groups in this sector. Where more major reforms have taken place, as in 1993, 2004 and 2007, they have therefore been possible only through consensus between the CDU/CSU and the SPD, who together have on occasion proved able to circumvent at least some of the organised resistance to change.

But in the most recent reform, in 2007, it was politics that clearly got in the way. As well as the usual goal of reducing costs, the Grand Coalition of CDU/CSU and SPD had to reconcile their own, ideologically driven models for financing healthcare to which they had each committed themselves in the 2005 election campaign. Thus, the SPD wanted to introduce a universal 'citizens' insurance scheme' (*Bürgerversicherung*) in order to bring high earners, who are currently able to opt out and go into the private system, under the umbrella of the statutory insurance schemes. By contrast, the CDU/CSU had in 2003 adopted a policy of a flat contribution rate on a per capita basis to the statutory schemes (*Kopfpauschale*). The final compromise was a messy and extremely complex hybrid of both models which is not only predicted to lead to rising costs in some areas, but will introduce an entire new layer of (costly) bureaucratic management in the form of the healthcare fund (*Gesundheitsfonds*). The upshot of this is that contributions to statutory health insurance rose once more in 2007 to an average of 13.9 per cent of salary, with the additional prospect of a gradually increasing subsidy from the federal budget over the coming years (see below). The goal of effectively containing costs therefore seems less attainable than ever.

In terms of reforms undertaken, four main trends may be identified here, too (see Streeck and Trampusch, 2005: 186–9). First, there have been a series of traditional cost-containment measures, such as capping budgets, reducing coverage for certain types of treatment and introducing a payment-by-results system (so-called Diagnosis Related Groups). These have tended to have only limited overall effect, yet they still require considerable political capital to overcome producer opposition. Second, as in pensions policy, there has been a growing emphasis on private contribution in the statutory schemes. As well as increasing prescription charges over the years, patients visiting their general practitioners were from 2004 required for the first time to pay a fee of ten euros per quarter. While this sum is arguably nominal for all but the poorest members of society, its introduction provoked a storm of protest from voters accustomed to the universal coverage of their health insurance. Third, there has been an initial move to shift financial responsibility for healthcare away from insurance contributions (in an effort to reduce non-wage labour costs) and on to general taxation. Although the level of subsidy in question is only a fraction of the amount spent on pensions, under the 2007 healthcare reform it is set to increase to around seven billion euros by 2011. By mid-2007, the question of how this sum was to be financed without further tax increases remained open, with the most likely option being via increased debt. Finally, and perhaps most importantly, healthcare was the first statutory insurance scheme to depart from the principle of parity in contributions from employers and employees. From 2005, a special supplement of 0.9 per cent of gross wages was introduced solely for employees – again with the official intention of easing pressure on non-wage labour costs for employers.

This has all been contentious, but the issue which has perhaps provoked the most public opposition has been the reform of unemployment insurance (see Streeck and Trampusch, 2005: 183–6). In post-unification Germany, high unemployment rates of around 10 per cent nationally have become the norm, and the cost implications of this for the unemployment insurance system have been extensive. Once again, unification has played a central role in creating this financial pressure: as Chapter 3 showed, unemployment rates in the new *Länder* are almost double those in the west, not including various government-funded and subsidised employment measures (Table 3.1). Yet governments of all persuasion have struggled to make any real inroads into this unemployment figure beyond short-term reductions due primarily to a cyclical increase in economic activity. Part of the problem has doubtless been the traditional level of insurance benefits: at around 70 per cent of last salary, with no requirement to take on any new employment at a lower status than the previous position (see Box 8.1), there has been little incentive for the unemployed to return to work, especially with the option of early retirement on the horizon for older people. But the tax system has also contributed, via the so-called 'welfare trap': by returning to work, individuals have tended to find themselves worse off overall, as they no longer qualify for a range of benefits. Finally, there has been an organisational dimension to this problem. In 2002, it transpired that the Federal Labour Office (*Bundesanstalt für Arbeit*) employed around six times as many administrators as it did advisers, and that it had systematically faked its statistics on the number of people it had helped back into employment (Busch, 2005b). The ensuing organisational shake-up of this organisation, as well as its renaming as the *Bundesagentur für Arbeit* (BA), offered Chancellor Schröder (of the SPD) the opportunity to seize the political initiative on unemployment in the run-up to the federal election later that year. He appointed a commission under the leadership of a VW board member, Peter Hartz, to examine the overall structures of labour market policy. The commission reported back that summer, shortly before the election, and its recommendations were enthusiastically endorsed by Schröder. Following his narrow election victory, the commission's report dropped out of the political spotlight, but it returned in March 2003, when, following the final failure of the Alliance for Jobs (*Bündnis für Arbeit*), Schröder announced his *Agenda 2010* programme to modernise the welfare state and particularly unemployment insurance. The centrepiece of this programme was a law which drew heavily on the Hartz Commission's recommendations and became known as *Hartz IV* (see Kemmerling and Bruttel, 2006).

Essentially, the Hartz commission had argued that long-term unemployment benefit (*Arbeitslosenhilfe*) and means-tested income support (*Sozialhilfe*) should be combined, and it was this change which lay at the heart of the *Hartz IV* law. The merger of these two elements of the welfare state certainly represented a drop in benefits, but the calculation was that this would provide a financial incentive for the long-term unemployed (i.e., those without work for over one year) to return to the active labour market. Following the United States and the UK, the Hartz commission thus advocated the introduction of so-called 'workfare' policies in Germany, to consist of both incentives ('carrots') and penalties ('sticks').

Cutting the benefits of some of the poorest members of society was always going to be controversial, and so it proved in the case of *Hartz IV*. In particular, Schröder faced considerable opposition both from within his own party, the SPD, and from the trade union movement. *Hartz IV* was also the catalyst for the foundation of the WASG by disaffected SPD members in 2004, which later went on to merge with the ex-communist PDS (Hough *et al.*, 2007; see also Chapter 5). At the same time, the CDU/CSU used its dominance of the *Bundesrat* to extract key concessions from the government. The law was passed only after a marathon all-night sitting of the conciliation committee between the *Bundestag* and *Bundesrat* in December 2004.

At least initially, the law has proved less successful than intended. The key problem has been that the original plans grossly underestimated how many people would apply for assistance under this new framework. As a result of this, the expected savings in terms of expenditure have not materialised; on the contrary, during its first year of operation, the new combined benefit cost the federal government some eleven billion euros more than planned. In the final analysis, this sum had to be financed through additional debt. This financial imbalance is set to continue over the coming years and puts further strain on the federal government's fiscal position.

The last element to be discussed here is family policy. As Bleses and Seeleib-Kaiser (2004: 79–89) show, successive governments have over time increased child benefit levels and parental leave arrangements for mothers, thereby greatly increasing the range of options open to them in terms of combining work with family life. But two major changes have occurred in 2007 under the Grand Coalition. Ironically, these were initiated not by the SPD, but by the CDU Family Minister, Ursula von der Leyen, herself a qualified doctor with seven children. First, a new form of financial parental support (*Elterngeld*) came into force in January 2007, which replaces two-thirds of household income for a period of between twelve and fourteen months after the birth of the child, up to a maximum of €1,800 per month. It thus draws on the traditional mechanisms of status preservation inherent in the 'conservative' welfare state, and stands in contrast to the previous, 'social democratic'-style universal benefit (*Erziehungsgeld*), which provided a flat rate payment for up to twenty-four months. But what is particularly noteworthy about *Elterngeld* is that it specifically provides for fathers to have the same rights as mothers in taking parental leave. Indeed, the full fourteen months' support is available only if fathers take at least two months off work. This policy therefore marks a first major shift in the way society and government perceive and structure gender roles in childcare.

Von der Leyen quickly followed this up with a serious attempt to increase the availability of state-run childcare facilities for the under-threes. However, the response these initiatives generated was indicative of the cultural environment in which parenthood in Germany remains embedded: thus, in February 2007, the Roman Catholic Bishop of Augsburg condemned von der Leyen's initiative for forcing women into becoming nothing more than 'birthing machines' (*Gebährmaschinen*). And many on the CDU/CSU's conservative wings see these proposals as a frontal attack on the party's commitment to family values. But that is not to say that the SPD is free of such views: in 1998, Schröder infamously referred to women's and family policy as 'hot air' (*Gedöns*). Two striking elements of this debate in Germany are its polarised nature (women are either full-time mothers and homemakers or self-obsessed harridans) and the fact that the role of fathers has, until very recently, tended to be mentioned only as an afterthought.

In terms of the political fault-lines, and leaving aside family policy, the three areas of pensions, healthcare and unemployment show remarkable similarities. Essentially, both *Volksparteien* are competing for the political centre ground, meaning that neither can afford to be portrayed as a socially 'cold' party (*Partei der sozialen Kälte*). Both are acutely aware of the fact that their electorates include pensioners and the less well off; precisely those voters who are most affected by any cuts in welfare. This has meant that any proposal by one of the large parties to restructure welfare state provision over the past decade has invariably been met by howls of indignation from the other. Ultimately, none of the reforms outlined above has been possible without a Grand Coalition between the *Volksparteien*, be it an ad-hoc alliance, as during the SPD–Green government, or a formal coalition, as since 2005 (see Schmidt, 2002). But party politics in this field has also been supplemented by powerful interest groups. Already, the role of producer interests in healthcare has been noted. But in pensions and unemployment policy (see Busemeyer, 2005), the trade unions have also adopted highly conservative positions on welfare state reform, which during the SPD–Green government's incumbency saw them on occasion aligned more closely with the CDU/CSU than with the SPD. The unions have thus been persistent opponents of welfare reform.

Conclusion

This chapter has sketched out the principal dimensions of, and the transformative challenges to, the welfare state in Germany. It has highlighted the problem of demographic change, as well as the huge pressures caused by unification. It has discussed the difficulties for women to combine careers and families in Germany, and staked out the dimensions of the key conundrum facing governments in Germany: how to fund increasing demand for the welfare state without increasing non-wage labour costs and without bankrupting the federal budget?

From this discussion, three key conclusions may be drawn. First, the cost pressures created by unification have played a major role in forcing governments to consider more radical changes to Germany's welfare state. But, crucially, the two key structural problems, demographics and the expansion of early retirement, which have been exposed by these cost pressures, can themselves be traced back to the 1970s. It is, of course, an open question to what extent cost pressures would have developed in any case if unification had not taken place; but as things stand at present, welfare policy is another example of where the western population is effectively being forced to pay for the population of the new *Länder* (see Chapter 3). In this area, therefore, the challenge of transformation is particularly acute.

Second, how extensive have the various changes been? By themselves, it is difficult to conclude that the reforms have done anything other than tinker at the edges of provision. The current scheduled reductions in pensions are extremely long term and may yet be overtaken by events. The changes to healthcare and unemployment, while imposing new costs on beneficiaries, have led to *increases* in state expenditure. In that sense, incremental policy change is very much in evidence in this sector. In turn, this can be put down to the key features of semi-sovereign governance, which are clearly visible in this policy field: the tradition of self-regulation within the sector means that the federal government has little direct power to impose solutions, which moreover usually require the approval of the *Bundesrat* (see Chapter 4). In addition, the area is populated by a range of highly influential and effective interest groups.

And yet, the cumulative effect of the various reforms has been considerable. As Bleses and Seeleib-Kaiser (2004: 89–93) argue, the German welfare state has undergone a 'dual transformation', under which the goal of 'status preservation', as defined by Esping-Andersen's (1990) model of a 'conservative' welfare state, has been weakened. At the same time, the shift towards more family-orientated policies indicates a further shift away from the 'strong male breadwinner' towards the 'moderate male breadwinner' model, under which women are viewed as wives, mothers *and* workers.

The third and final conclusion here concerns effectiveness. For, despite the gradual transformation in the *quality* of the welfare state outlined above, issues of *quantity* remain predominant. In particular, as has been argued here, the political aim of cutting non-wage labour costs to promote employment is attainable only if benefits are capped, or if costs are privatised or taken over by government itself. But as experience has shown, it has taken enormous political effort to achieve even a modest reduction in non-wage labour costs. Taking the 2007 reduction of unemployment insurance by two percentage points as an example, can this really generate significantly more employment if, on the one hand, the total non-wage labour costs for employers stand at over 20 per cent of gross wages and if, on the other hand, pensions and healthcare costs rise concurrently?

All future federal governments will thus continue to be faced with the conundrum of containing cost pressures while not alienating voters. At the same time, the extent of Germany's long-term welfare commitments is such that there is precious little room for public spending anywhere else, including defence (see Chapter 10) and, most importantly, education, where levels of expenditure remain below the OECD average (see Schmidt, 2003a). For an economy based on skills, such a persistent trend is potentially disastrous. It is for this reason that welfare state reform is set to remain the single most important political issue in Germany over the coming years.

Questions for discussion

1   **Is Germany's welfare state unaffordable?**
2   **How can Germany meet the demands of its pension system?**
3   **Is Germany a family-friendly society?**

Further reading

Bleses, P. and M. Seeleib-Kaiser (2004), *The Dual Transformation of the German Welfare State* (London: Palgrave). A comprehensive and definitive discussion of the development of German welfare policy over the past thirty years.

Czada, R. (2005), 'Social Policy: Crisis and Transformation', in S. Green and W. Paterson (eds), *Governance in Contemporary Germany: The Semisovereign State Revisited* (Cambridge: Cambridge University Press). An excellent summary of changes to welfare provision since unification.

Useful website

<http://www.sozialpolitik-aktuell.de/> provides a wealth of data on social policy (in German).

9 Germany and the European Union

A European Germany or a
German Europe?

Summary

Since the 1950s the European Union has played a central role in the development of the German state. European integration provided Germany with an institutional framework to rebuild its economy, regain its international standing and establish lasting, peaceful ties with its European neighbours. Along with the obvious benefits which EU membership has brought Germany, it has more recently presented the country with a number of challenges. This chapter outlines Germany's role in the EU and assesses whether the country's current European policy has changed in the light of unification.

Introduction

This chapter analyses the development of German policy towards European integration. For the most part, (West) Germany has benefited considerably from its membership of the European Union. Germany has traditionally been seen as one of the most pro-integration member-states, being a founder member of both the European Coal and Steel Community in 1952 and the more important European Economic Community that came into existence with the 1957 Treaty of Rome. Forging closer co-operation with its European neighbours was a vital aspect of achieving unification in 1990 and overcoming the Cold War division of Europe in the years since. In terms of the overall themes of this textbook, Germany, through European integration, has been able to work towards *reconciliation* with its past and with its EU partners, forging broad *consensus* on the centrality of the EU project for the German political elite and working towards *transformation* of itself and its regional milieu in order to meet the challenges of the twenty-first century (Bulmer *et al.*, 2000).

Germany has been a pivotal European power in terms of both its economic weight and its political influence. Its central position at the heart of the European landmass has meant that good relations with its neighbours have been an essential precondition for stability in post-1945 Europe. Following the Second World War attention turned to establishing a system which would prevent Germany from seeking to increase its relative power through the use of military force. The subsequent development of the European integration project had at its heart the establishment of close ties between Germany and its Western European neighbours. West Germany came to view European integration as vital to its national interest and as a means to help it recover after the war without fear or suspicion that it would repeat the mistakes of Hitler's Germany. Box 9.1 provides some of the key dates in European integration.

Writing in the early 1980s, Pierre Hassner raised the intriguing question of what kind of Germany would fit into what kind of Europe so as to be neither too strong nor too weak for its external environment (Hassner, 1982). Hassner was in part paraphrasing one aspect of the 'German Question' (see Box 1.1) that had traditionally been understood as how best to deal with the possibility of a strong, combative and powerful Germany. Behind this statement there was also a reference to the destabilising impact of German indecision at a time when the European integration process was relatively stagnant and the so-called 'Second Cold War', provoked by the Soviet Union's invasion of Afghanistan in 1979, demanded a clearer expression of the 'European voice' on the international stage. The implication of Hassner's comment was that the maintenance of European order was as much dependent upon the willingness of Germany to use its economic strength to demonstrate political leadership (in a manner that neither France nor the UK was able

---

BOX 9.1 KEY DEVELOPMENTS IN EUROPEAN INTEGRATION

1952	European Coal and Steel Community is established.
1957	Belgium, France, Italy, Luxembourg, the Netherlands and West Germany establish European Economic Community.
1966	'Luxembourg Compromise' ends French boycott of EEC institutions and effectively institutionalises the national veto.
1973	Accession of Denmark, Ireland and the United Kingdom to bring number of member-states to nine.
1981	Accession of Greece to bring number of member-states to ten.
1986	Accession of Spain and Portugal to bring number of member-states to twelve.
1987	Single European Act (1986) comes into force.
1993	Single European Market comes into force; Treaty on European Union ('Maastricht Treaty') (1992) comes into force -EEC becomes European Union.
1995	Accession of Austria, Finland and Sweden to bring number of member-states to fifteen.
1999	Economic and Monetary Union is launched; Treaty of Amsterdam (1997) comes into force.
2002	Euro notes and coins replace national currencies.
2003	Treaty of Nice (2000) comes into force.
2004	Accession of Cyprus, Czech Republic, Estonia, Hungary, Latvia, Lithuania, Malta, Poland, Slovakia and Slovenia to bring number of member-states to twenty-five; Constitutional Treaty signed.
2005	Constitutional Treaty rejected by Dutch and French voters.
2007	Accession of Bulgaria and Romania to bring number of member-states to twenty-seven.

to do) as on the containment of German economic power within a European framework. In a similar vein, Bulmer and Paterson (1987: 7) state that, 'without European integration as a political arena of co-operation, West German economic performance would have been perceived as a threat'.

European policy in Germany (*Europapolitik*) has nevertheless changed substantially in recent years. Although Germany's membership of the EU has largely been a success story, it still faces a number of challenges emanating from this. These challenges have resulted in pressures for both domestic and EU reform. Germany's poor recent economic performance has placed constraints on its actions within the EU (Jeffery and Paterson, 2003; Streeck and Trampusch, 2005). As a result, politics in Germany is currently marked by an end to unwavering domestic consensus on the EU and more questioning of the benefits which Germany accrues from membership. This has reduced the federal government's room for manoeuvre in finding compromises to political impasses at the EU level. The defining characteristic of German European policy, particularly since the Schröder era, is that it has become more conditional – or, as Harnisch and Schieder (2006) have put it, more 'contingent'. This makes the job of acting as an 'honest broker' within the EU more difficult, as the temptation to pursue German interests becomes stronger.

This chapter examines the historical development of German *Europapolitk* in order to outline why the EU became such a central institution for the German state. Following on from this, it examines the degree of 'Europeanisation' that has taken place within Germany. Finally, we look at a range of key issues and debates which affect German European policy today and in the future.

Background

The process of European integration was of central importance for the renewal of West Germany after 1949. With the end of the Second World War and failure of the victorious powers to agree on what a united Germany should look like, Germany found itself split into zones of occupation. While East Germany was integrated into the institutions of the Soviet sphere of influence, West Germany began a process of integration with Western states. As Chapter 2 (p. 25) outlined, West Germany's founding Chancellor, Konrad Adenauer, saw integration with the West, founded on the primacy of Franco-German and US–German relations, as a precondition for post-war rehabilitation, reconciliation and reconstruction. The pursuit of Western integration led to the birth of the European integration process with the European Coal and Steel Community in 1952 and the signing of the Treaties of Rome in 1957. Western European integration was in a number of national interests, including those of West Germany and its Western European allies. The defence umbrella of the North Atlantic Treaty Organisation, which reinforced the United States' presence in Europe, provided the security necessary in the face of the Soviet threat, enabling Western European states to pursue closer relations between themselves. The model of integration which emerged during the 1950s was founded on the assumption that France would provide the political leadership and West Germany would provide the economic might. This was an acceptable bargain for Adenauer, who had come to view German foreign policy based on unilateralism as a self-defeating project. The 1950s witnessed bold attempts to overcome the acrimony and agony of past conflicts and to act genuinely co-operatively. It was thus a remarkable decade as it saw real advances in trust between once hostile states. The EEC provided a framework for rebuilding West Germany, without fears that a resurgent Germany would pose a threat to its neighbours (Bulmer and Paterson, 1987). Flagship policies such as the Common Agricultural Policy (CAP) and the agreement on atomic energy co-operation reinforced the emerging interconnectedness of France and Germany and the readmission of West Germany into the civilised world.

The dynamism of the 1950s did not, however, last particularly long, and the 1960s witnessed a slowing of the European integration project. The concerns of the French President, Charles de Gaulle, over the growing supranational character of the Community led to the so-called 'empty-chair crisis' of 1965–6, when de Gaulle removed his ministers from EEC institutions. This difficult period was overcome only with the introduction of what was in effect a national veto for instances when a member-state felt that its interests were being compromised by EEC decisions. France's refusal to accept the United Kingdom's application to join the Community further dampened the integration dynamic. De Gaulle's concern that the UK's Atlanticist instincts would compromise the European integration project was not shared by Adenauer, who viewed the UK's membership as a chance to strengthen both European and transatlantic co-operation (as outlined in more detail in Chapter 10).

Despite these setbacks, West Germany played a central role in trying to maintain the integration momentum among the member-states. The 1969 Hague Summit signalled the emergence of European Political Co-operation, the first attempt at foreign policy co-ordination within the EEC. EPC offered West Germany the opportunity to widen its foreign policy networks alongside other member-states, something that was further enhanced by West Germany's and East Germany's membership of the United Nations from 18 September 1973 and the founding of the Conference on Security and Co-operation in Europe (CSCE) that same year. The widening of West Germany's multilateral links was founded on the efforts of Chancellor Willy Brandt's *Ostpolitik*, which went some way to reduce tensions between East and West. The creation of the CSCE and the two Germanies' joint accession to the United Nations cemented the thawing of the Cold War stand-off during the early and mid-1970s. West Germany also worked to overcome the institutional limitations of European integration. Chancellor Helmut Schmidt was influential, alongside French President Valerie Giscard D'Estaing, in the creation of the European Council in 1974, which raised the profile of discussions within the EEC by formally including heads of government for the first time.

Another significant Franco-German initiative, the European Monetary System, which came into force in 1979, sought to reduce inflation and stabilise exchange rates among member-states in order to promote trade and monetary stability within the EEC. From the 1950s onwards, West Germany sought to exploit opportunities to expand on economic co-operation within Europe to provide a market for its booming export economy. But by the 1980s, the European integration process had come to depend upon West German financial contributions which totalled approximately one-third of the entire EEC budget. German funds went towards paying for many new initiatives, such as the southern enlargement to include Greece, Spain and Portugal, as well as maintaining the CAP, which accounted for 70 per cent of total expenditure at the European level in the early 1980s. It was considered that neither West Germany nor the EEC could do without the other.

The 1986 Single European Act (SEA), which effectively relaunched the integration process, was an ambitious effort to try to remove all barriers to trade between member-states and thereby create a single economic area (the Internal Market). The lead-up to the SEA coincided with the emergence of West Germany as a senior partner within the EEC, rather than the junior political actor that it had traditionally been. West German leaders became more willing to undertake political leadership, but still remained committed to framing this leadership in partnership with France. The first sign of this growing role was the 'Solemn Declaration' at Stuttgart in 1983, which kick-started efforts to renew European integration and imbue the process with more dynamism. Chancellor Helmut Kohl and his long-serving Foreign Minister, Hans-Dietrich Genscher, were instrumental in putting the EEC back on track and pressing for the completion of a single market between member-states, which ultimately was covered by the SEA.

This was again the result of close Franco-German co-operation, now between President François Mitterrand and Chancellor Kohl, and their relationship also helped to shape the subsequent 1992 Treaty on European Union. The TEU fundamentally reorganised the structures of European integration and was a visible signal from the newly united Germany that it would remain committed to the European integration project, despite having thrown off the shackles of division (Anderson, 1999). Instead of weakening its ties, Germany committed itself to Economic and Monetary Union (see Dyson and Featherstone, 1999), as well as to developing the Common Foreign and Security Policy and a common policy on justice and home affairs. Kohl's commitment to ever closer union involved restating Germany's conviction to European integration in order to dispel fears that united Germany would use its increased relative power to pursue its national interests more overtly. Kohl, however, asserted that the lessons of West Germany's membership of what had now become the EU had ensured that German and European interests were compatible. Continuity rather than change was subsequently the hallmark of the united Germany's European policy.

Post-unification European policy

The map of Europe changed substantially with the end of the Cold War. Not only did the German population increase to eighty million, making it by far the largest EU member-state, but Germany was provided with an opportunity to turn eastwards and devote its attention to rediscovering its traditional markets in Central and Eastern Europe. The signing of the Maastricht Treaty in 1992 was in part a response to a perceived threat that Germany would exploit this advantageous position and subsequently increase its own power within the EU. Maastricht was intended to counteract this and to bind Germany ever more firmly into the Western European community. The federal government was well aware of this and remained an enthusiastic advocate of the creation of full political union between member-states, with Kohl declaring on several occasions that German unification and European integration were 'two sides of the same coin'. Nevertheless, there has been a growing debate over Germany's post-unification role in the EU. Whereas pre-1989 observers spoke about the 'Europeanisation' of Germany (see below), attention more recently has focused on whether there has been an increase in German efforts to push its own national interests within the Union.

Still, Kohl certainly viewed German unification and European integration as interconnected processes. Neither project could, or should, be achieved without the other. Through this, Kohl considered himself to be extending the legacy of Adenauer, who put all his faith in achieving German unification through integration with the West. Kohl was in effect Adenauer's political 'grandson' in continuing this policy, which had served

Germany so well during the Cold War (Mertes, 2002). This clear linkage between the achievement of German unification and ever-expanding political and economic co-operation within the European Union was central to Germany's continued commitment to the EU after the end of the Cold War.

German European policy during much of the 1990s focused on constructing both EMU in the short term and full political union in the long term, as well as working towards the inclusion of Central and Eastern European states after the collapse of the Soviet Union. Germany remained very much at the heart of debates over the future direction of the EU's integration process. Kohl firmly believed that enlargement should not come at the expense of internal cohesion among the member-states. One of the most significant German contributions to this debate was a paper written in 1994 by the CDU's leading thinkers on European policy, Karl Lamers and Wolfgang Schäuble. They called for the creation of a 'core Europe', centred on those states that wished to pursue deeper integration (Schäuble and Lamers, 1994). The paper was controversial as it failed to include Italy and the United Kingdom in the core as they were not considered committed enough to the EU. Fundamentally, the paper asserted the right of more pro-integration-minded states to pursue closer co-operation with one another, rather than the development of the EU being determined by the more Eurosceptic states. This idea found its way into the 1997 Treaty of Amsterdam and is commonly referred to in the literature as 'variable geometry', which points to the fact that some EU member-states choose to be involved in all aspects of the Union, while others select which areas they would rather avoid, such as the UK's decision not to adopt the euro. Germany has consistently remained within 'core Europe', which gives its government considerable influence over all aspects of EU policy.

The idea of a 'core Europe' was central to overcoming French concerns of a more powerful Germany after the fall of the Berlin Wall. The quality of Franco-German relations provides an interesting barometer of the state of EU affairs. Co-operation between the two countries has been responsible for many of the major advances in European integration. Likewise, when Franco-German relations hit difficulties, so too does the European Union. This relationship has been so central to the success of the EU that one academic has described it as 'co-operative hegemony' (Pedersen, 1998). The signing of the 1963 Elysée Treaty marked the institutionalisation of the bilateral relationship which has remained strong ever since. Since 2001, France and Germany have once again stepped up their bilateral contacts through the 'Blaesheim Process', the term for the informal meetings of the French President and the German Chancellor, along with their respective foreign ministers, which take place approximately every four weeks. The regularity of these meetings encourages joint initiatives and ensures that differences, when they emerge, are dealt with swiftly to prevent long-lasting damage to relations. At the same time, the outcomes of this very close relationship are not always positive for other member-states: in 2002, for example, France and Germany agreed to fix payments under the CAP, a key French national interest, outside the normal budget time-frame and negotiating process until the year 2013 in order to outmanoeuvre those member-states, such as the UK, who wished to secure a significant cut in agricultural expenditure.

EU enlargement was a particularly important issue for Germany as it promised to spread stability and prosperity to Germany's near neighbours in Central and Eastern Europe (Tewes, 2001). Germany was the key advocate of EU membership for all of these countries, seeking to integrate them into the EU in order to ensure that an unstable power vacuum did not emerge to its east. Initiatives such as the 'Weimar Triangle' – France,

Poland and Germany – were institutionalised in order to ensure that German efforts to stabilise the region were not considered as attempts to exert Germany's new-found power in the aftermath of the Soviet Union's collapse. The parallel processes of NATO and EU enlargement were therefore vital for Germany in order to demonstrate further its commitment to multilateralism after unification.

The end of the CDU/CSU–FDP government's sixteen years in power in 1998 marked a significant shift in the German government's attitude towards the EU. The new SDP–Green government represented a generational change at the head of the country, and it was less weighed down by the legacy of the past and more confident in expressing Germany's interests. Chancellor Schröder's maxim of being 'Europeans because we want to be' was subtly different to what had gone before. His stance was indicative of a more pragmatic agenda for German European policy as he sought, for example, to be more assertive about spreading the financial burden among the EU's member-states. Rather than the burden of history being the main driving force behind Germany's EU member-ship, the new determination to be more assertive vis-à-vis the other member-states seemed to become a defining characteristic of German European policy.

One key example of this changed dynamic has been Germany's reassessment of its own weight within the European institutions, which has been diminishing due to successive enlargements. Historically, the way in which member-states were represented at EU level has favoured smaller member-states, an arrangement which initially suited West Germany, as its own comparatively low weight in the institutions provided further proof of its desire not to dominate its neighbours. But as increasing numbers of small states have joined the EU, especially in the 2004 enlargement, Germany has seen its relative weight shrink even further, to the extent that today, relative to its population, it has fewer Members of the European Parliament and fewer votes in the Council of Ministers than any other member-state (see Box 9.2). In consequence, since the late 1990s, Germany has emphasised that EU decision-making mechanisms should reflect to a greater degree its own status as the most populous member-state. In the 2000 Treaty of Nice, for instance, Germany was successful in securing a provision that qualified majority votes in the Council of Ministers should additionally require the support of countries comprising at least 62 per cent of the EU's population. This so-called 'double majority' is clearly designed to favour larger, more populous member-states.

Interestingly, the return of the CDU/CSU to federal government in 2005 did not result in any significant change in European policy from that of its SPD–Green predecessor, suggesting that Schröder's departure from previous patterns of engagement was not simply a party political matter. One major difference has been evident, however. During the second SPD–Green term of office, between 2002 and 2005, Germany became less effective within the EU on account of its position on the 2002–3 Iraq crisis, which split opinion between member-states. Schröder's polarising position on this issue (see Chapter 10) ensured that Germany's policy no longer represented the middle ground, spanning European and transatlantic interests. As a result, he became less adept at forging agreements within the EU, and German influence subsequently waned. Following her election as Chancellor, Angela Merkel sought to reposition Germany as a consensus-builder within the EU on issues such as the Constitutional Treaty, environment policy and transatlantic trade. Reoccupying the middle ground has seen Germany regain influence in Brussels, but it continues to be more confident about stating its national interest when German preferences are threatened.

BOX 9.2 GERMANY IN THE EUROPEAN UNION

- The *European Commission* initiates EU legislation and supervises its implementation. Originally, in 1957, West Germany nominated two (formally independent) commissioners out of nine; in 2007, following successive enlargements, Germany nominated just one commissioner out of twenty-seven.
- The *Council of Ministers* is the main forum for member-states to be represented in the EU and is also its primary legislative body. In 2007, and in those cases where voting by a qualified majority is applied, Germany held 29 votes out of 345, or 8.4 per cent of the total votes for 27 member-states, despite accounting for 17 per cent of the total EU population. The fact that 255 votes (74 per cent of the total) were needed to constitute a qualified majority further reduced Germany's weight.
- In 2007, Germany was one of twenty-seven members of the *European Council*, which represents heads of state and government.
- Since unification, Germany has held the six-month *Presidency of the EU* on three occasions: during the second half of 1994, the first half of 1999 and the first half of 2007.
- The *European Parliament* is the only directly elected EU institution and is the EU's secondary legislative council. After the 2004 elections, 99 of the 732 Members of the European Parliament (MEPs), or 14 per cent of the total, came from Germany. In Germany, 820,000 voters elect each MEP; in Malta, the equivalent figure is just 71,000.
- Germany nominates one judge to sit on the *European Court of Justice* in Luxembourg.
- Although the *European Central Bank*, which sets unified interest rates for those countries participating in the single currency, is based in Frankfurt/Main, its president so far has not been German.
- In 2007, Germany was represented by 24 delegates out of 344 on each of two consultative bodies: the *Economic and Social Committee* and the *Committee of the Regions*.

Source: Nugent (2006: esp. 108–9; 258)

Issues

One of the central features of European integration is that, over time, the distinction in many member-states between what is viewed as EU policy and what is domestic policy has become blurred. The process through which Germany has adapted to being a member of the EU is generally termed 'Europeanisation'. Although this can be defined in a wide variety of (sometimes contradictory) ways, Robert Ladrech's (1994: 69) definition will suffice here: '[an] incremental process re-orienting the direction and shape of politics to the degree that E[U] political and economic dynamics become part of the organizational logic of national politics and policy-making'.

Germany has had to adapt to the processes that have developed out of the European integration project, but it has also played a major role in shaping the form and content of the EU since the signing of the Treaties of Rome. The concept of Europeanisation describes these twin processes as *downloading* and *uploading* (Bulmer and Burch, 2000; see Figure 9.1). As Bomberg and Peterson (2002: 7) have put it, 'European integration shapes domestic policies, politics and polities, but member-states also "project themselves" by seeking to shape the trajectory of European integration in ways that suit national interests'. Domestic political and economic contexts in EU member-states have major impacts on the scope and nature of Europeanisation. As Börzel and Risse (2000: 61) state, 'the lower the compatibility between European and domestic processes, policies and institutions, the higher the adaptational pressure'. Adaptational pressures are therefore very different in each member-state. The pressures felt by a new member-state with little or no experience of co-operation within EU structures are vastly different from those in established EU members, such as Germany, with long historical experience of both shaping and being influenced by EU-level policy developments.

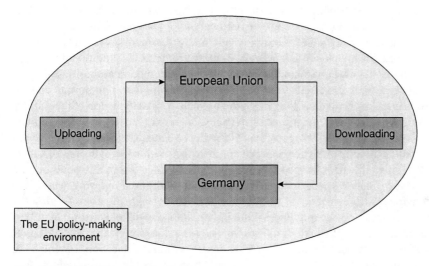

Figure 9.1 The Europeanisation process

As well as differences in policy-making at the member-state and EU levels, Europeanisation can be affected by how EU policies are interpreted within individual member-states. According to Olsen (2002: 936):

> European level developments do not dictate specific forms of institutional adaptation but leave considerable discretion to domestic actors and institutions. There are significant impacts, yet the actual ability of the European level to penetrate domestic institutions is not perfect, universal, or constant. Adaptation reflects variations in European pressure as well as domestic motivations and abilities to act. European signals are interpreted and modified through domestic traditions, institutions, identities and resources in ways that limit the degree of convergence and homogenization.

In the case of Germany, successive governments have sought to shape EU policies to fit with broad German policy goals and policy-making practices. Most obviously, the

European Central Bank, like the *Bundesbank* once was, is charged with controlling inflation without any political interference. Other high-profile examples of successful attempts to upload German policies to the EU level include the Schengen Agreement, which deals with border controls within most of the EU, and aspects of competition and environmental policies (Dyson, 2003). As Chapter 10 will demonstrate, Germany has also been quite influential in the development of the EU's foreign and security policy (Miskimmon, 2007). By shaping EU-level decisions, Germany has largely been able to limit the extent to which it has had to adapt its own policies and institutions as a direct result of its membership of the EU. Plus, it is not solely policies which Germany has uploaded. The EU's institutional structures and practices all reflect a particularly German (and French) bureaucratic style and tradition. This has been to Germany's advantage over the years in navigating the complexities of policy-making within Brussels.

However, in spite of the close fit between German and EU institutions, Germany has also been greatly influenced and affected by its EU membership. The implications of the Maastricht Treaty on Germany are a case in point. Not only did this treaty commit Germany to the creation of the Euro and the removal of the *Deutsche Mark*, but it called into question the extent to which Germany genuinely retained sovereignty over all aspects of its political system. In a landmark case, the Federal Constitutional Court in Germany ruled that states *did* remain the dominant decision-making authorities, despite the wide-ranging powers exercised by the EU. The treaty resulted in an important change in how European policy is made within Germany with the formal inclusion of the *Länder* in *Europapolitik*, which was enshrined in Article 23 of the Basic Law. The *Länder* successfully lobbied for the right to represent Germany in decisions taken by the Council of Ministers which directly influence regional competences within Germany (see Chapter 4, pp. 69–70). This radically changed German European policy. From this point on, the federal government had to co-ordinate European policy with the *Bundesrat*, while also trying to convince its EU partners of its policy initiatives, thus greatly complicating the policy-making process. As the influence of the EU on domestic policies within member-states has grown, so the role of the *Bundesrat* has increased in European policy (Bulmer *et al.*, 2000). The fundamental principle of subsidiarity within EU decision-making – the principle that decisions should be taken at the lowest possible level – which was reinforced within the 1997 Treaty of Amsterdam, has further strengthened the *Länder*'s hand in asserting their influence within Germany's European policy.

Model European or not, Germany has still come under increasing strain as a result of its involvement in the EU. It has been greatly affected by the onset of the so-called 'resource crunch', which, since unification, has narrowed Germany's traditional room to manoeuvre to forge agreements with its EU partners (Jeffery and Paterson, 2003; Miskimmon *et al.*, forthcoming). Previously, Chancellor Kohl's ability to encourage partners to sign up to EU agreements was aided by the use of 'chequebook diplomacy', offering financial incentives for assent on EU agreements. But the downturn in the German economy since the 1990s has limited subsequent German governments' ability to continue in this vein. Domestic economic pressures have also led to calls from Germany that it should contribute a fairer proportion to the EU budget and that other large states, such as France and the UK, should be willing to pay more. In addition, a sense within the German population that the EU is not helping Germany overcome its economic and fiscal difficulties has resulted in reduced support for European integration (Paterson, 2006). The SPD–Green government and the Grand Coalition have consistently dragged their feet on fulfilling their commitments to the Single European Market. As

Chapter 7 (p. 123) highlighted, Germany has sought to shield some national companies from EU competition, particularly in the energy market, and to continue to allow German public savings banks to operate under favourable national conditions. Germany has also attempted to water down proposals for an EU Services Directive for fear that this would undermine German competitiveness. In sum, financial and economic constraints during the early twenty-first century have resulted in Germany being more willing to push its national interest within the EU and to refuse initiatives which are considered contradictory to national policy preferences.

Economic underperformance has been central to the major challenges facing Germany within the EU. Added to this, the institutional commitments of EU membership in the field of monetary policy have reduced Germany's ability to adjust interest rates unilaterally to cope with short-term challenges. Germany, therefore, suffers from internal and external economic constraints; namely, the cost of the German welfare state and teething problems associated with the introduction of the euro and with finalising the Single European Market. Germany was a central actor in imposing an 'ordo-liberal' economic perspective at the EU level, reflecting its own domestic preferences for economic governance (see Dyson, 2005b; Dyson and Padgett, 2006). Despite this clear success, euro membership and the pressures of Single Market competition have not always been easy for Germany to manage. Chancellor Schröder regularly complained about the European Commission's challenge to German state-backed institutions such as regional banks and German companies. On account of diminishing tax revenues, Germany consistently undermined the Stability and Growth Pact criteria on public spending and government debt but faced few sanctions from fellow Eurozone members (see Chapter 7, p. 121).

Signs that Germany's economic problems are starting to ease have been evident since 2006. However, as a number of chapters in this book have argued, Germany still has considerable structural weaknesses in its economic and fiscal model. The federal government will also have to operate within the constraints of the Stability and Growth Pact. Thus, reforms such as *Agenda 2010* and *Hartz IV* have in part emanated from Germany's membership of the single currency. Significant portions of domestic public opinion have reacted angrily to cuts in government spending and blamed Germany's adoption of the euro for forcing the federal government's hand. Many in Germany still look back wistfully towards the *Deutsche Mark*, which was withdrawn from circulation on 31 December 2001. Public opinion polls have charted an incremental decrease in support for the EU within Germany: in the autumn 2006 Eurobarometer Survey, only 58 per cent of Germans polled responded that EU membership was a good thing, giving Germany only the tenth-highest positive response out of the twenty-seven members-states (Eurobarometer, 2006). More worryingly, and in the same survey, when asked whether Germany had benefited from its EU membership, only 49 per cent of those questioned replied in the affirmative. This downward trend has been mirrored in falling turnouts for European Parliament elections, a sign that the EU is becoming less relevant for ordinary Germans. This data suggests that while political elites remain supportive of the EU, German citizens are becoming less positive over time.

The long-running issue of Germany's excessive budget deficit has done little to improve the country's recent image in the EU, pitching the federal government against the European Commission. Germany's gradual economic recovery since 2006 has tempered Commission criticism of the federal government's economic management, but this does not mean that Germany has regained its position as the EU's self-declared 'model pupil' (*Musterknabe*). Indeed, evidence is mounting that Germany is not quite the 'good European' it likes to claim it is (see Box 9.3). For instance, Germany's position as the largest net contributor to the budget depends on how this is calculated. Similarly, Germany does not appear to be leading the field when it comes to either the implementation of EU legislation or the number of infringement proceedings initiated against it. Politically, Germany's blocking of negotiations on an EU-wide agreement on Value Added Tax went against the flow of majority opinion within the EU, while it has also been criticised for its poor record on carbon emissions – despite Angela Merkel's success in forging an EU agreement on tougher environmental standards during the 2007 German presidency of the EU.

These frictions should not cloud the fact that Germany remains very much within 'core Europe'. However, the enlargement of the EU since 2004 has been both a blessing and a curse for Germany's ability to influence the EU's development. Twenty-seven member-states mean that the EU is considerably more heterogeneous now than it has ever been. Therefore, Germany's ability to shape the course of the EU has been limited. As the next section will show, enlargement has also presented the EU with major challenges in terms of cohesion, which have severely slowed the integration process. This has significant consequences for Germany, which relies so much on co-operation with its EU partners, and it is one of the reasons why Germany proposed the European Constitutional Treaty:

BOX 9.3 IS GERMANY A GOOD EUROPEAN?

1   *Germany and the EU budget*

- Germany is regularly by far the largest net contributor to the EU budget in absolute terms – €5.068 billion in 2002.
- But in relative terms, the picture is different: when net contributions are calculated as a percentage of GDP, Germany's figure (0.24 per cent in 2002) lies fourth behind the Netherlands, Luxembourg and Sweden's (Wagner *et al.*, 2006: 429).

2   *Germany's compliance with EU law*

- Between 1978 and 2000, Germany ranked sixth among twelve EU member-states in the number of infringement cases initiated against it and referred to the European Court of Justice, with 136 cases.
- In the same period, Denmark, the Netherlands, Luxembourg, the UK and Ireland all had fewer infringement rates (Tallberg, 2002: 618)
- For the period between 1963 and 1999, Huelshoff *et al.* (2005) also find that Germany lies in the middle of EU member-states for compliance.

3   *Germany's implementation of EU law*

- During the 1990s, Germany's transposition rate, which measures the proportion of agreed directives to have been translated into national law, generally stood around the annual EU average of between 90 and 95 per cent.
- Among twelve member-states, Germany thus performed better than Greece, Italy and Portugal, but worse than Denmark and the Netherlands (Börzel, 2001: 815).

it hoped that institutional reform would help the EU deal with the considerable pressures of enlargement and would allow Germany to upload its views on the future of Europe to the EU level.

Debates

The debate over the future of the European Union has been an area in which Germany has had considerable influence in recent years. Previous unsatisfactory attempts to make the EU fit for enlargement, notably the Treaty of Nice in 2000, were dogged by in-fighting among member-states about the pecking order in any enlarged Union. Dissatisfaction with France's preparations as President of the European Council to deliver a more satisfactory treaty at Nice led to German Foreign Minister Joschka Fischer's call for a more ambitious debate over the future of the EU in light of the impending enlargement. In a now famous speech to the Humboldt University in Berlin on 12 May 2000, Fischer called for a 'federal Europe' which 'means nothing less than a European parliament and a European government which really do exercise legislative and executive power within the Federation. This Federation will have to be based on a constituent treaty' (Fischer, 2000). This federalist vision of centralised government and state-like institutions outlined in a constitutional treaty was met with scepticism by French President Jacques Chirac. In a speech before the Bundestag in Berlin on 27 June 2000, Chirac countered that 'the task of building Europe has, to too large an extent, been solely that of leaders and elites. It is time our peoples once more become the sovereigns of Europe. Democracy in Europe must be more dynamic, particularly through the European Parliament and the national parliaments' (Chirac, 2000: 76). Chirac's confederal outlook on the EU – the continued dominance of states, albeit within a more integrated federal structure – differed from the more centralised vision espoused by Fischer. These speeches highlight the differences in the European policies of the EU's two main states, with Germany being more comfortable with a traditional federal vision for the EU than France.

The debate sparked by Fischer and Chirac resulted in a commitment within the Treaty of Nice for a deeper discussion on the EU's future; the 2001 Laeken Declaration, under the Belgian EU presidency, then included an explicit commitment to establish a Convention on the Future of Europe. This 105-member Convention made up of representatives from current and prospective member-states in addition to members of EU institutions was chaired by former French President Valéry Giscard d'Estaing. It was tasked with writing a text which would make the EU more 'democratic, transparent and efficient' (cited in Nugent, 2006: 116). The resulting text, while unsatisfactory and representing a messy compromise between competing interests, was debated by EU heads of government and signed in Rome on 29 October 2004. The subsequent rejection of the treaty on 29 May 2005 in France and on 1 June 2005 in the Netherlands brought the constitutional process to a halt and heralded a period of soul-searching within the EU about how it could regain its direction and meaning.

Germany has consistently supported the proposed constitution, despite its faults, as it is an attempt to tidy up some of the EU's inefficiencies and quirks in order to equip the Union better to meet the challenges of its recent rapid growth in membership. This support stems from a deep desire to prevent enlargement from causing an unravelling of European integration into a series of loose, ad-hoc arrangements between member-states. The centrality of European integration for the German state means that any substantial weakening of it threatens to undermine an important aspect of German policy. The

CDU/CSU–SPD Grand Coalition has therefore aimed to revive the Constitutional Treaty in the face of widespread apathy elsewhere. As President of the European Council in the first half of 2007, Chancellor Merkel faced significant challenges when trying to provide a coherent and forward-looking agenda that had at least a chance of fostering some sort of political agreement in EU capitals. The Berlin Declaration of 25 March 2007 was an attempt to consolidate efforts to ratify the constitution and to re-engage European citizens with the workings of the EU. Although it failed to generate much enthusiasm among ordinary Germans, Merkel did achieve a significant breakthrough at the June 2007 European Council meeting, at which a new treaty focusing mainly on institutional amendments was agreed.

Central to current debates on the future of Europe within Germany has been the next round of EU enlargement. Most, but by no means all, of the EU enlargement debate has focused on the possibility of Turkey joining the Union. This issue has been particularly important within the ranks of the CDU/CSU, which has been largely hostile. Many conservative politicians fret about whether a large, poor, predominantly Muslim country will ever be able to integrate effectively with current EU members that are not just culturally homogeneous but much more affluent. Some also remain unconvinced that the EU will be able to adapt its institutions to bring Turkey successfully into its governance structures. Conversely, the SPD has been largely in favour of Turkish EU membership so long as Turkey can live up to the Union's tough entry requirements. The pro-Turkey arguments stress that the country as it is now will not be the one that ultimately enters the EU: it will have to prove itself much reformed, democratically secure and economically upbeat before it is allowed to join. The SPD is also well aware that it is generally the preferred party among those few Turks resident in Germany who have acquired the right to vote. Before becoming Chancellor, Angela Merkel tried to bridge her party's instinctive scepticism of Turkish accession with slightly more positive rhetoric, calling for a 'privileged partnership' rather than full membership. Edmund Stoiber – long-time leader of the conservative CSU in Bavaria – has been more vocal in outlining his objections to Turkish membership. At a CSU party convention in Augsburg in October 2006, in what was a typical expression of his party's reservations, he asserted that 'Europe is a community of values, and I say yes to close cooperation, to friendship with Turkey but if we want to make the European Union an intellectual centre, then I say Turkey has no place here' (Stoiber, 2006).

Since Merkel became Chancellor, the EU has opened membership negotiations with Turkey, forcing her to take a more diplomatic line and not openly oppose Turkey's efforts to join. Opposition to Turkish membership within Germany, however, takes political, cultural and economic forms, and clearly links with debates over the immigration and integration of Turkish nationals in Germany (see Chapter 6, pp. 100–2). The CDU/CSU has generally argued that Turkey is not European and does not hold the same cultural and religious values of EU member-states. The enduring tensions within Turkey between the secular state and Islam as the dominant religion is a further area of CDU/CSU concern. A major political complication has been the issue of Cyprus, an EU member-state since 2004: Turkey has occupied the northern half of the island since 1974. Finally, the economic costs of Turkish membership are considered almost too great to bear, given the current pressures on the EU budget caused by the enlargements in 2004 and 2007. The enlargement issue is also viewed within the pressures of the age-old debate on 'deepening versus enlarging' the EU – whether the member-states should concentrate more on making the EU work better (deepening), or work towards increasing the membership base of the organisation (widening) – and whether both can be achieved simultaneously. The fear abounds within Germany that enlargement has caused the dilution of European integration and threatens to undermine the principles which Germany and other like-minded pro-integration members-states have forged over the last fifty years.

To sum up, Germany views deeper EU integration to be in its best interests. The constitution was an attempt to resolve problems in existing EU treaties to ease the impact of enlargement and help connect the Union with its citizens. While this chapter has noted that German policy within the EU has become more contingent, Germany still remains committed to deeper co-operation with its EU partners. Deeper integration will also ensure that new member-states sign up to the policies which Germany, along with France and other EU partners, has shaped over the last fifty years. Looser co-ordination and a greater prevalence of national interests within the EU would undermine the policies and principles which Germany has sought to promote within Europe. Standing up for German interests while pursuing closer co-operation with EU partners has become the hallmark of German's *Europapolitik*.

Conclusion: still a good European?

The EU has changed substantially since the end of the Cold War. In 1990, the EEC had only twelve members. Just seventeen years later the EU had twenty-seven members. Germany remains a highly Europeanised state, despite its new-found penchant for pursuing its national interest within the EU in a more overt fashion. But the German public's growing scepticism over the benefits of EU membership reflects a change of attitude within Germany. Both this and growing assertiveness from the German government are due largely to the 'domestication' of European policy (Harnisch and Schieder, 2006). As EU integration has progressed over the course of the 1990s, the national impact of integration has resulted in the EU no longer being considered a foreign policy issue. Rather, European integration has become a matter of domestic political contestation in the same way as other areas of politics. This has meant that the German government can no longer gloss over the less palatable aspects of integration, and it is under pressure to deliver on German preferences in the Brussels policy environment.

The impact of this domestication is heightened by domestic economic pressures which have limited Germany's room for manoeuvre in European policy. The SPD–Green and Grand Coalition governments have stated their determination no longer to carry the main burden of the EU budget and both have been more assertive in countering the Commission's criticisms of economic protectionism and industrial subsidies within Germany. The country's underperforming economy, coupled with increased welfare payments due to high unemployment, have also meant that Germany has not been a model European, best seen in its regular flouting of the Stability and Growth Pact since the turn of the century. Moreover, Germany's record in its adherence to EU law is by no means that of a *Musterknabe*.

In spite of these pressures, the German government remains generally committed to European integration. Germany has been a major player in the operationalisation of the EU's military capabilities within the European Security and Defence Policy, as Chapter 10 will show. Chancellor Merkel has also tried to revive the Constitutional Treaty after it was rejected by the citizens of France and the Netherlands. Her determination to see the safe passage of the constitution signals a realisation within Berlin that Schröder's preference for close intergovernmental co-operation with France can achieve only so much within a vastly enlarged EU. Recent signs of growth within Germany suggest that its economic prospects look brighter, which will improve the country's position within the EU. Nevertheless, greater contingency will remain a hallmark of German *Europapolitik* for the foreseeable future.

Questions for discussion

1   **Why was Germany such a strong proponent of further EU integration?**
2   **How has German European policy changed since unification?**
3   **What are likely to be the key tenets of Germany's future EU policy?**

Further reading

Anderson, J. (2005), 'Germany and Europe: Centrality in the EU', in S. Bulmer and C. Lequesne (eds), *The Member States of the European Union* (Oxford: Oxford University Press). The most recent contribution reviewing Germany's approach to European integration.

Bulmer, S., C. Jeffery and W. Paterson (2000), *Germany's European Diplomacy: Shaping the Regional Milieu* (Manchester: Manchester University Press). An excellent discussion of Germany's European policy-making process and policy goals in European integration.

Dyson, K. and K. Goetz (eds) (2003), *Germany, Europe and the Politics of Constraint* (Oxford: Oxford University Press). A first-rate examination of Europeanisation and the German state.

Useful website

<http://www.deutsche-aussenpolitik.de/> – superb resource site in English on all aspects of German foreign and security policy.

10 Foreign and security policy

A new role for the twenty-first century?

Summary

Since 1949 German foreign and security policy has been dominated by the need to redefine the country's role in the world. It has been characterised by a firm commitment to co-operation within multilateral institutions and by a rejection of the use of military force as a tool of foreign policy. German foreign policy has, however, changed radically since unification. Politicians have pushed the armed forces to take on more responsibility in securing international stability, and German military personnel are now found in all corners of the world, alongside those of the country's multilateral partners. Yet, German foreign policy is now characterised by uncertainty in the face of a new and diverse set of challenges. This chapter examines the main pillars of German foreign policy and analyses the core international dilemmas facing Germany in the new millennium.

Introduction

Although Germany ranks among the most economically powerful states in the world, it is rarely seen as a heavyweight in international politics. In contrast to France and the UK, post-war German politicians have neither dabbled in belligerent international posturing nor sought to play an active role in shaping and maintaining the global order. The reasons for this have long-standing, historical roots. This chapter begins by examining the background that has shaped traditional German foreign policy, before analysing how the relative certainties of international politics in the Cold War era have been challenged by an event in Germany itself: unification. Initially, there was a real fear among some of Germany's partners that the unified country would come to dominate international affairs at the European level. By stressing that the principles of German foreign policy remained constant post-1990, federal governments repeatedly committed themselves to multilateral co-operation within the North Atlantic Treaty Organisation, the European Union and the United Nations. They did this both out of conviction and in order to avoid any suspicion that Germany would pursue a more unilateral foreign policy once unification had been achieved.

At the same time, German politicians also realised that Germany would inevitably become a more active international actor in the post-Cold War era. This change towards greater – if still hesitant – activism took place slowly and cautiously; and it was only the major shifts in international politics that took place post-11 September 2001 that prompted German foreign policy elites to redefine their positions once more – most notably, although not exclusively, towards the US-driven response to global terrorism. Germany has nevertheless sought refuge from these challenges within a traditional framework of multilateral institutions. It has also avoided clearly defining precisely what its new foreign and security policy should be. This is largely because, just as Germany was seeking to come to terms with unification and its role in Europe and the wider world, the world itself was moving on too.

Background

Seldom can it be said that a state fully achieves all of its foreign policy goals. Yet, in 1990, West Germany (and its Western allies – the United States, the UK and France) succeeded in achieving what had been its overriding international aim: bringing to an end the division of the country. Alongside repelling any possible Soviet military aggression from the East, the period 1949 to 1990 was dominated by efforts to achieve unification. Various chancellors adopted a variety of strategies in attempting to do this, but the overarching goal remained constant. When unification finally arrived, it had rather a different effect on Germany's international politics than many had envisaged. It certainly did not trigger the beginning of a new, tranquil era free of threats and enemies. The fall of the Berlin Wall saw Germany's foreign policy environment, as well as German citizens' perceptions of their country's place and role within this, become less certain when compared with the way they had felt during the Cold War period. Germany was no longer faced with a visible enemy or overriding purpose for its foreign policy. Given the absence of a clearly defined threat to national security, there have subsequently been a number of relatively high-profile debates on the country's future foreign policy direction.

Germany emerged from the Second World War defeated and discredited. It lacked international standing as well as trusted partners in the international community. The country's catastrophic defeat meant that its fate lay initially in the hands of the victorious Allied powers (the United States, the USSR, the UK and, to a lesser extent, France), not in the hands of the German people. The consequences of the Potsdam Summit in the summer of 1945 and the emerging tensions between East and West resulted in the division of the country in 1949, with the drawing of an iron curtain through Germany's geographic heart. This set the context for the West German foreign and security policy that emerged after the foundation of the Federal Republic in 1949. Subsequently, this focused on recovering some international credibility with the ultimate aim of unifying the divided nation. West German politicians attempted to achieve this through forging strong ties with the United States and pursuing closer co-operation with other states in Europe, distancing themselves from the bankrupt principles of German foreign policy of the late 1930s.

Acutely aware of its gruesome past, the principle of non-violence became central to Germany's foreign policy development. Reinforced by all post-1949 governments, enshrined in the Basic Law and supported by the overwhelming majority of West German citizens, it became an incontestable pillar of all of West Germany's strategy for conducting international affairs. West Germany replaced expansionism and imperialism with policies that stressed building institutional co-operation on both European and global levels. Such was the belief in the rejection of military force to achieve foreign policy objectives that the Federal Republic became closely associated with the concept of what Hanns Maull (1990) called 'civilian power' (see also Harnisch and Maull, 2001). However, since the terrorist attacks on the United States on 11 September 2001, the core principle that aggressive military force would not be used as a tool of German foreign policy has posed a significant challenge for German foreign policy-makers as they have found themselves under increased pressure to act militarily in international crisis management. Despite the growing deployment of German troops overseas, the country's foreign policy nevertheless remains characterised by the use of 'soft power' and the rejection of 'hard power' in the pursuit of German interests.

Germany's relationship with the EU and with other European countries was analysed in detail in Chapter 9. This highlighted the centrality of Germany within Europe as well as its undoubted (primarily economic) influence across the region. Linked to this is a clear reluctance to take full advantage of its national power resources in pursuing unilateral national interests. Helga Haftendorn (2006) characterises German foreign policy as being a balance between self-limitation and self-assertion. The first of these has been most evident in Germany's multilateralist strategy, most clearly demonstrated in its membership of NATO and the EU. Despite Germany's central position and obvious power resources, Konrad Adenauer chose to pursue a policy of 'binding to the West' (*Westbindung*) to affirm West Germany's commitment to partnership with the United States and its Western European neighbours. Above all, during the Cold War, successive West German chancellors from Adenauer to Kohl stressed Germany's alliance compatibility (*Bündnisfähigkeit*) in pursuing its foreign and security policy goals. NATO became the bedrock of this and the guarantor of the United States' commitment to the continent of Europe in the face of the Soviet threat. During the Cold War, reflexive multilateralism therefore became the hallmark of German foreign policy (Paterson, 1992). NATO, the EEC, the Conference on Security and Co-operation in Europe (CSCE) and, from 1973, the United Nations, provided the settings for the re-emergence of Germany as an international actor. These institutions also served as arenas through which West German diplomacy sought to counteract the negative consequences of the Cold War division of Europe and of Germany. Through membership of NATO and the EEC/EU, West Germany was consequently able to balance its European and transatlantic interests.

Despite these self-limitations, Haftendorn (2006) also highlights how Germany was able to assert itself in these same multilateral settings. One example of this was Ostpolitik (Germany's policy towards the East), which is most clearly associated with Willy Brandt's time as Chancellor. Brandt sought to forge closer relations with the Soviet Union and its satellite states through bilateral relations and through the establishment of the CSCE, the first serious attempt to institutionalise relations between East and West during the Cold War. *Ostpolitik* went some way to easing the tensions between West Germany and the countries of the Warsaw Pact, most notably the Soviet Union, Poland and, most importantly, the GDR. It was undertaken under a shroud of secrecy for fear of upsetting the USA and to avoid the danger of threatening the delicate Cold War stand-off between East and West. Germany's policy towards the East was responsible at least in part for improved relations between West Germany and the countries of Eastern Europe and it played a significant role in opening up a dialogue between the opposing sides.

West Germany also sought to create particularly close and productive relations with both the USA and France. The FRG's support for the European integration project offered it a way to reconnect with Western Europe and to foster economic growth and political co-operation. The Franco-German relationship was central to this, as no

European project from the European Coal and Steel Community to the Single European Act succeeded without their co-operation. The bilateral relationship with the USA stemmed from the latter's security guarantee and from Germany's desire to influence the superpower in finding a solution to the Cold War stand-off.

The Franco-German relationship is crucial in understanding both the development of European integration after 1945 and how the Federal Republic was able to regain the trust and support of its neighbours. Developing a working relationship between these states was of key importance in the post-war push towards greater integration among all the states of Europe. The impetus for an improved Franco-German relationship in the aftermath of the Second World War was given by Konrad Adenauer and Charles de Gaulle, whose collective efforts resulted in the signing of the Elysée Treaty of 1963. This outlined the areas of co-operation that the two states would undertake in an effort to improve relations and work towards building a common European home. Later, in the 1980s, Helmut Kohl and François Mitterrand sought to deepen relations by establishing a Franco-German Defence Council and a Franco-German Corps, which became the nucleus of the multinational Eurocorps, established in 1992. As was mentioned in Chapter 9, Franco-German co-operation and co-ordination within the EU reached such a level that it could be described as 'co-operative hegemony' (Pedersen, 1998). This was evident in the Franco-German motor's ability to push for ever-greater integration and to generate a dynamic for closer co-operation in the field of foreign policy. The post-1945 Franco-German relationship is the most obvious example of one of the main character traits of German foreign policy: Germany has consistently attempted to forge bilateral relationships with its key partners on a long-term basis, and it has been less worried about short-term calculations in the interest of long-term stability. This strategy of long-term commitments to bilateral relationships ensured that even during times of tension, Germany was never left exposed and without partners with which to forge wide international agreement in the pursuit of its interests.

Multilateral institutions were also critical for the development of West German foreign policy. NATO, and the emerging foreign policy of the European Community, provided West Germany with a highly institutionalised setting in which to re-engage internationally without the risk of criticism for following a unilateralist course. West Germany's entry into NATO in 1955 marked a significant moment for Adenauer and the country as a whole, because it had conceded the need to militarise in order to play its role in defending its borders to the east. The integration of the new armed forces, the *Bundeswehr*, into NATO command structures and a constitutionally enshrined limiting of those forces to the role of defending the state and the Atlantic alliance demonstrated West Germany's commitment to multilateralism as well as a limited conception of the use of force in international affairs. Supporting NATO was in West German interests as it helped maintain the USA's nuclear umbrella as well as American influence in Western Europe. Furthermore, West Germany was forbidden from possessing atomic, biological or chemical weapons, reinforcing Bonn's reliance on the USA for its nuclear arsenal.

West Germany also participated actively in the development of the foreign policy of the European Economic Community. European Political Co-operation (EPC), which emerged after 1970, was the informal co-ordination of foreign policy among the member-states. While EPC did not deal with security and defence policy, it enabled West Germany to widen its international links under the cover of (yet another) multilateral endeavour, and once more facilitated the development of West German foreign policy without fear of claims of German unilateralism. It also provided a forum for expressing differences within the transatlantic community without upsetting the cohesion of the NATO alliance.

Some authors have seen the Federal Republic's reliance on myriad international organisations as an instinctive 'exaggerated multilateralism' (Anderson, 1997), resulting in the country becoming 'particularly interested in, and increasingly adept at, not clearly articulating distinctive national positions, but rather feeding its own special German concerns and priorities into a common approach' (Garton Ash, 1993: 262). This principle of multilateralism remains a central tenet of foreign policy in post-unification Germany and is at the core of the remarkable continuity seen in the post-Cold War era. Post-1989, foreign policy has focused on developing and expanding both NATO and the EU in order to secure peace and stability within Europe through the enlargement of both organisations. NATO and the EU have also proved important institutions through which Germany has sought to find answers to the challenges facing the transatlantic community since the end of the Cold War.

Who makes German foreign policy?

Foreign policy is made by a number of difference actors. The *Auswärtiges Amt* – Foreign Ministry – is responsible for the day-to-day conduct of Germany's foreign relations. The Foreign Minister is responsible for the policy direction of the ministry and is usually, though not always, the leader of the junior coalition partner in government as well as Deputy Chancellor. The Foreign Ministry is a conservative organisation which is interested in cultivating Germany's medium- to long-term interests rather than the short-term policy calculations which often characterise other government ministries. The influence of the Foreign Minister is highly dependent on his (or her, although every one thus far has been a man) skill in influencing German policy. Perhaps the person most associated with the office is Hans-Dietrich Genscher (of the FDP), who was Foreign Minister between 1974 and 1992. Genscher's influence is still discernible in Germany's predilection for multilateral co-operation. The other major player in German foreign policy is the Chancellor, who can take a leading role in the area and often appears to take it over. During the 1990s, Helmut Kohl dominated German foreign policy, leaving his Foreign Minister, Klaus Kinkel (of the FDP), to play something of a secondary role. The *Bundestag*'s role in foreign policy is as a forum to debate its direction as well as to help craft government policy. This can be done in plenary sessions of the parliament, but is more generally undertaken within the Foreign Affairs Committee, the Defence Committee and the European Committee of the *Bundestag*. Most notably, the *Bundestag* must agree to any deployment of the *Bundeswehr* in international crisis management, which is an important constraint on the government's ability to deploy German armed forces.

Four other ministries play important roles in German foreign policy. The Defence Ministry tends to be much less visible than some of the others. It largely implements decisions taken by the Foreign Ministry, the Federal Chancellery and the *Bundestag*, and it has spent most of its time since unification on the onerous task of reforming the *Bundeswehr* for the post-Cold War international environment and improving the armed forces' capabilities in international crisis management. In contrast to the massive influence and the defence budget within the United States' Department of Defense commands, the German Defence Ministry's policy influence remains restricted, while its budget is limited by Germany's poor economic situation and by the reluctance of political elites to consider significant military build-up. The Federal Finance Ministry, therefore, plays an important role in holding the budgetary purse strings of funds which are designated for this area. The Defence Ministry has been significantly underfunded since unification, which compromises its ability to develop the German armed forces to co-operate with their main allies. The Finance Ministry's profile in foreign policy has also increased in light of the introduction of the euro and Germany's efforts to abide by the conditions of the Stability and Growth Pact. The Federal Ministry for Economic Co-operation and Development (BMZ) has sought to play a proactive role in forging international co-operation and implementing aid programmes in developing states. It has been closely associated with the UN's Millennium Development Goals and with efforts to reduce the debt burden on developing states. Under the SPD–Green government (1998–2005) the minister at the head of the BMZ formally became a member of the Federal Security Council, a governmental co-ordinating body for foreign and security policy issues. This signalled a raising of the profile of development issues within the framework of Germany's foreign policy formulation. However, despite government rhetoric on the importance of develop- ment issues, the amount of financial aid available declined on account of Germany's financial troubles, thus limiting the influence of these issues within overall foreign policy. Finally, the Federal Ministry for Economics (BMWi) has historically played an important co-ordinating role in German European policy, making it an important foreign policy player overall. Beyond the question of formal competencies, the role of the Chancellor in setting the tone of foreign policy remains a key factor and his/her ability to build strong personal relationships with the leaders of Germany's main partners can have a major bearing on how German policies are received.

Debates

Continuity has, for the most part, governed German foreign policy since 1990. Germany has tried to manage the adaptational pressures impacting upon it in order to keep to the well-versed method it developed in the Cold War era. However, by maintaining relative continuity in its foreign policy Germany has not always adapted well to new international challenges, especially since 11 September 2001. It has been unable to outline the direction in which its foreign policy is going, nor to suggest a solution to one of the main challenges to maintaining cohesion within the transatlantic community – Iraq. The German position on Iraq was clear: it would not participate in military action against Iraq under any circumstances. More significant, however, was the manner in which Chancellor Schröder presented his opposition to the war, which angered US President George W. Bush and severely damaged relations with the USA (Szabo, 2004). Schröder's decision to use the Iraq issue in the federal election of 2002, thereby making German– American differences explicit, was a clear break from past behaviour. US Secretary of State Condoleezza Rice's promise to 'punish France, ignore Germany and forgive Russia' was an indication of the Bush administration's disapproval of the German position (*Daily Telegraph*, 2 June 2003). Her chastisement was also an obvious sign from the Americans that Germany does not yet rank highly enough in international affairs to merit too much consideration when its politicians behave in a recalcitrant manner.

Germany had united with France and Russia in opposing the use of force against Iraq, which many Americans viewed as inevitable after the passing of UN Resolution 1441. Of most interest in the position taken by Schröder was that as early as September 2002 he had ruled out any German involvement in military action against Iraq *even if* a UN Security Council mandate was forthcoming. In adopting such an oppositional stance,

Schröder took a position in line with Germany's traditional post-1945 strategic culture of not being drawn in to military operations outside the NATO area, despite the fact that this foreign policy taboo had been broken by Germany's involvement in the NATO action against Slobodan Milosevic in the former Yugoslavia in 1999. But many saw Schröder's strategy as being deeply flawed. By his early refusal to consider any German involvement in a military operation in Iraq he lost any ability to influence Washington. It also left Germany as very much the junior partner in relations with France, as the latter maintained considerable room for manoeuvre in the debate by refusing to rule out any option until it was clear that Washington had abandoned all efforts to seek a second UN Security Council resolution in January 2003.

Schröder's tactics came under further scrutiny in a series of newspaper reports outlining the role of two agents from the *Bundesnachrichtendienst* (BND) – Germany's overseas intelligence agency – in allegedly helping the American military operation against Baghdad. The agents, it was claimed, provided the US forces with plans of Saddam Hussein's defensive strategy for the Iraqi capital. This greatly compromised Schröder's position and the (non-)role which Germany sought to play in the conflict. The Chancellor's stance was coupled with his growing interest in foreign policy matters and the emergence of a more self-confident discourse in foreign and security policy. His self-assured pronouncements of Germany's national position and his alliance with France and Russia on the Iraq issue threatened to unsettle the traditional German strategy of balancing European and American interests. Such a strident tone also raised issues of a new, potentially more unilateralist 'German way' in foreign and security policy, less tied to the principles of the second half of the twentieth century and more prepared to articulate German interests in public. The Iraq issue nevertheless highlighted the weaknesses of German and European foreign policy as a whole: Germany, France and Russia proved unable to influence the US-led coalition in any way, nor even to suggest a credible alternative strategy for dealing with Iraq. It also showed that Germany is faced with a dual challenge in conducting its foreign and security policy. It is likely to have to continue to develop its own capabilities and to be prepared to deploy them more readily in the event of new challenges. At the same time, however, it remains to be seen how effective Germany will be in influencing foreign and security policy within an EU of twenty-seven member-states, many of which frequently adopt contrasting positions in international debates. The 'Letter of the Eight' of 30 January 2003 is a prime example of this. Published in the *Wall Street Journal* and entitled 'Europe and America must stand united', it was signed by a pro-American set of countries (the Czech Republic, Denmark, Hungary, Italy, Portugal, Spain, Poland and the UK). Meanwhile the 'Vilnius Ten' – comprising Germany and states from Central and South-eastern Europe drafted a rival letter that expressed concern about US policy in Iraq. Here was a clear demonstration that Germany could not mobilise a consensual majority around its own policy goals.

Schröder's new style of foreign and security policy raises an interesting paradox. In the twenty-first century, multilateralism offers Germany 'equality' with other, more powerful states. However, Germany is less adept at exerting influence within international institutions at a time when Berlin has fewer international constraints on it than was the case during the Cold War era. Germany aspires to a greater role and influence in the international community, but it does not yet have the economic, political or military resources necessary to achieve this.

The impact of unification

The unification of Germany in 1990 sparked a lively debate concerning the future course of German foreign policy and Germany's role in international affairs. Germany came under intense scrutiny from the international community for fear that it would pursue a more unilateral foreign policy now that the constraints of the Cold War no longer existed. Even among Germany's closest allies, suspicions abounded that the new, larger and more powerful Germany would come to dominate Europe. Shortly after the Berlin Wall was breached John Mearsheimer (1990) claimed that Germany would strive to attain Great Power status and actively pursue its national interests. He suggested it would do this by increasing investment in its military forces and acquiring nuclear weapons. Successive German policy-makers since unification have gone out of their way to refute Mearsheimer's predictions by doing neither of these things. Germany has not acquired the status of a Great Power alongside the United States, largely preferring to eschew unilateralism and to continue its commitment to multilateral institutional co-operation.

One of the defining moments of post-unification German foreign policy came in December 1991, when Germany decided to break ranks from the rest of the European Union to recognise unilaterally the breakaway former-Yugoslav republics of Croatia and Slovenia (Crawford, 1996). Germany's decision to do so, before its European partners, raised concerns that it was indeed becoming more assertive after unification. This action caused such controversy because other member-states believed that Germany had undermined any attempts to forge a cohesive European response to the crisis in the Balkans. It damaged Germany's foreign policy role in the region and proved a setback for the emergent Common Foreign and Security Policy of the European Union, agreed at Maastricht earlier that month (Ginsberg, 2001). By rejecting multilateralism and embarking on a unilateral course, the decision to recognise Croatia and Slovenia seemed to fly in the face of the orthodoxies of German foreign policy. In failing to work within the EU to find a common approach to the crisis, it seemed that united Germany had failed its first major foreign policy challenge and proved Mearsheimer's predictions correct. For most of the 1990s, the Balkans remained a highly controversial issue within the EU and in transatlantic relations. Germany and the other major regional powers – the United States, the UK and France – have often held divergent policies on this troubled area which have themselves contributed to many of the problems this region continues to face (Glenny, 1999; Holbrooke, 1998). Germany's geographical proximity to the Balkans, the large number of refugees from there who settled in Germany during the early 1990s and the regional instability caused by the break-up of Yugosalvia have ensured that this area remains a foreign policy priority for Germany, culminating in its participation in the Kosovo air campaign of 1999.

With unification and the return of full sovereignty to Germany came increased demands on it from its partners to play a more active role in security stability. This necessitated a substantial reassessment of foreign and security policy within Germany to adapt to these requirements. But any such reassessment was also going to take place within the context of Germany's myriad memberships of influential international organisations. The culture of reflexive multilateralism lived on, and Germany's continued membership and (re)commitment to NATO, the EU, the CSCE (from 1995, the Organisation for Security and Co-operation in Europe) and the UN ensured that these institutions remained central fora as Germany slowly began to adapt some of its foreign policy positions. Yet, as Hanns Maull (1994: 114) states, 'the upshot of all this is a Germany which is both old and new, both more powerful (or rather "weighty") and more vulnerable. Its policies want to emphasise continuity at all cost, yet they have inevitably been pushed off their trajectory and in new directions by changed interests and changed circumstances.'

The aftermath of unification was marked by a lack of German foreign policy rather than a reformulation of Germany's aims in light of new geopolitical realities. The period from 1990 to 2006 was marked by Germany's determination to keep Europe secure through the twin enlargements of NATO and the EU, culminating in the accession of twelve new member-states to the latter in 2004 and 2006. Outside of the EU, Germany's foreign and security policy has come under a number of pressures, mainly revolving around the country's participation in military crisis management and, since 2001, its reaction to America's position on international terrorism.

Post-unification continuity in German foreign and security policy was reinforced by Helmut Kohl's time in office, during which the centrality of NATO and the EU was repeatedly stressed. The election of 1998, which ushered in the first SPD–Green admini-stration, coupled with the federal government's move from Bonn to Berlin, signalled a possible change and an end to German foreign policy provincialism. The new govern-ment also represented a generational change as it comprised ministers with no personal recollection of Hitler's regime. Germany significantly expanded its international com-mitments under the SPD–Green government, and became more assertive, as was seen in Schröder's frequent rhetorical outbursts on world affairs. Since 1998, Germany has undergone an internal reassessment of its international role and its contribution to the use of military force in international affairs, culminating in its involvement in NATO's military operation against Serbia in 1999, in NATO's Operation Enduring Freedom/the UN's operation in Afghanistan and in the SPD–Green government's decision to break with tradition and openly oppose US foreign policy towards Iraq in 2003.

Germany and the use of military force in the post-Cold War order – pressures to go 'out-of-area'

One of the most controversial aspects of Germany's new foreign policy has been framing the country's contribution to international crisis management. The restrained German policy of the Cold War period was, over the course of the 1990s, replaced by a more engaged role alongside its allies in crisis management. Signalling this change, former Defence Minister Peter Struck declared in Germany's *Defence Policy Guidelines* of 2003 that 'Germany's security environment is characterised by changed risks and new opportunities. At present, and in the foreseeable future, there is no conventional threat to German territory. The *Bundeswehr*'s spectrum of operations has changed fundamentally' (Struck, 2003: paragraph 6). This statement pointed to the acceptance of a new, proactive and interventionist German foreign and security policy. No longer will Germany shirk its commitment and responsibility to maintaining security across the globe. Added to this, Struck declared that German foreign policy interests are defended as far away as at the Hindu Kush, a break with the previously held reluctance to consider what former CDU Defence Minister Volker Rühe termed 'exotic missions' (*Orchideen Einsätze*). The beginnings of this development began in the early 1990s, with German deployments to the former Yugoslavia and Somalia.

Germany's involvement in military crisis management has focused on two central institutions: NATO and the emerging European Security and Defence Policy of the EU. The major debates over the future of European security co-operation during the 1990s focused on the issue of 'burden-sharing': that is, the division of labour between Europe and the USA in matters relating to military crisis management and defence. The increased role of European states in providing for the continent's security has had important consequences. Germany has accepted the necessity for an increased role in maintaining global security through its participation in NATO and ESDP (which has been operational since 2003).

The development of the EU's Common Foreign and Security Policy has also been important in Germany's attempts to deal with the implications of the end of the Cold War – most notably the break-up of the former Yugoslavia. Throughout the 1990s Germany sought to develop CFSP as part of an overall aim to establish full political union and a commitment to build a common European defence, while maintaining NATO as the cornerstone of the European security framework. Indeed, Berlin's strong support for CFSP has led some commentators to describe Germany as having a Europeanised foreign policy (Miskimmon, 2007).

Changes in Germany's international role have had a significant impact on the role of the country's armed forces. The size of the *Bundeswehr* has almost halved since the late 1980s, from a peak of around 500,000 troops to currently around 250,000. But now, the development within both NATO and the ESDP of rapidly deployable military capabilities has had a major impact on the Germany military. The *Bundeswehr* has begun to change from an army solely for the defence of the homeland to a force designed for international crisis management across the globe. These organisational changes have taken place in conjunction with a domestic debate about the *Bundeswehr*'s role on the international stage. In general, the development of EU military capabilities and calls for a more active German role in maintaining international security have acted as a cover or facilitating milieu for *Bundeswehr* reform by giving successive defence ministers (Volker Rühe, Rudolf Scharping, Peter Struck and Franz Josef Jung) a new strategic vision for the German armed forces. Scharping and Struck (both of the SPD) initiated wide-ranging reform of the *Bundeswehr* in order to improve its ability to work alongside its allies in crisis management.

One issue has lain at the heart of these debates over the structure of the *Bundeswehr*: conscription. As Chapter 2 (p. 27) noted, the notion that the armed forces should be fully integrated into society as a whole has been a core feature of Germany's post-1945 military ethos and an excellent example of the country's determination to break with the traditions of the past. To this end, the conscription of young men (not women) to serve alongside professional soldiers has been an integral feature of German security policy. However, two important trends have served to make it more difficult for the armed forces to maintain this form of recruitment. First, the number of conscientious objectors, the right to which is enshrined in the Basic Law, has been high since the late 1960s and generally exceeds the number performing military service. Second, in line with the overall reduction in the size of the armed forces, the duration of military service has fallen sharply since 1990, from twenty months to currently just nine. Taken together, these two trends have certainly raised the question of whether conscription remains appropriate to helping the *Bundeswehr* meet its new challenges, and the smaller political parties (the FDP, Greens and Left Party) have all come out in favour of a professional army. Ultimately, though, conscription is so engrained in Germany's military culture and defence policy that the *Bundeswehr* is unlikely to become an all-volunteer force in the foreseeable future, despite pressure from Germany's major partners to do precisely this (see Longhurst, 2003).

A major impetus for *Bundeswehr* reform has been the development since 1999 of EU foreign and security policy. Germany has been a major player in the development of ESDP, which equips the EU for the first time with military forces for crisis management operations around the globe. Since ESDP has come into effect, Germany has taken the lead in flagship missions in the Balkans, Africa and elsewhere. Of most significance has been the EU's presence in Bosnia-Herzegovina, in which it took over responsibility for peacekeeping from NATO, and its 2006 mission in the Democratic Republic of Congo to support UN troops in their attempt to enforce stability during the 2006 presidential election. Here, Germany, alongside France, provided the largest contingent of troops for the mission, and German generals were in overall command. This 'lead nation' role highlighted the German armed forces' transition from a defensive force focused on the NATO area to a truly mobile force, ready to be deployed even in areas where Germany has had little prior interest. The development of ESDP has also shed light on the responsibilities for burden-sharing which Germany faces in the enlarged EU.

Germany's increasing responsibilities in military crisis management have underlined two central pressures relating to the use of force in German foreign and security policy. The first relates to Germany's ability to afford the investment in the defence budget that will allow the government to equip the armed forces to play a global role. German defence spending has declined steadily since the end of the Cold War. While this has been a general trend across NATO countries, the reduction in German spending has been more pronounced than elsewhere (see Table 10.1). Wedded to this is the relatively poor performance of the German economy and the pressure which this has exerted on public finances overall. Germany currently cannot afford simply to ratchet up defence spending to plug the capability gaps in its armed forces, which will constrain them in their attempts to play a more active part in international crisis management. The second major issue relating to the use of force in Germany is the continued sensitivity within German society concerning the deployment of the *Bundeswehr* for anything other than defensive duties. Successive German governments since the end of the Cold War have sought gradually to increase the range of activities of the *Bundeswehr* in crisis management, while attempting to limit its exposure to high-intensity military operations. Afghanistan has been a case in point. While the German armed forces played a key role in removing the Taliban from power, Chancellor Merkel has been reluctant to deploy the *Bundeswehr* in areas of Afghanistan where high-intensity clashes with the Taliban are most common. So, while the principle of Germany's responsibilities in burden-sharing multinational crisis management operations has become embedded within society, concerns remain about putting German troops in harm's way.

Table 10.1 Average annual defence expenditure as percentage of GDP (current prices), 1985–2004

Year	Germany	UK	France	Italy	United States
1985–9	3.0	4.5	3.7	2.3	6.0
1990–4	2.1	3.7	3.3	2.1	4.6
1995–9	1.6	2.7	2.9	1.9	3.3
2000–4	1.5	2.4	2.5	2.0	3.4

Source: NATO (2005: 7)

Kosovo and Afghanistan

Ironically, the SPD–Green government which took office in the autumn of 1998 was responsible for the decision to deploy West German military forces aggressively for the first time since the Second World War. These parties had both been highly critical of developments under Chancellor Kohl which opened up the possibility of a greater role for the *Bundeswehr* in international crisis management. Also, there was a significant pacifist wing within the Greens which rejected the evolving German involvement in international military crisis management on principle. Kosovo was therefore a defining moment in post-Cold War German foreign and security policy as it broke many of the German taboos surrounding the use of force. Foreign Minister Fischer was very vocal in explaining Germany's responsibility to take part in the military operation against Serbia. He framed his argument along the following lines: whereas the legacy of the Second World War meant that Germany in the past had lived by the maxim 'no more war' (*nie wieder Krieg*), it was now faced with the responsibility for a military operation to prevent the killing and displacement of thousands of Kosovars precisely due to the legacy of German history in the first part of the twentieth century. 'Never again genocide' (*nie wieder Völkermord*) was a much more pressing concern for Germany at the dawn of twenty-first century than avoiding the use of military force at all costs. Thus, humanitarian responsibility became the bedrock of Fischer's thinking on international intervention during his time in office.

Germany's involvement in the military operation against the Taliban in Afghanistan was equally controversial. Schröder's unqualified support and solidarity with the American people following the attacks on New York and Washington on 11 September 2001 left the SPD–Green government with little room for manoeuvre when asked for support by the US government. Germany balanced hard security in the form of *Bundeswehr* participation in Operation Enduring Freedom with significant diplomatic efforts, in the form of the Petersberg Declaration of December 2001, to foster a post-conflict settlement among the main players in Afghanistan. On 16 November 2001, the *Bundestag* agreed to deploy up to 3,900 troops as part of Operation Enduring Freedom. In addition, it agreed on 22 December 2001 to send troops within the United Nations' International Security Assistance Force (ISAF) mission to Afghanistan. Germany has since played a significant role in the reconstruction effort in Afghanistan, maintaining around 2,900 troops in the north of the country in mid-2007. However, it came under criticism for not participating enough in the more intense fighting against Taliban forces in the south of the country. Over time, it seems certain that pressure will grow on the German government to play a more active role in burden-sharing, even in the most dangerous missions. Even so, the current extent of Germany's military commitments abroad should not be underestimated, as the figures from spring 2007 illustrate (Figure 10.1).

Germany's wider foreign policy

Germany's wider foreign policy interests have grown as a result of its global economic reach and through it membership of the EU, NATO and the UN. Since the early 1990s Germany has sought, without success, to secure a permanent seat on the United Nations Security Council. This lack of a permanent seat puts Germany at a relative disadvantage with respect to the UK and France, which have traditionally had more globally engaged foreign policies. That said, Germany's membership of the EU goes some way to lessening this apparent disadvantage, as the EU's Iran diplomacy has demonstrated in recent years. Germany, in tandem with France and the UK, has fronted the EU's diplomatic efforts to

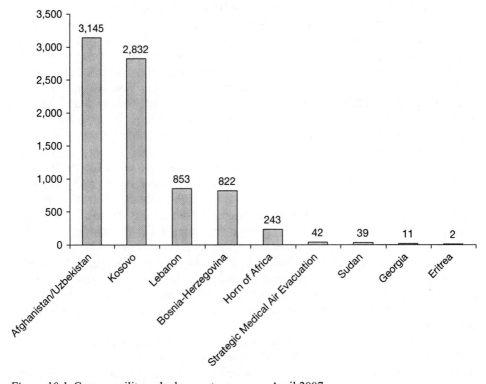

Figure 10.1 German military deployments overseas, April 2007
Source: adapted from www.bundeswehr.de

try to dissuade the Iranian government from pursuing plans to develop a nuclear weapon capability. This close co-operation with France and the UK allows Germany to have a major say in international affairs and provides an example in foreign policy of the EU's big three countries succeeding in forging a common position.

The Middle East remains a top priority for Germany, whose engagement with the region stems from attempts to reconcile with Israel in the 1940s. The legacy of the Holocaust remains a leitmotif of German–Israeli relations. Chancellors from Adenauer to Merkel have reinforced Germany's commitment to defending Israel's right to exist in the face of opposition from regional challengers, such as Iran. Germany's participation in enforcing peace in the Lebanon after the outbreak of violence between Israeli forces and Hezbollah in the summer of 2006 illustrated both Berlin's commitment to the region and the continued singularities of Germany's relationship with Israel. The latter were most obvious in the negotiation of Germany's military deployment as part of the UN's subsequent peacekeeping operation, ensuring that German troops would not come into active combat with Israeli forces. But running alongside Germany's commitments to Israel, the federal government has been a vocal advocate, along with its EU partners, for the claims of Palestinians to establish their own state. The EU has historically been the largest donor of aid to the Palestinian Authority, much of which has come from German coffers. Regional stability in the Middle East is a major goal for German foreign policy, and Germany's membership of such institutions as the Middle East Quad, made up of Russia, the UN, the United States and the EU, is a visible sign of the country's commitment to finding a lasting solution to the Israel–Palestine issue and securing wider regional stability. In the same vein, German criticisms of the US-led invasion of Iraq in 2003 focused on its negative impact on regional stability.

Another major issue for German foreign policy has been its bilateral ties with Russia (Timmins and Gower, 2007). Germany's relations with Russia under Chancellors Schröder and Merkel have come under increased scrutiny. Under Schröder, relations took on a new significance driven by shared views on the Iraq War of 2003 and shared interests in terms of energy policy. While Schröder was widely criticised for developing overly close relations with President Putin, on assuming power Angela Merkel called for a more pragmatic relationship on energy issues with the Russian leader. Rising energy prices, instability in the Middle East and Germany's increasing reliance on Russia for its energy supplies have highlighted the growing importance of maintaining strong German–Russian relations. However, Germany realises that a more coherent EU approach towards Russia is necessary if it is to be more successful in influencing Russia's behaviour, in order to stem Russian influence in the region. In the enlarged EU, sensitivities are evident in Central and Eastern European states over closer German–Russian relations which are often interpreted as ignoring the interests of smaller countries. Europeanising these relations would therefore have the dual advantages of lessening potential exposure to unwanted Russian influence on account of Germany's energy reliance and reducing the concerns of smaller EU member-states who fear they have little influence over issues which concern Russia.

German–Russian relations also highlight tensions in the transatlantic community over the United States' plans for a missile shield which could eventually cover much of Europe. Germany has been caught between Moscow's protestations that the American plans will lead to a return to an East–West arms race and Washington's determination to enforce its current military-industrial advantage before nuclear weapons proliferate further. The renegotiation of the EU–Russia Partnership and Co-operation Agreement, which came to the end of its initial ten-year period in 2007, is a vital diplomatic tool to institutionalise relations between the EU and Russia, and by association NATO and the United States, in order to reinforce patterns of co-operation between Russia and the West. Germany alone cannot shape Russian behaviour and must seek to institutionalise relations in a wider European and transatlantic context to prevent tensions becoming ingrained.

A final area in which there is a discernible German interest is Africa. For years, Germany was content to let former major colonial states such as France and the UK take the lead on discussions in the EU involving the African continent. But this has begun to change in recent years thanks largely to Germany's involvement in the EU's foreign policy activities. The EU is the largest aid donor in the world, and a large part of its aid budget is directed towards African states. Germany has also been involved in crisis management operations in the region, most notably in the Democratic Republic of the Congo in 2006. Since taking office in 2005, President Horst Köhler has been influential in raising the profile of Africa within the German political community. Germany's policy in the continent is largely targeted through the EU to combat political instability, to help African states to deal with the challenges of globalisation, and to support the efforts of those states most badly affected by the AIDS virus. The Federal Ministry for Economic Aid and Development and the Foreign Ministry are the lead institutions for dealing with Germany's relations with African states both bilaterally and within the EU. While the German government has set out substantial goals for helping African states fulfil their potential, these policies have lacked sufficient resources to be implemented effectively (Molt, 2006).

Nevertheless, Germany's engagement with Africa is likely to continue to grow in the foreseeable future. A clear sign of this was the inclusion of Africa on the German presidency's agenda for the G8 summit of leading industrial nations at Heiligendamm in June 2007.

Conclusion

Germany has consistently been described as a middle-ranking power in the international system. This persists despite the country throwing off the shackles of the Cold War system and overcoming the 1949 division of the country, which left Germany, in relative terms, a more powerful state, particularly vis-à-vis France and the United Kingdom. Some theorists explain Germany's power status as being the result of persistent policies which preclude unilateral, power-seeking behaviour. This contrasts with realist writings which predicted the rise of German aspirations to Great Power status once the restrictions of the Cold War had been overcome. The true answer to the puzzle of the limitations of German influence and power in the world fall somewhere between these two positions. In practice, Germany continues to have a restricted view of its ability to exert power in the international community and has therefore failed to attain the label 'Great Power'.

Within Germany there has been a noticeable absence of debate on Germany's foreign policy direction in response to the events of 11 September 2001. Now that the Cold War is over and Europe is largely at peace, foreign policy ranks lower in importance for a Germany that is surrounded by friendly states. In addition, the major domestic difficulties which Germany faces have meant that its politicians are more concerned with kick-starting the economy and reducing unemployment than thinking about what Germany's foreign and security policy should be. As a result, Hanns Maull (2006) has written of Germany's 'uncertain power', highlighting the country's continued hesitation over its foreign policy direction and its increasing inability to influence major developments on the international stage. While Germany may indeed be trying to be more assertive, the economic resource crunch that it now labours under has had a clear effect on investment in military hardware.

Germany needs effective and efficient multilateral institutions to make its presence felt in world affairs. Its lack of a permanent seat on the UN Security Council limits its ability to persuade the highest levels of global politics and its foreign policy therefore remains heavily reliant on its ability to persuade other states within multilateral frameworks. US President George W. Bush's policy of bypassing multilateral institutions in favour of more flexible, ad-hoc co-operation with allied states has therefore created problems for Germany. However, it has found ways around difficulties in forging multilateral agreement through its involvement in small-group co-operation with leading states, such as in the NATO Quad (USA, UK, France, Germany) or in the so-called *directoire* (leading group) of the CFSP, with France and the UK, which has been active in seeking a solution to the Iran nuclear question on behalf of the EU.

Questions for discussion

1 **What sort of power is Germany?**
2 **Why does Germany continue to resist having a fully professional army?**
3 **Why does Germany continue to rely so much on multilateral institutions in its foreign and security policy.**

Further reading

Haftendorn, H. (2006), *Coming of Age: German Foreign Policy since 1945* (London: Rowman and Littlefield). An overview of the factors behind the development of German foreign policy since the Second World War.

Maull, H. (ed.) (2006), *Germany's Uncertain Power: Foreign Policy of the Berlin Republic* (Basingstoke: Palgrave). A comprehensive and accessible examination of the current state of German foreign policy.

Useful website

<http://www.deutsche-aussenpolitik.de/> an excellent source for up-to-date analysis and primary sources in English and German dealing with German foreign and security policy.

11 Conclusion

Three themes reassessed

The preceding chapters have provided a survey of the key issues and debates that make up the politics of the new Germany. Inevitably, a textbook such as this has not been able to cover every single aspect and nuance of such a broad field: issues of judicial politics, the role of religion and of the media, as well as the structure of public administration, have, for example, received relatively little attention. Moreover, the issue of gender, although touched upon in Chapters 5 and 8, could be addressed only tangentially and not as a topic in its own right. Perhaps most of all, two key policy areas, namely education and the environment, could also not be included here for simple reasons of space.

Yet, even without these areas, the three main themes of the book – reconciliation, consensus and transformation – are clearly in evidence. The theme of reconciliation, for example, particularly characterises European policy (Chapter 9), as well as underpinning Germany's continued preference for conscription (Chapter 10). It explains Germany's approach, at least initially, to asylum policy (Chapter 6). It also impacts on institutional structures (Chapter 4): Germany's federalism, its central government and its civil society all bear the unmistakable hallmark of history and the desire to achieve reconciliation by learning from the mistakes of the past. The main historical point of reference remains Nazi Germany, but it is not the only one: the principle that the central bank (the *Bundesbank* and now the European Central Bank) should have operational independence in controlling inflation, arguably one of the secrets of West Germany's economic success, is, for example, an explicit response to the trauma of hyperinflation in the early 1920s.

Consensus, too, is clearly visible, and can simultaneously be considered as a corollary of the process of reconciliation. In Germany, as Chapter 4 illustrated, outright majoritarian politics, where the political majority simply imposes its will on the minority in the way that is common in, say, Great Britain, remains very much the exception; instead, the 'politics of centrality' still tends to be, broadly speaking, the yardstick (Smith, 1976). Often, this degree of consensus has extended to tacit co-operation between the parties. The party political appointment of key positions in public broadcasting is, for instance, a key element of the characterisation of Germany as a *Parteienstaat* (as discussed in Chapter 5). Consensus is also one of the traditional features of *Modell Deutschland*, for instance in industrial relations, which have been generally harmonious. Lastly, consensus even extends to Germany's international relations, where its actions have largely been defined by acting in concert with partner states in an instinctively multilateralist approach (Chapter 10).

But, equally, the preceding chapters tell a tale of transformation. Germany is facing a range of very significant challenges, of which three principal examples can be identified.

First, its international environment has changed fundamentally. Germany, as a major trading nation, is now exposed to the full forces of economic globalisation with all that this entails for the *Standortdebatte* (Chapter 7). It has also transformed its security and defence policy to play a more active role in crisis management within the context of the EU and NATO, and has had to take more responsibility for European security since Europe became less of a priority for the United States in the post-9/11 era (Chapter 10). In essence, Germany is now required to take on a much greater degree of active responsibility than in the past, not only for its own security but for shaping Europe and the wider world.

Second, Germany's social structure is undergoing far-reaching change. As Chapter 6 showed, in the coming thirty years Germans will become, on average, older, and the country will in all likelihood experience a reduction in the number of people who live there. In addition, Germany will have a much more diverse population in ethnic and cultural terms. But social change also extends into areas of employment and voting behaviour. Thus, changing employment patterns are reflected in the decline in union membership; in turn, this is mirrored in the decline of the SPD's core electorate. Indeed, the 'dealignment' of voting patterns (Chapter 5) can in general be linked to this gradual transformation of German society. Together, these changes in social structure constitute a real challenge to the organisation of politics at all levels in Germany, which has hitherto been predicated on and legitimated by strong social organisations, such as unions and political parties. So far, a new (possibly even postmodern) constellation of organised interests has failed to emerge; instead, traditional mass-membership organisations in Germany remain firmly on the retreat.

The third and arguably most important challenge is that of public finance (see Streeck, forthcoming). The implications of the resource crisis in state income and expenditure cannot be overstated. They affect and stymie all areas of domestic and foreign policy: without adequate resources, Germany is unable to pursue any meaningful goals in foreign policy and European integration (Chapters 9 and 10); nor is it able to invest in vital areas for the future, such as education. More immediately, the effects of the sustained squeeze on public finance, whether at federal, *Land* or municipal level, are becoming increasingly visible to the casual observer. This is especially the case in the western part of the country, where the public infrastructure, much of which dates back to the 1960s and is now showing its age, has not been replaced due to the priority the new *Länder* have taken in public investment plans. On a purely anecdotal level, university buildings are often in very poor condition, playground equipment has not been renewed and potholes remain unfilled in municipal road surfaces up and down the country.

The extent of the crisis in public finances is typified by the fact that Germany fell foul of the EU's Stability and Growth Pact for four consecutive years between 2002 and 2005 (Chapter 7). Indeed, an ever-increasing level of public debt appears now to be politically entirely acceptable: when it transpired in early 2007 that Germany had not transgressed the Stability and Growth Pact in 2006, this was heralded as a major success and immediately led to new demands for more spending from across the political spectrum. But in the clamour of self-acclamation, what got lost was that the public sector still incurred new debt to the tune of 1.7 per cent of GDP in 2006 (see Table 3.1) – in other words, debt was still increasing, just at a slower rate than before. Moreover, there is no guarantee that this upward trend in government finances and GDP growth during 2007 can be sustained over several, as opposed to individual, years: first, economic growth may slow again; second, interest rates may rise, with each quarter of a percentage point rise costing the federal government almost €1.9 billion in additional debt servicing annually (cited in Streeck, forthcoming); and, lastly, substantial new tax-financed commitments were included in the 2007 healthcare reform, which have yet to be incorporated into spending plans (Chapter 8). Tellingly, while the 2006 deficit level by itself would be of no concern, other EU member-states (Denmark, Ireland and Finland) actually ran up budget *surpluses* in every year between 2003 and 2006. The German state is thus living beyond its means, and is getting used to doing so.

As Chapter 8 showed, the underlying problem with public finances is that the federal government's hands are effectively tied in terms of addressing the fundamentals of the issue. On the one hand, two items dominate the federal budget: welfare and debt. In particular, the federal subsidy to the pension funds constitutes an enormous drain on resources, and it is all the more notable because the pension system is in principle supposed to be financed from contributions alone. Yet the principles of *Vertrauensschutz* and *Verhältnismäßigkeit* leave the federal government, whatever its political complexion, practically no room for manoeuvre in terms of cutting its own expenditure in this area, except in the very long term. On the other hand, the only other option in the short term, namely raising contribution rates to make the system truly self-financing, would inevitably lead to a further major increase to the already high levels of non-wage labour costs. With significant political costs attached to all proposals for reform, it is not surprising that political parties have preferred incremental policy change to a root-and-branch review of pensions in particular, and welfare in general. In practice, these three challenges are interlinked. Thus, the crisis in public finance is a major impediment to Germany playing its proper role on the international stage; at the same time, the changes in its social structure, including demographic change, make it more difficult for governments to solve the fiscal conundrum in a lasting fashion.

The impact of unification

Of course, in the context of the above discussion, the 'elephant in the room' is unification. This has undoubtedly had a seminal effect on Germany in the new millennium, in two specific ways. First, it has changed the structures that shape policy preferences, both internally and externally. Internally, as Chapter 4 demonstrated, the addition of five new *Länder* and eastern Berlin has served to complicate the formation of politically aligned majorities in both the *Bundestag* and the *Bundesrat*, thereby contributing decisively to the notion of *Reformstau*. It has also led to increased diversity within the party landscape, with a quite different party system to the rest of the country, underpinned by different political values, crystallising in eastern Germany (Chapter 5). Externally, unification (and the end of the Cold War more broadly) has changed Germany's entire international context (Chapter 10), unleashed significant new levels of immigration (Chapter 6) and provided a decisive impulse towards the single-currency project at Maastricht in 1991 (Chapter 9). Lastly, unification removed one of the principal obstacles to the modernisation of German citizenship (Chapter 6) – without the collapse of the GDR, it is difficult to see how the 1999 Citizenship Law would ever have been passed.

As well as changing the structures of the Federal Republic, unification has posed a significant challenge to Germany. Most obviously, this has been in the form of an economic shock so great that it is a testament to the massive underlying strength of the German economy that it coped with it as well as it did; it is certainly doubtful whether any other country in the world would have had the resources to have done any better.

Nonetheless, high unemployment and low GDP growth in the east have taken their toll on German economic performance over the past fifteen years (see Chapter 3), and they are likely to continue to do so for decades to come. A further economic shock linked to unification and the end of the Cold War has been the growing impact of globalisation. Suddenly, German companies are no longer in competition with counterparts just from the USA or the rest of Western Europe, but from all over the world. In comparison with countries such as China and India, German labour costs (including the non-wage element) are prohibitively uncompetitive.

In turn, the economic impact of unification lies at the heart of Germany's current fiscal crisis. By increasing its total public debt by almost 50 per cent in the space of less than ten years, Germany has effectively taken out a huge, indefinite mortgage in order to finance unification. The implications of this in terms of interest payments will also be felt in public finances for many years to come. Even more importantly, unification has placed formidable pressure on welfare expenditure in Germany (see Chapter 8), which has disproportionately been spent in the east. But because the statutory insurance schemes are financed through contributions by employers and employees, in other words by making welfare effectively a tax on employment, rising welfare expenditure has simultaneously increased the incentive for employers to reduce their costs by restructuring their workforces into different types of employment, such as mini- or midi-jobs, or outsourcing production to cheaper countries (Chapter 7). The real challenge for governments in the future will be to move away from the current contributions-based system towards a tax-based system of financing welfare without bankrupting the German state.

In addition to the economic challenges, unification has, perhaps unexpectedly, created a new challenge of identity in united Germany, which rather supersedes the unanswered question it inherited from West Germany as to whether it was a country of immigration (Chapter 6). It has become clear that, despite all official rhetoric to the contrary, western Germans and eastern Germans are divided by significant differences, not only in material terms, but in terms of values and identities (Chapter 3). In truth, whether or not Germany in 2007 possesses 'enough' inner unity is perhaps the wrong question to ask: there is an overwhelming consensus that supports the country's constitutional settlement, its political order and, broadly speaking, the social market economy; the days of significant parties seeking to overthrow the state are long since gone. But serious socio-economic and political divisions are rarely seen as positive forces in creating societal cohesion; something Germany has not always had in abundance since 1990. The success (or otherwise) of the drive to drag the eastern German economy into the twenty-first century therefore remains pivotal to increasing levels of social satisfaction in that region.

One further impact of unification needs to be mentioned here. The scale and extent of the economic challenges thrown up by unification, which pervade practically all aspects of public policy, have fundamentally challenged the consensual nature of politics in Germany. Chapter 7 showed how the established patterns of partnership within *Modell Deutschland* have been breaking up since the mid-1990s, with large companies adopting a much more 'shareholder value'-orientated approach to business. This inevitably produces a more confrontational pattern of interactions with other stakeholders, especially unions. Furthermore, the twin challenges of unemployment and welfare state reform have stretched consensual patterns of policy-making, both between the established parties and between government and civil society, to breaking point. Both the failure of the Alliance for Jobs in 2003 and Chancellor Schröder's subsequent announcement of

Agenda 2010, which brought his government into direct conflict with the unions, normally the SPD's traditional allies, can be seen in this light. In parallel, as Chapter 8 pointed out, pensions and healthcare have now become highly contested party political battlegrounds. Consensus politics has clearly come under strain in the new Germany.

At the same time, one of the central messages of this book is that unification in several key cases did not *cause* the challenges facing Germany, but merely *amplified* them. As Chapter 6 showed, immigration to West Germany began long before unification, and the roots of the challenges linked to it stretch back to this time. Similarly, the demographic trends identified here were clearly visible in the 1980s. Indeed, the politicisation of immigration as an issue also dates back to this time (Green, 2004). Likewise, the dealignment of the party system and the decline in union membership (Chapters 5 and 7) can both be traced back to the same period. Most notably, as Chapter 8 showed, the problems of the welfare state, especially in pensions, date back to the 1970s and even the late 1950s. However, in all three areas, the pressures of unification have revealed traditional responses and established patterns of incremental policy-making (Chapter 4) to be inadequate to the scale of the challenge.

Taken together, the preceding chapters therefore provide a multi-layered picture of the politics of the new Germany. On the next page, Table 11.1 provides a summary of how the various themes which have been raised in the course of this book impact on the areas discussed in individual chapters.

Conclusion

What does the future hold for Germany and its politics? By focusing on broad issues and debates, the intention of this book has been to highlight the themes and challenges that affect all German governments, regardless of their party political composition. And evidently the economic impact of unification, the fiscal crisis of the state, the demographic transformation and the reform of the welfare system will all remain recurring themes over the coming ten to twenty years. Put differently, the political agenda, barring the unexpected, is more-or-less established for a generation.

The real question is whether established patterns of policy-making, as summed up by the notion of the semi-sovereign state producing incremental policy outcomes (Chapter 4), can generate plausible solutions to Germany's ongoing, and arguably increasing, problems. Here, the evidence is inconclusive. Certainly, the cumulative effect of (individually incremental) reforms should not be underestimated. Thanks to several moderate wage rounds, German labour has become highly competitive internationally and the unexpectedly strong economic growth in 2007, combined with a drop in unemployment, indicate that reforms such as *Hartz IV* may be starting to have a tangible effect. Some authors, notably Peter Katzenstein (2005), also believe in the resilience of semi-sovereignty as a normative notion, in other words as a pattern of governance to which Germany *should* aspire. On the other hand, it remains to be seen whether Germany's economic recovery is sustainable over time in light of two key pressures which affect both policy outputs and the social foundations on which semi-sovereignty is constructed. First, demographic change not only affects the welfare state but also the structure of the electorate by spawning a new young-versus-old 'cleavage'. Second, the long-term changes in employment and work patterns (Chapter 7) fundamentally affect two central constituent elements of the semi-sovereign state, namely political parties and interest representation. How will this affect policy outcomes? On top of these, the long-term fiscal crisis of the

Table 11.1 Thematising the politics of the new Germany

Area	Role of history/ reconciliation	Evidence of consensus politics	Structural changes through unification	Transformation pressures		
				Unification as an external shock	Fiscal resource pressures	Changes in social structure
German unity (Chapter 3)	High	High	Yes	Yes	Yes	Yes
The political system (Chapter 4)	High	High	Yes	No	Yes	No
The party system (Chapter 5)	Medium	High	Yes	No	No	Yes
Economic management (Chapter 6)	High	Low	Yes	Yes	Yes	Yes
Immigration and demographics (Chapter 7)	Medium	Medium	No	Yes	No	Yes
Welfare state (Chapter 8)	Medium	Medium	No	Yes	Yes	Yes
European policy (Chapter 9)	High	High	Yes	No	Yes	No
Foreign and security policy (Chapter 10)	Medium	High	Yes	No	Yes	No

state is such that any new policy initiative to reflect the changing nature of German society, such as family policy, can only rarely be financed without major political effort.

Ultimately, this leads us to the question of whether Germany is heading towards a major 'tipping point' – a juncture in the future at which problems will have accumulated, albeit gradually, to such an extent as to lead to a more fundamental reorientation of policy or structures (see Dyson, 2005b). While the answer to this question is undoubtedly speculative, it is notable, based on current trends of fertility and migration, that Germany's population is predicted to start falling from around 2020 onwards. This might therefore seem a plausible future tipping point. That said, much can change before then. In particular, the impact of external factors such as globalisation, something which has certainly affected Germany already (Chapter 7) is potentially significant, yet also difficult to predict. Equally, globalisation need not always constitute a threat to Germany: indeed, the 2007 economic upturn was, as has traditionally been the case, linked to strong growth in exports by German companies.

One final overarching theme which has been touched upon at various points in this book remains to be addressed: is Germany now a *normal* state (see Pulzer, 1996; Cooke and Taberner, 2006)? Inevitably, how this question is answered depends on the definition that is adopted. Certainly, Germany is normal in that it is now inconceivable that any German government should threaten other European nation-states through expansionist aggression in the way it has done in the past. German governments in the 'Berlin Republic' may act slightly differently to those of the Bonn era, but there is little evidence of the belligerence that some feared. In that sense, it has mastered its history and has taken its place among those countries in the world lucky enough to benefit from exceptionally high levels of wealth. But, on the other hand, all countries are defined by their history: the UK's imperial legacy and France's republicanism are just two examples of how no country can escape its past. Perhaps the simplest test to this question lies in the constellation of issues on the political agenda. In that context, the fact that politics in Germany is now defined more by mundane issues such as unemployment and public finances than by the spectre of national socialism is a testament to how far the country has come since 1945.

Questions for discussion

1   **Is Germany in a crisis and is it unsolvable?**
2   **Is united Germany a 'normal' state?**

References

This book has made extensive use of official data from electronic sources. Unless otherwise stated, we have used data from the German statistical office (Statistisches Bundesamt – <http://www.destatis.de>) and the EU's statistical agency, Eurostat (<http://ec.europa.eu/eurostat>) throughout. Although websites inevitably change in terms of content, we would hope that data from these sources will remain more or less constantly available. Where other data have been used, we have made every effort to use reputable sources, such as respected election reporting websites or opinion poll agencies. See the references in the text and below for more details.

Albert, M. (1992), *Capitalism against Capitalism* (London: Whurr).

Almond, G. and S. Verba (1963), *The Civic Culture: Political Attitudes and Democracy in Five Nations* (Princeton, NJ: Princeton University Press).

Anderson, B. (1991), *Imagined Communities: Reflections on the Origin and Spread of Nationalism* (London: Verso).

Anderson, J. (1997), 'Hard Interests, Soft Power, and Germany's Changing Role in Europe', in P. Katzenstein (ed.), *Tamed Power: Germany in Europe* (Ithaca NY: Cornell University Press).

—— (1999), *German Unification and the Union of Europe: The Domestic Politics of Integration Policy* (Cambridge: Cambridge University Press).

—— (2005), 'Germany and Europe: Centrality in the EU', in S. Bulmer and C. Lequesne (eds), *The Member States of the European Union* (Oxford: Oxford University Press)

Assman, J. (1999), *Das kulturelle Gedächtnis: Schrift, Erinnerung und politische Identität in frühen Hochkulturen* (Munich: Verlag C.H. Beck).

Augstein, R. *et al.* (1987), *Historikerstreit. Die Dokumentation der Kontroverse um die Einzigartigkeit der nationalsozialistischen Judenvernichtung* (Munich: Piper).

Aust, S. (1998), *Der Baader-Meinhof Komplex* (Munich: Goldmann).

Bade, K. (1994), *Ausländer, Aussiedler, Asyl* (Munich: Verlag C.H. Beck).

Bandelow, N. (2007), 'Health Policy: Obstacles to Policy Convergence in Britain and Germany', *German Politics* 16/1: 150–63.

Barker, P. (ed.) (2000), *The GDR and Its History* (Amsterdam: Rodopi).

Basic Law (2005), <http://www.constitution.org/cons/germany.txt> (viewed 11 November 2005).

Beschloss, M. (2002), *The Conquerors: Roosevelt, Truman and the Destruction of Hitler's Germany, 1941–1945* (London: Simon and Schuster).

Beyer, J. and M. Höpner (2003), 'Corporate Governance and the Disintegration of Organised Capitalism in the 1990s', *West European Politics* 26/4: 179–98.

Blankenburg, E. (1996), 'Changes in Political Regimes and Continuity of the Rule of Law in Germany', in H. Jacob, E. Blankenburg, H. Kritzer, D. Provine and J. Sanders, *Courts, Law and Politics in Comparative Perspective* (New Haven, CT: Yale University Press).

Bleses, P. and M. Seeleib-Kaiser (2004), *The Dual Transformation of the German Welfare State* (Basingstoke: Palgrave).

Blondel, J. (1968), 'Party Systems and Patterns of Government in Western Democracies', *Canadian Journal of Political Science* 1/2: 180–203.

BMAS (2006), *Statistisches Taschenbuch 2006: Arbeits- und Sozialstatistik* (Berlin: Bundesministerium für Arbeit und Sozialordnung).

Bomberg, E. and J. Peterson (2000), 'Policy Transfer and Europeanization: Passing the Heineken Test?', *Queens Papers on Europeanisation*, 2/2000 (Belfast: Queens University).

Börzel, T. (2001), 'Non-compliance in the European Union: Pathology or Statistical Artifact?', *Journal of European Public Policy* 8/5: 803–24.

Börzel, T. and T. Risse (2000), 'When Europe Hits Home: Europeanization and Domestic Change', European University Institute, RSC Working Paper, 56/2000.

Brockmann, S. (1990), 'The Politics of German History', *History and Theory* 29/2: 179–89.

Brubaker, R. (1992), *Citizenship and Nationhood in France and Germany* (Cambridge, MA: Harvard University Press).

Bulmer, S. and M. Burch (2000), 'Coming to Terms with Europe: Europeanisation, Whitehall and the Challenge of Devolution', *Queen's Papers on Europeanisation*, 9/2000 (Belfast: Queens University).

Bulmer, S., C. Jeffery and W. Paterson (2000), *Germany's European Diplomacy: Shaping the Regional Milieu* (Manchester: Manchester University Press).

Bulmer, S. and W. Paterson (1987), *The Federal Republic of Germany and the European Community* (London: Allen and Unwin).

—— (1996), 'Germany in the European Union: Gentle Giant or Emergent Leader?', *International Affairs* 72/1: 9–32.

Busch, A. (2005a), 'Globalisation and National Varieties of Capitalism: The Contested Viability of the "German Model"', *German Politics* 14/2: 125–39.

—— (2005b), 'Shock-Absorbers under Stress: Parapublic Institutions and the Double Challenge of German Unification and European Integration', in S. Green and W. Paterson (eds), *Governance in Contemporary Germany: The Semisovereign State Revisited* (Cambridge: Cambridge University Press).

Busemeyer, M. (2005), 'Pension Reform in Germany and Austria: System Change versus Quantitative Retrenchment', *West European Politics* 28/3: 569–91.

Campbell, A., P. Converse, W. Miller and D. Stokes (1960), *The American Voter* (Chicago: University of Chicago Press).

Chirac, J. (2000), 'Our Europe', Speech to the *Bundestag*, Berlin, 27 June, reproduced in B. F. Nelson and A. Stubb (eds) (2003), *The European Union: Readings on the Theory and Practice of European Integration* (Basingstoke: Palgrave).

Cooke, P. (2005), *Representing East Germany: From Colonisation to Nostalgia* (Oxford: Berg).

Cooke, P. and S. Taberner (eds) (2006), *German Culture, Politics and Literature into the Twenty-first Century: Beyond Normalisation* (Columbia, MD: Camden House).

Crawford, B. (1996), 'Explaining Defection from International Cooperation: Germany's Unilateral Recognition of Croatia', *World Politics* 48/4: 482–521.

Czada, R. (2005), 'Social Policy: Crisis and Transformation', in S. Green and W. Paterson (eds), *Governance in Contemporary Germany: The Semisovereign State Revisited* (Cambridge: Cambridge University Press).

Dahrendorf, R. (1968), *Society and Democracy in Germany* (London: Weidenfeld and Nicolson).

Dalton, R. (1996), 'A Divided Electorate', in G. Smith, W. Paterson and P. Merkl (eds), *Developments in German Politics* (Basingstoke: Macmillan).

—— (2002), *Citizen Politics* (New York: Chatham House).

—— (2003), 'Voter Choice and Electoral Politics', in S. Padgett, W. Paterson and G. Smith (eds), *Developments in German Politics 3* (Basingstoke: Palgrave).

Deeg, R. (2005), 'The Comeback of "Modell Deutschland": The New German Political Economy in the EU', *German Politics* 14/3: 332–53.

Dennis, M. and N. LaPorte (2003), *The Stasi: Myth and Reality* (London: Longman).

'In der Falle', *Der Spiegel*, 19 March 2007.

'Kollektiv verantwortungslos', *Der Spiegel*, 3 July 2006.

Deutscher Bundestag (2006), *Bericht der Bundesregierung über die Entwicklung der Finanzhilfen des Bundes und der Steuervergünstigungen für die Jahre 2003 bis 2006 (20. Subventionsbericht)*, Bundestagsdrucksache 16/1020, <http://dip.bundestag.de/btd/16/010/1601020.pdf> (viewed 13 March 2007).

Dornberg, J. (1996), 'Five Years after Unification – Easterners Discover Themselves', *German Life*, January 1996, <http://www.germanlife.com/Archives/1995/9512_01.html> (viewed 10 January 2007).

Duckenfield, M. and N. Calhoun (1997), 'Invasion of the Western Ampelmännchen', *German Politics* 6/3: 54–69.

Dümcke, W. and F. Vilmar (eds) (1996), *Kolonialisierung der DDR* (Münsher: Agenda).

Dyson, K. (1982), 'West Germany: The Search for a Rationalist Consensus', in J. Richardson (ed.), *Policy Styles in Western Europe* (London: Allen and Unwin).

—— (2003), 'The Europeanisation of German Governance', in S. Padgett, W. Paterson and G. Smith (eds), *Developments in German Politics 3* (Basingstoke: Palgrave).

—— (2005a), 'Binding Hands as a Strategy for Economic Reform: Government by Commission', *German Politics* 14/2: 224–47.

—— (2005b), 'Economic Policy Management: Catastrophic Equilibrium, Tipping Points and Crisis Interventions', in S. Green and W. Paterson (eds), *Governance in Contemporary Germany: The Semisovereign State Revisited* (Cambridge: Cambridge University Press).

Dyson, K. and K. Featherstone (1999), *The Road to Maastricht* (Oxford: Oxford University Press).

Dyson, K. and K. Goetz (eds) (2004), *Germany, Europe, and the Politics of Constraint* (Oxford: Oxford University Press/British Academy).

Dyson, K. and S. Padgett (eds) (2006), *The Politics of Economic Reform in Germany* (London: Routledge); special issue of *German Politics* 14/2.

Elias, N. (1996), *The Germans: Power Struggles and the Development of Habitus in the Nineteenth and Twentieth Centuries* (Cambridge: Polity Press).

Esping-Andersen, G. (1990), *The Three Worlds of Welfare Capitalism* (Cambridge: Polity Press).

Eurobarometer (2006), *Eurobarometer Survey*, 66, <http://ec.europa.eu/public_opinion/archives/eb/eb66/eb66_en.htm> (viewed 10 April 2007).

Feldman, G. (1997), *The Great Disorder: Politics, Economics, and Society in the German Inflation, 1914–1924* (Oxford: Oxford University Press).

Fischer, J. (2000), 'From Confederacy to Federation: Thoughts on the Finality of European Integration', speech to the Humboldt University, 12 May, available at <http://www.jeanmonnet program.org/papers/00/joschka_fischer_en.rtf> (viewed 10 April 2007).

'France Will Be Punished', *Daily Telegraph*, 2 June 2003.

Frankland, E. and D. Schoonmaker (1992), *Between Protest and Power: Green Party in Germany* (Boulder, CO: Westview).

Frei, N. (2003), *Hitlers Eliten nach 1945* (Munich: DTV).

Friedrich, J. (2002), *Der Brand: Deutschland im Bombenkrieg* (Munich: Propyläen).

Fulbrook, M. (1997), *Anatomy of a Dictatorship: Inside the GDR, 1949–89* (Oxford: Oxford University Press).

—— (2000), *Interpretations of the Two Germanies, 1945–1990* (Basingstoke: Palgrave).

—— (2002), *History of Germany, 1918–2000* (Oxford: Blackwell).

Garrett, C. (2001), 'Towards a New Model of German Capitalism? The Mannesmann–Vodafone Merger and Its Implications', *German Politics* 10/3: 83–102.

Garton Ash, T. (1993), *In Europe's Name* (London: Vintage).

—— (1994), 'Germany's Choice', *Foreign Affairs* 73/4: 65–81.

—— (1997), *The File: A Personal History* (London: Random House).

Ginsberg, R. (2001), *The European Union in International Politics: Baptism by Fire* (Oxford: Rowman and Littlefield).

Glenny, M. (1999), *The Balkans, 1804–1999: Nationalism, War and the Great Powers* (London: Granta).

Goldhagen, D. (1997), *Hitler's Willing Executioners: Ordinary Germans and the Holocaust* (London: Little, Brown).

Görtemaker, M. (2004), *Geschichte des Bundesrepublik Deutschland: Von der Gründung bis zur Gegenwart* (Frankfurt/Main: Fischer).

Green, S. (2004), *The Politics of Exclusion: Institutions and Immigration Policy in Contemporary Germany* (Manchester: Manchester University Press).

—— (2005), 'Between Ideology and Pragmatism: The Politics of Dual Nationality in Germany', *International Migration Review* 39/4: 921–52.

—— (2007), 'Divergent Traditions, Convergent Responses: Immigration and Integration Policy in the UK and Germany', *German Politics* 16/1: 95–115.

Green, S. and W. Paterson (eds) (2005), *Governance in Contemporary Germany: The Semisovereign State Revisited* (Cambridge: Cambridge University Press).

Grix, J. (2000a), 'East German Political Attitudes. Socialist Legacies vs. Situational Factors: A False Antithesis', *German Politics* 9/2: 109–24.

—— (2000b), *The Role of the Masses in the Collapse of East Germany* (Basingstoke: Macmillan).

Habermas, J. (1986), 'Eine Art Schadensabwicklung: Die apologetischen Tendenzen in der deutschen Zeitgeschichtsschreibung', *Die Zeit*, 18 July.

—— (2001), *The Postnational Constellation: Political Essays* (Cambridge, MA: MIT Press).

Haftendorn, H. (2006), *Coming of Age: German Foreign Policy since 1945* (London: Rowman and Littlefield).

Hall, P. and D. Soskice (2001), *Varieties of Capitalism: The Institutional Foundations of Comparative Advantage* (Oxford: Oxford University Press).

Hamilton, D. (1989), 'Dateline East Germany: The Wall behind the Wall', *Foreign Policy* 76: 176–97.

Harding, R. (2007), 'The Unmovable Elephant: Germany and the UK's Competitiveness Jungle', *German Politics* 16/1: 137–49.

Harnisch, S. and H. Maull (eds) (2001), *Germany – Still a Civilian Power? The Foreign Policy of the Berlin Republic* (Manchester: Manchester University Press).

Harnisch, S. and S. Schieder (2006), 'Germany's New European Policy: Weaker, Leaner, Meaner', in H. Maull (ed.), *Germany's Uncertain Power* (Basingstoke: Palgrave).

Hassner, P. (1982), 'The Shifting Foundations', *Foreign Policy* 48/3: 3–20.

Hay, C. and D. Marsh (eds) (2001), *Demystifying Globalization* (Basingstoke: Palgrave).

Hellmann, G. (ed.) (2006), *Germany's EU Policy on Asylum and Defence: De-Europeanization by Default?* (Basingstoke: Palgrave).

Helms, L. (2004), *Presidents, Prime Ministers and Chancellors: Executive Leadership in Western Democracies* (Basingstoke: Palgrave).

Henson, P. and N. Malhan (1995), 'Endeavours to Export a Migration Crisis: Policy Making and Europeanisation in the German Migration Dilemma', *German Politics* 4/3: 128–44.

Herbert, U. (2001), *Geschichte der Ausländerpolitik in Deutschland* (Munich: C.H. Beck).

Hirschman, A. (1993) 'Exit, Voice and the Fate of the German Democratic Republic: An Essay in Conceptual History', *World Politics* 45/2: 173–202.

Hodge, C. (1998), 'Botching the Balkans: Germany's Recognition of Slovenia and Croatia', *Ethics and International Affairs* 12/8: 1–18.

Holbrooke, R. (1998), *To End a War* (New York: Random House).

Hough, D. (2002), 'The Many Faces of Europeanization', *Journal of Common Market Studies* 40/5: 921–52.

—— (2005), 'The Programmatic Development of the Eastern German PDS: Learning What from Whom and under What Conditions?', *Journal of Communist Studies and Transition Politics* 21/1: 142–60.

Hough, D. and C. Jeffery (2006), *Devolution in Comparative Context* (Manchester: Manchester University Press).

Hough, D., M. Koß and J. Olsen (2007), *The Left Party in Contemporary German Politics* (Basingstoke: Palgrave).

Huelshoff, M., J. Sperling and M. Hess (2005), 'Is Germany a Good European? German Compliance with EU Law', *German Politics* 14/3: 354–70.

Huntington, N. and T. Bale (2002), 'New Labour: New Christian Democracy', *Political Quarterly* 73/1: 44–50.

Hutton, W. (1996), *The State We're In* (London: Vintage).

Infratest Dimap (2005a), <http://www.infratest-dimap.de/?id=51> (viewed 11 November 2005).

—— (2005b), <http://www.tns-infratest.com/03_presse/Presse/ 2005_01_20_TNS_Infratest_ Reputation.pdf> (viewed 11 November 2005).

Jacoby, W. (2000), *Imitation and Politics: Redesigning Modern Germany* (Ithaca, NY: Cornell University Press).

—— (2005), 'Institutional Transfer: Can Semisovereignty be Transferred? The Political Economy of Eastern Germany', in S. Green and W. Paterson (eds), Governance in Contemporary Germany: The Semisovereign State Revisited (Cambridge: Cambridge University Press).

Jarausch, K. (2006), *After Hitler: Recivilizing Germans, 1945–1995* (Oxford: Oxford University Press).

Jeffery, C. (1995), 'The Non-Reform of the German Federal System after Unification', *West European Politics* 18/2: 252–72.

—— (1999), 'Party Politics and Territorial Representation in the Federal Republic of Germany', *West European Politics* 22/2: 130–66.

—— (2005), 'Federalism: The New Territorialism', in S. Green and W. Paterson (eds), *Governance in Contemporary Germany: The Semisovereign State Revisited* (Cambridge: Cambridge University Press).

Jeffery, C. and D. Hough (2001), 'The Electoral Cycle and Multi-Level Voting in Germany', *German Politics* 10/2: 73–98.

—— (2006), 'Germany: An Erosion of Federal–Länder Linkages', in D. Hough and C. Jeffery (eds), *Devolution in Comparative Context* (Manchester: Manchester University Press).

Jeffery, C. and W. Paterson (2003), 'Germany and European Integration: A Shifting of Tectonic Plates', *West European Politics* 26/4: 59–75.

Joppke, C. (1995), *East German Dissidents and the Revolution of 1989: Social Movement in a Leninist Regime* (New York: New York University Press).

Katzenstein, P. (1987), *Policy and Politics in West Germany: The Growth of a Semisovereign State* (Philadelphia, PA: Temple University Press).

—— (2005), 'Conclusion: Semisovereignty in United Germany', in S. Green and W. Paterson (eds), *Governance in Contemporary Germany: The Semisovereign State Revisited* (Cambridge: Cambridge University Press).

Katzenstein, P.J. (ed.) (1997), *Tamed Power: Germany in Europe* (Ithaca, NY: Cornell University Press).

Kelek, N. (2005), *Die fremde Braut: Ein Bericht aus dem Innern des türkischen Lebens in Deutschland* (Cologne: Kiepenheuer & Witsch).

Kemmerling, A. and O. Bruttel (2006), '"New Politics" in German Labour Market Policy? The Implications of the Recent Hartz Reforms for the German Welfare State', *West European Politics* 29/1: 90–112.

King, I. (2005), 'The 2005 German General Election', *Debatte* 13/3: 229–41.

Kirchheimer, O. (1966), 'The Transformation of the Western European Party Systems', in J. La Polombara and M. Weiner (eds), *Political Parties and Political Development* (Princeton, NJ: Princeton University Press).

Klusmeyer, D. (2001), 'A "Guiding Culture" for Immigrants? Integration and Diversity in Germany', *Journal of Ethnic and Migration Studies* 27/3: 519–32.

Kolb, H. (2005), 'Die Green Card: Inszenierung eines Politikwechsels', *Aus Politik und Zeitgeschichte* B27/2005: 18–24.

Kommers, D. (1997), *The Constitutional Jurisprudence of the Federal Republic of Germany* (Durham, NC: Duke University Press).

Kopstein, J. (1997), *The Politics of Economic Decline in East Germany, 1945–1989* (Chapel Hill: University of North Carolina Press).

Ladrech, R. (1994), 'Europeanization of Domestic Politics and Institutions: The Case of France', *Journal of Common Market Studies* 32/1: 69–88.

Lees, C. (2005), *Party Politics in Germany: A Comparative Politics Approach* (Basingstoke: Palgrave).

Lehmbruch, G. (2002) [1976], *Parteienwettbewerb im Bundesstaat* (Wiesbaden: Westdeutscher Verlag).

Leonardy, U. (1991), 'The Working Relationships between Bund and Länder in the Federal Republic of Germany', in C. Jeffery and P. Savigear (eds), *German Federalism Today* (Leicester: Leicester University Press).

Lewis, J. (1992), 'Gender and the Development of Welfare Regimes', *Journal of European Social Policy* 3: 159–73.

Lijphart, A. (1999), *Patterns of Democracy: Government Forms and Performance in Thirty-six Countries* (New Haven, CT: Yale University Press).

Lindenberger, T. (1999), *Herrschaft und Eigen-Sinn in der Diktatur* (Cologne: Böhlau).

Longhurst, K. (2003), 'Why Aren't the Germans Debating the Draft? Path Dependency and the Persistence of Conscription', *German Politics* 12/2: 147–65.

—— (2004), *Germany and the Use of Force: The Evolution of German Security Policy 1989–2003* (Manchester: Manchester University Press).

McAdams, J. (1997), 'Germany after Unification: Normal at Last?', *World Politics* 49: 282–308.

McKay, J. (1998), *The Official Concept of the Nation in the Former GDR: Theory, Pragmatism and the Search for Legitimacy* (London: Ashgate).

—— (2004), 'Women in German Politics: Still Jobs for the Boys?' *German Politics* 13/1: 56–80.

Maier, C. (1997), *Dissolution: The Crisis of Communism and the End of East Germany* (Princeton, NJ: Princeton University Press).

Maull, H. (1990), 'Germany and Japan: The New Civilian Powers', *Foreign Affairs* 69/5: 91–105.

—— (1994), 'Germany at the Summit', *International Spectator* 29/2: 113–39.

—— (ed.) (2006), *Germany's Uncertain Power: Foreign Policy of the Berlin Republic* (Basingstoke: Palgrave).

Mearsheimer, J. (1990), 'Back to the Future: Instability in Europe after the Cold War', *International Security* 15/4: 5–56.

Menz, G. (2005), 'Old Bottles – New Wine: The New Dynamics of Industrial Relations', *German Politics* 14/2: 196–207.

Mertes, M. (2002), 'Helmut Kohl's Legacy for Germany', *Washington Quarterly* 25/4: 67–82.

Miskimmon, A. (2007), *Germany and Common Foreign and Security Policy of the European Union: Between Europeanisation and National Adaptation* (Basingstoke: Palgrave).

Miskimmon, A., W. Paterson and J. Sloam (eds) (forthcoming), *The German Crisis and the 2005 Federal Election* (Basingstoke: Palgrave).

Molt, P. (2006), 'Germany's Development Policy since 1998', in H. Maull (ed.), *Germany's Uncertain Power* (Basingstoke: Palgrave).

Moltke, J. von (2005), *No Place Like Home: Locations of Heimat in German Cinema* (Berkeley: University of California Press).

Moore, C. (2006), '"Schloss Neuwahnstein"? Why the Länder Continue to Strengthen Their Representations in Brussels', *German Politics* 15/2: 192–205.

Murray, L. (1994), 'Einwanderungsland Bundesrepublik Deutschland? Explaining the Evolving positions of German Political Parties on Citizenship Policy', *German Politics and Society* 33: 23–56.

NATO (2005), *NATO–Russia Compendium of Financial and Economic Data Relating to Defence*, <http://www.nato.int/docu/pr/2005/p05-161.pdf> (viewed 7 September 2006).

Nolte, E. (1986), 'Die Vergangenheit, die nicht vergehen will. Eine Rede, die geschrieben, aber nicht gehalten werden konnte', *Frankfurter Allgemeine Zeitung*, 6 June 1986.

Nugent, N. (2006), *The Government and Politics of the European Union* (Basingstoke: Palgrave)

O'Dochartaigh, P. (2003), *Germany since 1945* (Basingstoke: Palgrave).

Padgett, S. (2001), 'The German *Volkspartei* and the Career of the Catch-All Concept', *German Politics* 10/2: 51–72.

—— (2003), 'Political Economy: The German Model under Stress', in S. Padgett, W. Paterson and G. Smith (eds), *Developments in German Politics 3* (Basingstoke: Palgrave).

Paterson, W. (1992), 'Gulliver Unbound: The Changing Context of Foreign Policy', in G. Smith, W. Paterson and S. Padgett (eds), *Developments in German Politics* (Basingstoke: Macmillan).

—— (2006), 'Does Germany Still Have a European Vocation?', *European Research Institution Working Papers*, 15, University of Birmingham, September 2006, <http://www.eri.bham.ac.uk/research/WP15Paterson.pdf> (viewed 4 April 2007).

Paterson, W. and J. Sloam (2005), 'Gerhard Schröder and the Unlikely Victory of the German Social Democrats', in D. Conradt *et al.* (eds), *A Precarious Victory: The 2002 German Federal Election and Its Aftermath* (Oxford: Berghahn).

Pearce, C. (2007), *Contemporary Germany and the Nazi Legacy. Remembrance, Politics and the Dialectic of Normality* (Basingstoke: Palgrave).

Pedersen, T. (1998), *Germany, France and the Integration of Europe: A Realist Interpretation* (London and New York: Pinter).

Peters, B. (1999), *Institutional Theory in Political Science: The New Institutionalism* (London: Pinter)

Petrov, V. (1967), *Money and Conquest: Allied Occupation Currencies in World War II* (Baltimore, MD: Johns Hopkins Press).

Poguntke, T. (1993), *Alternative Politics: The German Green Party* (Edinburgh: Edinburgh University Press).

Pulzer, P. (1995), *German Politics: 1945–1995* (Oxford: Oxford University Press).

—— (1996), 'Model or Exception: Germany as a Normal State?', in G. Smith, W. Paterson and S. Padgett (eds), *Developments in German Politics 2* (Basingstoke: Macmillan).

—— (1997), *Germany, 1870–1945: Politics, State Formation and War* (Oxford: Oxford University Press).

Reinberg, A. and M. Hummel (2004), 'Fachkräftemangel bedroht Wettbewerbsfähigkeit der deutschen Wirtschaft', *Aus Politik und Zeitgeschichte* B28/2004: 3–10.

Rist, R. (1978), *Guestworkers in Germany: The Prospects for Pluralism* (New York: Praeger).

Roberts, G. (1991), '"Emigrants in Their Own Country": German Reunification and Its Political Consequences', *Parliamentary Affairs* 44/3: 373–88.

Ross, C. (2000), *Constructing Socialism at the Grass-Roots: The Transformation of East Germany, 1945–65* (Basingstoke: Macmillan).

Rudzio, W. (2003), *Das politische System der Bundesrepublik Deutschland* (Opladen: Leske+Budrich).

Saalfeld, T. (2005), 'Political Parties', in S. Green and W. Paterson (eds), *Governance in Contemporary Germany: The Semisovereign State Revisited* (Cambridge: Cambridge University Press).

Sally, R. and D. Webber (1994), 'The German Solidarity Pact: A Case Study in the Politics of the Unified Germany', *German Politics* 3/1: 19–46.

Scarrow, S. (2006), 'Beyond the Scandals? Party Funding and the 2005 German Elections', *German Politics* 15/4: 376–92.

Schäuble, W. and K. Lamers (1994), *Überlegungen zur europäischen Politik*, <http://www.wolfgang-schaeuble.de/positionspapiere/ schaeublelamers94.pdf> (viewed 10 April 2007).

Scharpf, F. (1988), 'Joint-Decision Trap: Lessons from German Federalism and European Integration', *Public Administration* 66: 239–78.

Scharpf, F., B. Reissert and F. Schnabel (1976), *Politikverflechtung: Theorie und Empirie des kooperativen Föderalismus in der Bundesrepublik* (Kronberg: Scriptor).

Schmidt, M. (1987), 'West Germany: The Policy of the Middle Way', *Journal of Public Policy* 7/2: 135–77.

—— (1989), 'Learning from Catastrophes: West Germany's Public Policy', in F. Castles (ed.), *The Comparative History of Public Policy* (Cambridge: Polity Press).

—— (2001), 'Still on the Middle Way? Germany's Political Economy at the Beginning of the Twenty-first Century', *German Politics* 10/3: 1–12.

—— (2002), 'Germany: The Grand Coalition State', in J. Colomer (ed.), *Political Institutions in Europe* (London: Routledge).

—— (2003a), 'Ausgaben für Bildung im internationalen Vergleich', *Aus Politik und Zeitgeschichte* B21-22/2003: 6–11.

—— (2003b), *Political Institutions in the Federal Republic of Germany* (Oxford: Oxford University Press).

—— (2007), *Das politische System Deutschlands* (Munich: Verlag C.H. Beck).

Schmidt, M. and R. Zohlnhöfer (2006), 'Rahmenbedingungen politischer Willensbildung seit 1949', in M. Schmidt and R. Zohlnhöfer (eds), *Regieren in der Bundesrepublik Deutschland: Innen- und Außenpolitik seit 1949* (Wiesbaden: VS Verlag).

Schmitter, P. and G. Lehmbruch (eds) (1979), *Trends toward Corporatist Intermediation* (London: Sage).

Schomaker, G. (2006), 'Ehemalige Stasi-Kader schreiben Schulen an', *Die Welt*, 26 March 2006.

Sesselmeier, W. (2006), 'Die demographische Herausforderung der Alterssicherung', *Aus Politik und Zeitgeschichte* B8-9/2006: 25–31.

Shonfield, A. (1965), *Modern Capitalism: The Changing Balance of Public and Private Power* (Oxford: Oxford University Press).

Smith, G. (1976), 'West Germany and the Politics of Centrality', *Government and Opposition* 11/4: 387–407.

Soysal, Y. (1994), *The Limits of Citizenship: Migrants and Postnational Membership in Europe* (Chicago: University of Chicago Press).

Sperling, J. (2003), 'The Foreign Policy of the Berlin Republic: The Very Model of a Post-Modern Power? A Review Essay', *German Politics* 12/3: 1–34.

Statistisches Bundesamt (2006a), *Im Blickpunkt: Deutschland in der EU 2006* (Wiesbaden: Statistisches Bundesamt).

—— (2006b), *Bevölkerung Deutschlands bis 2050. 11. koordinierte Bevölkerungsvorausberechnung* (Wiesbaden: Statistisches Bundesamt).

Steingart, G. (2004), *Deutschland: Abstieg eines Superstars* (Munich: Piper).

Stevenson, P. and J. Theobald (eds) (2000), *Relocating Germanness: Discursive Disunity in Unified Germany* (Basingstoke: Macmillan).

Stoiber, E. (2006), 'Stoiber Speaks out against SPD and Turkish EU Membership', *Deutsche-Welle Online*, 16 October, <http://www.dw-world.de/dw/article/0,2144,2205390,00.html> (viewed 12 March 2007).

Stone Sweet, A. (2000), *Governing with Judges: Constitutional Politics in Europe* (Oxford: Oxford University Press).

Streeck, W. (2005), 'Industrial Relations: From State Weakness as Strength to State Weakness as Weakness: Welfare Corporatism and the Private Use of the Public Interest', in S. Green and W. Paterson (eds), *Governance in Contemporary Germany: The Semisovereign State Revisited* (Cambridge: Cambridge University Press).

—— (forthcoming), 'Endgame? The Fiscal Crisis of the German State', in A. Miskimmon, W. Paterson and J. Sloam (eds), *The German Crisis and the 2005 Federal Election* (Basingstoke: Palgrave).

Streeck, W. and A. Hassel (2003), 'The Crumbling Pillars of Social Partnership', *West European Politics* 26/4: 101–24.

Streeck, W. and C. Trampusch (2005), 'Economic Reform and the Political Economy of the German State', *German Politics* 14/2: 174–95.

Struck, P. (2003), *Defence Policy Guidelines*, 21 May, Berlin, <http://www.bmvg.de/portal/ PA_1_0_LT/PortalFiles/C1256F1200608B1B/W268AHEH510INFOEN/VPR_en.pdf?yw_re pository=youatweb> (viewed 21 January 2007)

Sturm, R. (1992), 'The Changing Territorial Balance', in G. Smith, W. Paterson, P. Merkl and S. Padgett (eds), *Developments in German Politics* (Basingstoke: Macmillan).

Sturm, R. and H. Pehle (2005), *Das neue deutsche Regierungssystem: Die Europäisierung von Institutionen, Entscheidungsprozessen und Politikfeldern in der Bundesrepublik Deutschland* (Wiesbaden: VS Verlag).

Stürmer, M. (1986), 'Ein Land ohne Geschichte', *Frankfurter Allgemeine Zeitung*, 25 April 1986.

'"Ich möchte keine zweisprachigen Ortsschilder haben": Otto Schily zum Zuwanderungs- und Integrationsgesetz', *Süddeutsche Zeitung*, 27 June 2002.

Szabo, S. (2004), *Parting Ways: The Crisis in German–American Relations* (Washington, DC: Brookings Institution)

Tallberg, J. (2002), 'Paths to Compliance', *International Organisation* 56/3: 609–43.

Tewes, H. (2001), *Germany, Civilian Power and the New Europe: Enlarging NATO and the European Union* (Basingstoke: Palgrave).

Timmins, G. and J. Gower (eds) (2007), *Russia and Europe in the Twenty-first Century: An Uneasy Partnership* (London: Anthem).

Tooze, A. (2006), *The Wages of Destruction: The Making and Breaking of the Nazi Economy* (London: Allen Lane).

Tsebelis, G. (1995), 'Decision Making in Political Systems: Veto Players in Presidentialism, Parliamentarism, Multicameralism, and Multipartism', *British Journal of Political Science* 25: 289–326.

United Nations Population Division (2000), *Replacement Migration: Is It a Solution to Declining and Ageing Populations* (New York: United Nations Population Division).

Veen, H.J. (1997), '"Inner Unity" – Back to the Community Myth? A Plea for a Basic Consensus', *German Politics* 6/3: 1–15.

Wachendorfer-Schmidt, U. (2005), *Politikverflechtung im vereinigten Deutschland* (Wiesbaden: VS Verlag).

Wagener, H.-J., T. Eger and H. Fritz (2006), *Europäische Integration* (Munich: Vahlen).

Webber, D. (ed.) (2001), *New Europe, New Germany, Old Foreign Policy? German Foreign Policy since Unification* (London: Frank Cass); special issue of *German Politics* 10/1.

Weizsäcker, R. (1985), *Rede zum 8. Mai 1995*, <http://www.bundestag.de/geschichte/parlhist/ dokumente/dok08.html> (viewed 19 December 2006).

Whittall, M. (2005), 'Modell Deutschland under Pressure: The Growing Tensions between Works Councils and Trade Unions', *Economic and Industrial Democracy* 26/4: 569–92.

Wink, R. (2002), 'Labour Market Strategies for Ageing European Societies', in L. Funk and S. Green (eds), *New Aspects of Labour Market Policy* (Berlin: Verlag für Wissenschaft und Forschung).

Winkler, H. (2002), *Der lange Weg nach Westen* (Munich: C.H. Beck).

Wolff, S. (2003), *The German Question since 1919: An Analysis with Key Documents* (Westport, CT: Praeger).

Wüst, A. (2004), 'Naturalised Citizens as Voters: Behaviour and Impact', *German Politics* 13/2: 341–59.

Zohlnhöfer, R. (2006), 'Vom Wirtschaftswunder zum kranken Mann Europas? Wirtschaftspolitik seit 1945', in M. Schmidt and R. Zohlnhöfer (eds), *Regieren in der Bundesrepublik Deutschland: Innen- und Außenpolitik seit 1949* (Wiesbaden: VS Verlag).

Index